Young Chinese Migrants: Compressed Individual and Global Condition

Youth in a Globalizing World

Series Editors

Vincenzo Cicchelli (*Ceped, Université Paris Descartes/IRD*)
Sylvie Octobre (*GEMASS, Université Paris Sorbonne / CNRS and la DEPS au Ministére de la Culture, France*)

Editorial Board

Valentina Cuzzocrea (*University of Cagliari, Italy*)
Ratiba Hadj-Moussa (*York University, Canada*)
Claudia Jacinto (*prejet-Instituto de Desarrollo Económico y Social, Argentina*)
Jeylan Mortimer (*University of Minnesota, United States of America*)
Andrea Pirmi (*Universitá di Genova, Italy*)
Dan Woodman (*University of Melbourne, Australia*)
Chin-Chin Yi (*Academic Sinica, Taiwan*)

VOLUME 14

The titles published in this series are listed at *brill.com/ygw*

Young Chinese Migrants: Compressed Individual and Global Condition

By

Laurence Roulleau-Berger

Translated by

Matthew Glasgow

BRILL

LEIDEN | BOSTON

Cover illustration: *Chinese Migrants* by Francis Berger (YEAR). Courtesy of the artist.

Library of Congress Cataloging-in-Publication Data
Names: Roulleau-Berger, Laurence, 1956- author. | Glasgow, Matthew, translator.
Title: Young Chinese migrants : compressed individual and global condition/ by Laurence Roulleau-Berger ; [translated by Matthew Glasgow].
Description: Leiden ; Boston : Brill, [2021] | Series: Youth in a globalizing world, 2212-9383 ; volume 14 | Includes bibliographical references and index.
Identifiers: LCCN 2021012430 (print) | LCCN 2021012431 (ebook) | ISBN 9789004462861 (hardback) | ISBN 9789004463080 (ebook)
Subjects: LCSH: Migration, Internal–China. | Teenage immigrants–China. | Rural-urban migration–China. | Internal migrants–China–Social conditions.
Classification: LCC HB2114.A3 R68 2021 (print) | LCC HB2114.A3 (ebook) | DDC 331.3/4089951–dc23
LC record available at https://lccn.loc.gov/2021012430
LC ebook record available at https://lccn.loc.gov/2021012431

Typeface for the Latin, Greek, and Cyrillic scripts: "Brill". See and download: brill.com/brill-typeface.

ISSN 2212-9383
ISBN 978-90-04-46286-1 (hardback)
ISBN 978-90-04-46308-0 (e-book)

Copyright 2021 by Laurence Roulleau-Berger. Published by Koninklijke Brill NV, Leiden, The Netherlands.
Koninklijke Brill NV incorporates the imprints Brill, Brill Nijhoff, Brill Hotei, Brill Schöningh, Brill Fink, Brill mentis, Vandenhoeck & Ruprecht, Böhlau Verlag and V&R Unipress.
Koninklijke Brill NV reserves the right to protect this publication against unauthorized use. Requests for re-use and/or translations must be addressed to Koninklijke Brill NV via brill.com or copyright.com.

This book is printed on acid-free paper and produced in a sustainable manner.

A Côme, Jeanne, Margaux et Arsène

Contents

Preface IX
Acknowledgements XI
List of Figures, Maps and Tables XII

Introduction: Young Chinese Migrants, the *Compressed Individual* and Global Condition 1
1 Compressed Modernity, Time and Space 2
2 Chinese Experience and Young Migrants 4
   2.1 *Chinese Experience and Internal Migration* 5
   2.2 *Chinese Migration and Transnationalism* 6
3 Work and "Emotional Capitalism" 8
4 *Compressed Individual* and Inequalities 11
5 Compressed Modernity, Subpolitics and Collective Action 13

1 Young Chinese Migrants, Subalternity and the *Compressed Individual* 17
1 New Urban Boundaries and Migratory Ordeals in China 17
2 Young Migrants and Urban Segregation 21
3 Labour and Subalternity 25
4 Employment and Social Discrimination 31
5 *Floating Labour*, Hegemonic Labour Regimes and Emotions 34
6 Social Conflicts, Collective Action and Dormitory Regimes 43
7 Multi-Compressed Modernity and Mobility 50
8 Compressed mobilities and Subalternity 53
   8.1 *Strong Subalternity* 54
   8.2 *Integrative subalternity* 55
   8.3 *Weak Subalternity* 56

2 The Fabric of "Heroes" and Emotional Capitalism 59
1 Young Migrant Graduates and Employment 59
2 Compressed Modernities and Migratory Careers 65
   2.1 *Disaffiliative Mobility and Weak Integration* 68
   2.2 *Affiliative Mobility and Strong Integration* 70
   2.3 *"Alternative" Mobility and the Distancing of Compressed Modernity* 71
3 Moral Economies and the *Compressed Individual* 73
4 "Being a Hero" and Restricted Autonomy 76

5	*Guanxi* and Professional Relationships	80
6	Socialist Heritage, Compressed Modernities and Work	82
7	Compressed Modernity and Resistance to Emotional Capitalism	88

3 Young Chinese Migrants, Economic Cosmopolitanism and Globalisation 93

1	Young Chinese Migrants and Local Cosmopolitanisms	93
2	Compressed Society, Migration and the Digital Economy	97
3	Retail Traders, Entrepreneurs and Workers	100
4	Inter-Ethnic Relations, Muslim Solidarity and Discrimination	102
5	Transmigration and Economic Assemblages	106

4 Young Chinese Migrants and World Society 112

1	Work, Employment and Young Chinese Graduates in Europe	112
2	Ethnic Niches, Violence and Suffering	117
3	Chinese Economic Elites and the *Cosmopolitan Spirit*	121
4	Discrimination, Racism and Skills	125
5	Ethnic Enclaves and Multiple Affiliations	129

5 The *Compressed Individual* and *Polygamic Biographies* 135

1	Social Networks, Spatial Capital and Migratory Circulations	135
2	*Compressed Individual* and Family Governmentality	138
3	Polygamic Biographies and the Translation of Resources	142
4	Multi-Compressed Modernity and the *Spiral of Downward Mobility*	148
5	Ownership, Maintenance and Loss of Self	150
6	*Compressed Individual*, Re-migration in China and to China	152

Conclusion   158

Bibliography   165
Index   180

Preface

This book is the result of a very successful and quite long cooperation with my Chinese colleagues started in 2006 when I was Invited Professor at the Institute of Sociology of the Chinese Academy of Social Sciences (Beijing) during one year. I would like to thank so warmly Li Peilin, Professor and Director of the Academic Division of Law, Social and Political Studies and Former Vice-President of the Chinese Academy of Social Sciences (Beijing); we have long enjoyed rich and excellent scientific exchanges. The Centre National de la Recherche Scientifique (CNRS), the Chinese Academy of Social Sciences (CASS) and the Ecole Normale Supérieure de Lyon signed an agreement to jointly establish our International Associated Laboratory (LIA)[1] *Post-Western Sociology in Europe and in China* in 2013, in partnership with the department of sociology Beijing University, the department of sociology and political science of Shanghai University and the School of Social and Behavioral Sciences of Nanjing University. Professor Li Peilin and I are in charge of this laboratory for China and France respectively.

Many thanks are given to my colleagues at the Chinese Academy of Social Sciences: Professors Chen Guangjin, Wang Chunguang, He Rong, Yang Yiyin, Li Chunling, Shi Yunqing, Luo Hongguang; at the Department of Sociology, Beijing University: Professors Xie Lizhong, Liu Shiding, Qu Jingdong, Qiu Zeqi, Liu Neng, Tong Xin and Sun Feiyu; at the School of Sociology and Political Sciences, Shanghai University: Professors Li Youmei, Zhang Wenhong, Liu Yuzhao, Ji Yingchun, Zhen Zhihong, and Dr Yan Jun; at the Department of Sociology, Tsinghua University: Professors Guo Yuhua and Shen Yuan; at the School of Social and Behavioral Sciences, Nanjing University: Professors Chen Boqing, Fan Ke and Zhou Xiaohong; at the School of Social Development East China Normal University: Professors Wen Jun and Zhao Yeqin; at Tongji University Professors Zhe Weijue and Dr Chen Jin.

This book is also the result of several research programs I have conducted in China and in France, and of a long cooperation with Chinese sociologists since 2002:

– *Migration, segregation and disqualification in Chinese Cities* with Shi Lu, University Jean Moulin in cooperation with Shi Xiuyin, Institute of sociology, Chinese Academy of Social Sciences, Peking, financed by Department of International Cooperation, CNRS and MSH Rhône-Alpes (2002–2005).

---

1 In 2021 the LIA has changed of name and is called International Advanced Laboratory (IAL).

In Shanghai, 140 biographical interviews were conducted with young low-skilled Chinese migrants in agricultural product markets, shops and restaurants, construction and furniture manufacturing companies.

- *Work and globalisation in China: mobility and cooperation in French enterprises in China and joint-ventures* with Tang Jun, Polytechnic University of Peking, financed by French Ministry of Labour and Employment (2006–2008).

  Within the framework of this program 85 biographical interviews were conducted with young migrant workers in the automobile industry in Wuhan, 62 biographical interviews were conducted with young migrant men and women employed in retail companies in Beijing and Harbin, 40 biographical interviews were with young migrant cleaning women in the hotel sector in Wuhan

- *Young skilled Chinese migrants and work in Paris, Lyon and Shanghai* CMIRA Program, financed by the Rhône-Alpes Region in cooperation with Zhen Zhihong and Yan Jun, School of Political Science and Sociology, Shanghai University (2012–2015)

  Within the framework of this program, quantitative and qualitative surveys—including 50 biographical interviews—were carried out in companies in Shanghai with 150 young Chinese migrant graduates. In France, quantitative and qualitative surveys of 84 young graduated Chinese migrants—including 43 biographical interviews—were conducted in companies in Paris and Lyon.

- *Young Chinese migrants, subaltern work and urban competencies in China*, Program financed by the Rhône-Alpes Region with Béatrice Zani, Triangle, ENS Lyon (2015-2019)

  Within the framework of this program 40 biographical interviews were conducted with young female migrant workers and young migrant workers in Shanghai, Ningbo and Zhongshan.

- *International migration and global economies in Yiwu*, Program IDEX University of Lyon (2017–2021) with Marie Bellot and Li Yong, Triangle, and in cooperation with Zhao Yeqin, ECNU (Shanghai) in the framework of the JORISS Program. Within the framework of this program, the realisation of migratory and professional careers were carried out with 35 young Chinese entrepreneurs and traders and 25 young entrepreneurs from the Middle East, India, Pakistan, Iraq, Afghanistan, Syria, sub-Saharan Africa etc.

Acknowledgements

Firstly, I would like to thank so warmly Vincenzo Cicchelli and Sylvie Octobre, Editors-in -Chief of "Youth in a Globalizing World", for their invitation to publish this manuscript in their prestigious serie, their confidence and the richness of the exchanges we had around this text.

I would like to thank very much Ecole Normale Supérieure of Lyon, the Region Rhône-Alpes, and Triangle UMR 5206 CNRS for their strong support in the cooperation with China.

I would like to thank so warmly Drs Béatrice Zani, Marie Bellot, Verena Richardier, Li Yong, Marie-Astrid-Gillier from Triangle and Dr Su Liang from Shanghai University for their so precious and so rich contribution to research programs.

I also would like to thank warmly translator Matthew Glasgow for his rigorous translation in English.

I would like so much to thank warmly all young Chinese migrants in China and in Europe who have given me their confidence, shared their migratory experience and told me about their lives.

Figures, Maps and Tables

Figures

1 Evolution of migrant worker occupations with a Shanghai hukou in 2000 and 2010. Source: China Labour Bulletin   27
2 Occupations of migrants aged 18–30 years without a Shanghai hukou 2017 (%). Source: Shanghai Urban Neighbourhood Survey (SUNS) (N=874)   28
3 Economic sectors of young migrant graduates in Shanghai. Source: Shanghai Urban Neighbourhood Survey (SUNS) 2017 (N=424)   63

Maps

1 Map of China. Source: Nations Online Project, nationsonline.org   xiv
2 Collective protests recorded on CLB's Strike Map from January 2015 to December 2017. Source: maps.clb.org.hk   45

Tables

1 Three types of pathways for *balinghou, jiulinghou* and *linglinghou* young migrants   54
2 Education level of immigrants by geographic origin in 2018   113
3 Socio-professional categories of immigrants by geographic origin in 2018   114

MAP 1   Map of China
SOURCE: NATIONS ONLINE PROJECT, NATIONSONLINE.ORG

Introduction: Young Chinese Migrants, the *Compressed Individual* and Global Condition

In China, strong economic growth over the past four decades, accelerated urbanisation and multiple inequalities between urban and rural worlds have driven the escalation of internal and international migrations. This has occurred in a context of *compressed modernity*: according to Chang Kyung-Sup (2018), "*compressed modernity* is a civilisational condition in which economic, political, social and/or cultural changes occur in an extremely condensed manner in respect to both time and space and in which the dynamic coexistence of mutually disparate historical and social elements leads to the construction and reconstruction of a highly complex and fluid social system".

According to Li Peilin (2018) in the history of global modernisation, there has never been such a large movement of people (hundreds of millions of people) from agriculture to industry, from the countryside to the cities and from underdeveloped areas to developed areas in such a short period of time. Although the flow of migrant workers is internal, it differs from the urban population in terms of household registration, lifestyle, economic and social status, ideological perspectives. The internal migration of workers represents a unique phenomenon in the history of Chinese modernisation and the creation of global factories since the reform and opening of China (Li Peilin, 2019a). Young Chinese migrants have strongly internalised the idea of being the "heroes" of the new Chinese society, if not society in general, and are fascinated by the cult of success and excellence. Internal and international migrations intersect and intertwine to produce economic cosmopolitanisms. Young internal and international migrants from China invent new, local and global economic systems in a local and multi-ethnic society through discreet globalisation, top-down and bottom-up globalisation (Portes, 1999), and intermediary globalisation. *Compressed* modernity contains the effects of economic and social collisions where social, economic, moral processes, linked to regimes of premodernity, modernity and postmodernity, clash and hybridise. The resulting forms of individuation are both situational and, as they are active in Western societies, global. The young Chinese migrant incarnates the Global Individual, what we labeled here as the *Compressed Individual*: a Homo Sentimentalis living in an environment of what Eva Illouz refers to as "emotional capitalism" (2006). This individual has internalised the injunction to create a narrative of self-improvement and to become a hero of Chinese society and globalisation. The *Compressed Individual* also is adept at developing strategies to distance,

© LAURENCE ROULLEAU-BERGER, 2021 | DOI:10.1163/9789004463080_002

circumvent and resist the injunction to become an adherent of emotional capitalism.

Nevertheless, we are all *Compressed Individuals* living in different compressed modernities.

1 Compressed Modernity, Time and Space

Chang Kyung-Sup (2010) identified different regimes of *compressed modernity* based on reflexive cosmopolitisation: *low order-compressed modernity in advanced capitalist societies, high-order compressed modernity in non-Western societies, and compartmentalised compressed modernity* in transition societies. China has different regimes of compressed modernity in its urban, rural, coastal zones and its central western provinces, which is why this author can speak of internal multiple modernities in China and so multi-compressed modernities (Chang, 2020) in the world. Nonetheless, the regime of high-order compressed modernity remains dominant and is assembled via different temporalities.

In China, industrialisation and urbanisation processes have strongly accelerated in recent times causing clashes between economic and social sequences. While certain European approaches consider them related to a first modernity, others view them as related to a second modernity, to use the term coined by Ulrich Beck (1992). In order to examine the Chinese experience, Li Peilin (2015) applied the concept of Eastern modernisation. He sought to demonstrate how the elasticity of societal structures simultaneously produces upward social mobility, inequality and uncertainty. This influences the social fate of vulnerable social groups in China, especially migrants and youth in a new economy heading towards a *sui generis* capitalism (Aglietta, Guo, 2012). Historical, social, political and economic as well as individual and collective temporalities tighten and intertwine in regimes of compressed modernity which generate a plurality of temporal rationalities that come into conflict with each other. We introduce compressed temporalities that give rise to increased social, economic, environmental and health risks. However, while the effects of temporal contraction play a key role in the production of compressed modernity, they are in constant dialogue with social, geographic, cultural and economic spaces. Temporalities and spaces combine in internal and international Chinese migrations to produce mobility and intense circulations. The regimes of compressed modernity create interferences which produce societal and biographical bifurcations.

INTRODUCTION   3

In compressed modernity, *we* identified four forms of objective temporalities: historical, social, political and economic (Roulleau-Berger 2018).
Historical temporalities refer to different eras in Chinese society: traditional,
modern and postmodern. They tighten where forms of modernity and postmodernity disrupt traditional rural society through the introduction of new
technologies, migratory circulations and social networks. Historical temporalities also contract when Chinese cities, which differ greatly in morphology and
size, produce forms of modernity and postmodernity that generate tension or
conflict with segments of traditional Chinese society, especially the lives of
internal migrants.

Social temporalities refer to the social stratification process that has rapidly developed since 1979 and created increasingly distinct social strata in
the "upper" middle class, the "lower" middle-class and the new urban working class. Social temporalities are compressed by the simultaneous production of an *enrichment economy* (Boltanski, Esquerre, 2017) and an economy of
stark poverty. This brings about a new globalised economic elite and rural and
urban underclass, largely comprised of young migrants.

Political temporalities refer to the competition and organisation of societal
structures inherited from communism and those closer to sui generis capitalism, and even global capitalism. State and public economic institutions
account for just one-fourth of urban employment, giving private companies
a key role in China's growth. Political temporalities contract where there is a
coexistence of an authoritarian state and the development of public spaces
that may gain autonomy more or less covertly. They also give way to micromobilisations which result in public micro-arenas and intermediate spaces
where flexible citizenship emerges (Ong, 1999) and where democracy is built
from the "bottom-up" in an authoritarian context.

Economic temporalities refer to the transition from a planned economy
to a market economy structured by economic institutions. These institutions
were both differentiated from, and connected, to its socialist past and new
forms of globalised capitalism. The contraction of economic temporalities
can be identified through the coexistence and competition of market, non-
market and monetary economies—be they "informal", invisible, multipolar or
globalised—at the heart of which stands the young Chinese migrant.

Finally, we identify subjective temporalities referred to here as experienced temporalities. These refer to an individuals' experiences located in
different identifiable spaces in a young migrants' biographical sequence. For
young migrant workers, time spent in rural zones rapidly builds tension with
time spent in urban zones. They must constantly shift from one temporality

and space to another at a pace dictated by resources: more constrained for migrants with poor social, economic and symbolic resources and at a more desirable speed for those with more. Furthermore, individuals in the Chinese labour market, particularly migrants, are subject to flexible working hours that can see them placed in a form of servitude.

Temporalities contract in exacerbated accelerations and removal of restrictions in urban and rural spaces at various levels, amplifying economic, social and moral insecurity. The construction of young Chinese migrants' mobility skills is characteristic of factors that develop "the art of making do" in different regimes of compressed modernity.

In China, the regime of high-order compressed modernity prevails over low compressed modernity and compartmentalised compressed modernity. In contrast, in Europe the regime of low-order compressed modernity takes precedence over high-order compressed modernity and compartmentalised compressed modernity. Young Chinese migrants create *multi-compressed modernity* through circulating in different regimes of compressed modernity. Spaces and temporalities severely contracting high-order compressed modernity and then loosen in low-order compressed modernity but remain in a constant state of flux.

In China, young Chinese migrant graduates are increasingly implicated in *internal multiple modernities* (Chang Kyung Sup, 2020). They are born to a culture imbued with tradition, have transitioned into a modern, industrial era and must survive in a postmodern, post-industrial era. Consequently, they must continually juggle new forms of restricted autonomy that force them to acquire strong adaptability skills and creates a sense of fatigue (Ehrenberg, 1998) regarding being oneself. The product is the *Compressed Individual*, confronted with manifold double-binds, uncertainty and mobility in the acceleration and multiplicity of local and global spaces, temporalities and diverse situations.

2 Chinese Experience and Young Migrants

The contraction of Chinese temporalities cannot be disassociated from that of spaces. The experience of internal and international migration demonstrates the simultaneous contraction of both space and time. Compacted temporalities produce multimobilities in China and in the global space via transnational migrations. As *high-order compressed modernity* accelerates and removes restrictions in space and time, temporalities constrict in exacerbated accelerations and limitations are removed in urban and rural spaces at various levels. This in turn amplifies situations of economic, social and moral insecurity.

INTRODUCTION

2.1 *Chinese Experience and Internal Migration*

Before 1979, the implementation of the 户口 *hukou* (household and civil registration system) policy deterred migration and controlled rural to urban migratory movements. It is a system which came into effect in 1958 during a time of grain shortages and migration to cities. This anti-migration policy was implemented to control the geographic mobility of individuals outside their registered household. The *hukou* system put in place in the 1950s meant an assigned place of residence, that is, no mobility is allowed without prior authorisation from the local administration. Two *hukou* have been distinguished: a rural *hukou* and a non-rural *hukou* for urban residents. Rural *hukou* provide access to land and employment in rural areas and urban *hukou* guarantee access to social rights in housing, employment and education (Thireau, 2006). Migration continued to be structured and organised until the mid-1980s, but has subsequently increased in continental China since 1985. Then the weakening of the *hukou* policy then favoured widespread, open mobility through individual migration that rivaled organised migration. In China, the escalation of internal migration correlates with the commodification of work and the circulation of poor, low-skilled youth. Frequently from rural areas, they are at risk of being treated as indentured servants. According to the 2016 China Mobile Population Development Report, more than 247 million Chinese migrate internally, equating to 18% of the total population (1 in 6 citizens). These figures, sourced from the UN, are not far off the 244 million international migrants that moved around the world in 2015. Internal migration has increased in terms of numbers and complexity in continental China since 1990.

The regimes of compressed modernity in China are characterised by a Chinese experience (Li Peilin, 2012) in particular by high levels of internal migration. In 1982, the migrant population totaled only 6.6 million. The sixth national census revealed urban migrants accounted for 19.72% of the total migrant population, up 7.5 percentage points compared to 2005 (12.23%). The number of new-generation urban migrants is estimated to have more than doubled in 2010. Data published in the 1% National Population Sample Survey report indicated the number of migrants was growing in each city. In 2019, more than 236 million Chinese migrated internally in China, a number that now appears to be slowly decreasing.

In the years leading up to 2010, the number of young migrants expanded rapidly. Between 2005 and 2010, the number more than doubled from 16 to 33 million migrants. This 5-year period also saw the number of urban migrants rise to 83% of the floating population. In contrast, the percentage of urban-rural and rural-urban migrants decreased. Young migrants mostly originated from rural zones and gathered in Chinese megalopolises located on the east coast. In 2015, 87.4% of young migrants lived in Chinese cities and young migrants accounted for 33.2% of total urban youth populations, i.e. one in three youths.

In 2015, according to data from the 1% National Population Sample Survey, individuals aged 16 to 30 years represented 77% of the new migrant generation, or almost 91 million individuals. The number of young migrants aged 10 to 19 years was 27.48 million, or 18.8% of the country's total youth population. In short, almost one in five Chinese youth are migrants. This ratio is one percentage point higher than that of the national floating population (17.9%), an indicator of the high mobility of Chinese youth. In 2015, the new generation of migrant workers born in 1980 (*80 后 balinghou*) or later represented 50.4% of the country's total migrant workers, an increase of one percentage point on the previous year. *90 后 jiulinghou* (post-1990) migrant workers represented 43.2% and the *00 后* linglinghou (post-2000) accounted for 6.4%.

In this book we will focus on *80 后* balinghou, *90 后 jiulinghou* and *00 后 linglinghou* migrant workers.

In 2005, the average number of years of schooling was 9.5. This rose to 10.4 in 2011, an increase of 1.6 years on the previous generation. The average for young urban migrants was 13.23 in 2014, while the average for rural migrants remained below the minimum standard of 9 years set by the State. Mass education and compulsory education for young people has increased their time spent in school. In 2015, of young migrants aged 16–30, 54% had only lower-secondary education, 27.1% had secondary education, 12.2% had opted for vocational pathways, 3.7% had attained a general baccalaureate (secondary school diploma) equivalent and 0.3% had a graduate degree. Thus, young migrants' educational level has improved substantially.

2.2 *Chinese Migration and Transnationalism*

Forty million Chinese nationals live abroad. Since the introduction of the Reform and Opening Up policy in 1978, over 10 million migrants have moved from China to Europe. Chinese migration is first and foremost a multipolar phenomenon. In 2018, the origins of France's immigrant population were 33.5% European, 46.1% African and 14.5% Asian (including 1.6% Chinese).

Over the past 30 years, increasing migratory movements and the expanding population of high and low skilled Chinese workers have shaped transcontinental and transnational frameworks in the economic and social spaces of European labour markets. Chinese migration is not new phenomenon; it has

INTRODUCTION

grown against a backdrop of transforming national labour markets as well as new emigration policies within China. New Silk Roads have opened, and the Chinese and European governments have established cooperation policies by promoting economic trade and increased migratory movements.

While Chinese migration has always been a powerful force in international migration, it is today characterised by its expansion and increasing multipolarity. In a globalised world, Chinese migrations cannot be isolated from internal movements that can be precursors to transcontinental mobility to the Americas, Europe and, more recently, Africa. If Chinese migrants continue to preference countries with large, existing Chinese communities (i.e. the UK, the Netherlands, France and Germany), they are also establishing themselves in new countries such as in Southern Europe (Italy, Spain, Portugal, etc.), Austria and Eastern Europe (Ambrosini, 2007, 2020; Roulleau-Berger, 2007). In the past 20 years, Chinese nationals have migrated to Bulgaria, the Czech Republic, Serbia, Russia and Hungary. These countries are now places of transit and settlement for migrant populations. New Chinese migrations such as from Wenzhou have also emerged, mostly made up of youth who are frequently from urban areas; in addition, the past 30 years have also seen the arrival of Northern Chinese populations (Pieke, 2007).

Chinese migrations to France have grown steadily, increasing by 25% from 80,000 migrants in 2008 to over 100,000 in 2013.[1] These migrations are increasingly visible and new Chinese migrants represent a growing proportion of arrivals in France. This wave of migration is young in age: in 2013, 64% of Chinese migrants were between 25 and 64 years. For the most part, they come to study with 69% of residence permits in 2010 were granted for this reason.[2] Despite their education (86% had the equivalent of a general baccalaureate diploma in 2014), they experience greater difficulty finding employment than their European counterparts. In 2013, Chinese migrants were overrepresented in three branches of activity: 18% of Chinese men were employed as chefs and 15% worked in the hotel-hospitality sector, trade (13% of female Chinese workers); and the manufacturing industry.[3] Chinese women do not migrate

---

1 Source: INSEE (French National Institute of Statistics and Economic Studies), 2008 population census data: http://www.insee.fr/fr/themes/tableau_local.asp?ref_id=IMG-1B&nivgeo=FE&codgeo=1&niveau=2&millesime=2008 (publication october 2013); 2013 population census data *http://www.insee.fr/fr/themes/tableau_local.asp?ref_id=IMG-1B&nivgeo=FE&codgeo=1&niveau=2&millesime=2013* (publication: 30 June 2016).

2 Source: http://www.insee.fr/fr/ffc/docs_ffc/ref/IMMFRA12_h_Flot2_flu.pdf.

3 Source: INSEE, census data of 2007 population; conducted by: CAS and DSED-SGII cited in Immigrants' employment and occupations, Cécile Jolly, Frédéric Lainé, Yves Breem,

primarily for family reasons and are equally represented in the student population (6,000 up from 3,700 in 2010 respectively).

According to the French National Institute of Statistics and Economic Studies, in 2018, 17.1% of Chinese active migrants in France were listed in the socio-professional categories (CSP) as agricultural workers, artisans, traders and company directors. A total of 23.9% were in management positions, 8.8% were employed in intermediate professions, 31.3% were employees and 19% were manual labourers. In this book, we will focus on young Chinese migrants from these various socio-professional categories.

Therefore, the young Chinese migrant plays a central role in explaining how internal multiple modernities are produced. In seeking to understand the intertwining regimes of modernity in China and abroad, we will consider the intracontinental and international mobility of young Chinese migrants in a continuum of multiple spaces and temporalities.

3 Work and "Emotional Capitalism"

Internal multiple compressed modernities in China restructured Chinese labour markets around the concept of manufacturing consent (Burawoy, 1979). This occurred via the production of hierarchies based on domination, flexibility and symbolic violence that gave rise to an enrichment economy. This economy replaced the planned socialist economy that provided workers with structure and protection through the 单位 *danwei* (labour unit), communist work organisation systems. As a result, Chinese workers, in particular young migrants, were forced to commodify themselves, i.e. be both the trader and the commodity. The indefinite extension of working hoursup to 14 hours a day is not compensated in material and economic rewards for workers. This is especially true for migrant workers who may receive no wages for months on end. The enrichment economy is part of a regime of high-order compressed modernity that causes extreme social inequality. It eliminates worker solidarity and obligates them to agree to violence and domination in labour markets. The process of widening inequality appears to be unpredictable and limitless under a global capitalism. These formations are assemblages of powerful economic agents, markets, technologies and governments

---

Work document, Strategic analysis centre, February 2012 available online: http://www.immigration.interieur.gouv.fr/Info-ressources/Statistiques/Etudes-et-publications/Etudes/L-emploi-et-les-metiers-des-immigres.

INTRODUCTION 9

as it constantly restructures itself under a regime of high-order compressed modernity. The hyper commodification of Chinese labour markets drives a perpetual conquest of new domestic and international sectors of economic activity.

For Chang Kyung-Sup (2020) time compression involves the phenomena of intense competition, collision, disjuncture and compounding between post-modern elements and traditional elements. On the one hand, the Chinese migrant is a flexible complex traditional-modernised-post-modernised Subject and, on the other, an indigenous-Westernised-cosmopolitan figure. This results in a local and global Individual. Young Chinese migrants must manage the effects of collisions between employment and work situations in traditional, "modern" and "postmodern" work cultures.

Multi-compressed modernity features "predatory formations" that are assemblages of powerful economic agents, markets, technologies and governments and produce violences, brutality and expulsions (Sassen, 2014). So multi-compressed modernity also features the hyper commodification of emotions converted into *emodities* (Illouz, 2019). This takes place in the hegemonic labour regimes created by authoritarian structures linked to "emotional capitalism" (Illouz, 2006), and is experienced differently by young graduate and low-skilled migrants. Multi-compressed modernity gains ground by normalising the intimate and economic spheres and by situations of domination through the emotional confiscation of young migrants in subaltern positions via depersonalisation techniques (Goffman, 1963). Compressed modernity triggers strong emotions in young graduate migrants aspiring to become "heroes" of Chinese society. They are subjected to controlled personalisation techniques as part of managerial strategies that produce maximum exploitation in labour markets.

Migrants with more resources internalise to differing degrees the injunction to join the cult of excellence that affects their professional and personal lives in different ways. While the search for recognition and happiness at work becomes a key element in the production of emotional capitalism, a portion of young graduates respond "positively" to these injunctions. The most qualified perform emotional labour to conform to these social expectations and may overexert themselves by internalising norms of competition. The wide range of work situations slightly alters their relationship to labour founded on overinvestment and the search for excellence and self-realisation. We can clearly see that the gap between emotions experienced and those imposed by a social order produce an intense emotional labour. Another category of young Chinese migrant graduates who are tired of being themselves (Ehrenberg, 1998) distance themselves from work and criticise the injunction to internalise the norms of success and excellence, perceived as impeding their self-realisation. Here the gap between emotions experienced and those imposed by a social order is reduced and less intense emotional work is produced.

Low-skilled migrants must adapt to emotional sub-cultures specific to different professional segments. To a varying degree, these enforce silence and censure emotions through the strong internalisation of the injunction to consent and through false consent or the refusal of forced silence. In an authoritarian environment, this emotional confiscation comes about through the implementation of systems in the labour division department. Such systems dispossess the subaltern of any form of reflexivity on their work and any possibility of self-fulfillment and freedom in the workplace. Young low-skilled Chinese migrants are forced into emotional work that, in an authoritarian context and in hegemonic labour regimes, represents accepting, adapting to or resisting the confiscation of their emotions through angry protest and the refusal to be humiliated or mistreated.

Multi-compressed modernity restricts the development of forms of emancipation for individuals from a subaltern condition by placing them in a plurality of double-bind situations. Pun Ngai (2016) demonstrated that in a hegemonic labour regime, migrant workers are overexposed to the ordeal of not being themselves and the loss of family and community ties. These tests toothier sense of self impede the process of partial individuation. This in turn creates identity trauma and fractures that may lead to suicide as an act of resistance to *compressed modernity*. Political and economic temporalities in Chinese society combine to produce violent processes of overexposure for the most vulnerable individuals in situations of subalternity, resulting in social or even physical death.

The young migrant workers that committed suicide in the Foxconn Factory, for example, were violently subjected to this transformation. They were confronted by situations of immense solitude, cut off from families and support networks, and forced into economic over productivity in working conditions that failed to take their rights or identities into account. While autonomy entails independence in a democratic context, it can never take on this form in an authoritarian society. The construction of social and moral autonomy in China must be viewed through the lens of Chinese history and the politics of Chinese society. Luo Jarde and Yeh K. (2012) found that Chinese individuals were both collectivist and individualist in their affiliation to different social circles, namely family, community and social networks. Nonetheless, the "cult of excellence" has reached its zenith in China. It has led to situations where youth have no social support and experience the ordeal of a loss of self and loneliness. They experience anxiety in spaces where they are alienated,

INTRODUCTION

indentured, deprived of self, stripped of future aspirations and rendered invisible.

As young Chinese migrants move to Europe, Africa or North America, they transition from a multi-compressed modernity where *high-order compressed modernity* regimes take precedence to spaces where *low-order compressed modernity* is the dominant form. In the process of socialisation attached to different regimes of modernity, they have internalised various ways of becoming Compressed Individuals. These are redefined in the context of the societies of arrival in transmigration. Young Chinese migrants apply the rules and norms of *high-order compressed modernity* to regimes of *low-order compressed modernity*. For this reason, young Chinese migrants emerge as emblematic figureheads of the global condition of the Compressed Individual. During the international migration process, young graduates often encounter situations of social disqualification and racial discrimination that stymy their dream of becoming the "heroes of globalisation". After being subjected to injunctions to become "heroes" under emotional socialism, they dream of becoming entrepreneurs in their own right within the framework of "emotional capitalism". The least qualified rapidly become "those left behind by globalisation" when confronting situations of economic, moral and social captivity in ethnic niches or enclaves in international cities.

4   *Compressed Individual* and Inequalities

In China under internal compressed modernities individuation processes linked to regimes of premodernity, modernity and postmodernity clash and hybridise. They thus give rise to forms of individuation that are both situated and, given that they are active in Western societies, globalised. Individuals remain highly dependent on the authoritarian state and continue to consider themselves a member, all the while developing individual and collective strategies to emancipate themselves.

To visualise the *Compressed Individual*, the notion of "partial individuation" (Yan Yunxiang, 2010) must be brought into play. This contributes to the image of a young migrant caught between political control imposed by the State and reclamation of individual rights and emancipation in a regime of contradictory modernity. Individuals have grown up in compressed and differentiated temporalities linked to stages of the modernisation and urbanisation process. First, they had to prove their loyalty to the government during the socialist movements of the 1950s and later, they had to adapt to a market economy structured around the injunction to be oneself.

Shi Yunqing (2015) defined *compressibility* as lying between tradition and modernity, the coexistence of socialism, capitalism, social and political freedom for individuals ruled by an authoritarian State. Creating the *Compressed Individual* in China requires a State-Individual relationship be established, despite Chinese society increasingly being shaped by the State's retreat from individuals' private lives and the assertion of a growing number of dissenting voices. A process of partial individuation defined by Chinese sociologists is taking place under the control of the central State. Relations between individuals, local and central governments arise in spheres linked to interpersonal networks. Boundaries here are permeable and allow individuals a varying degree of *self-empowerment* (Shi Yunqing, 2018).

The effects of collisions between temporalities, spaces and situations specific to multi-compressed modernity produce bifurcations, unpredictability and reversibility in individual and collective biographies. Constant clashes occur between spaces, temporalities and situations, simultaneously giving rise to a growing number of zones of uncertainty. Each time Chinese youth migrate, a new biographical crossroads appears with a vast number of possible choices, fuelling further uncertainty. The individual must undergo a series of identity changes due to spatial and professional mobility and changes in their situation, thus becoming increasingly multi-compressed.

The Chinese migrant reveals the effects of collisions intrinsic to compressed modernity which manufacture "successful" individuals that have acquired a home, a social place and property in different spaces and temporalities. Thus, we will present the successful *Compressed Individual* who features as "a hero", equipped with strong emotional capacities and forced into a cycle of self-improvement. If, according to Eva Illouz (2006), emotional capitalism is a culture where emotional and economic practices and discourses influence each other and where feelings and emotions become commodities, we can say that a "emotional socialism" exists in China. The *Compressed Individual* has internalised the injunction to invent a narrative of self-improvement, giving rise to young Chinese entrepreneurs and executives in both China and abroad.

Successful and unsuccessful *Compressed Individuals* coexist, the latter being excluded from, or unable to become part of, collective schemes and the safety of community collectives. They lack resources and support networks and have decreased self-ownership (Castel, Haroche, 2001). The unsuccessful *Compressed Individual* emerges as the "loser" in emotional capitalism and cannot create a narrative of self-improvement. They are deprived of all forms of public recognition in the plurality of spaces and temporalities. The effects of collisions inherent in compressed modernity bolster moral economies of shame

INTRODUCTION

and contempt. It is in this category that low-skilled young Chinese migrants, undocumented migrants, sex workers, etc. are located.

In *high-order compressed modernity*, the effects of collisions strengthen the position of the successful Compressed Individual seeking perpetual self-improvement. The unsuccessful Compressed Individual, however, is driven down a path of self-deterioration. Social conflicts reveal tensions in the widening gap between these two Compressed Individuals in *high-order compressed modernity*, a catalyst for acts of individual and collective resistances, i.e. protests and suicide.

In *low-order compressed modernity*, the effects of collisions strengthen the position of the successful *Compressed Individual* seeking controlled self-improvement, while reinforcing a pattern of self-deterioration for unsuccessful Compressed Individuals. While the gap between these two figures is narrower in a regime of low-order compressed modernity, internal tensions and conflicts emerge nevertheless.

Young Chinese migrants are restricted to a plurality of temporalities and spaces where they develop forms of action, mobilisation and reflexivity, including practical skills adapted to each new migratory stage. Under multi-compressed modernities, they continuously engage undergo a process of *identity alternation*; they must re-socialise when faced with the dismantling of their preceding nomic structure of subjective reality (Berger, Luckmann, 1986). This identity alternation process calls on emotional skills and produces moral careers that, if applied to self-improvement, create anchor points, attachment and social affiliations. However, if applied to self-deterioration, they produce disassociations, stigmatisation and social expulsion.

5 Compressed Modernity, Subpolitics and Collective Action

In China, multi-compressed modernity also creates a growing number of public spaces in which individuals mobilise. Different modes are utilised and subaltern groups, in this case young migrants, produce subpolitical narratives through negotiated solidarities. Although in the past public and political spaces tended to intermingle (Zhang Jing, 2012), today these two spaces are increasingly distinct. This is leading to the emergence of public micro-arenas and autonomous public spaces located in different places in Chinese societies: namely in neighbourhoods or small co-dwelling spaces suitable for mobilisations of various kinds, and in small groups that gather at different times to produce different types of activities. These spaces remain under the control of the government. Norms of cooperation, agreement and action are thus negotiated with the political norms of state structures. This gives rise to adjustments, transactions, arrangements and disputes between institutional and non-institutional forms.

In the authoritarian context of *high order compressed modernity*, a number of active and interactive public micro-arenas established in collective temporalities facilitate *flexible citizenship* (Ong, 1999). A discontinuous process is thus set in motion, creating forms of public participation in diverse social groups that voice anti-establishment ideas, especially young migrants. While Chinese authorities implement a range of hard control and surveillance measures, including directives and enforced consent, they also promote the expansion of forms of" interactional citizenship" (Colomy, Brown, 1996). These public micro-arenas emerge through social networks and ordered interactive and participative spaces for expression and discussion (Cefaï, 2007). They are set up and dismantled in step with events and political restrictions and foster the construction of public identities by drawing on individual and collective creativity and social solidarity systems.

In China today, younger generations are mobilising new repertoires of action to organise spaces of limited democracy. Furthermore, small groups of youth, notably young migrants, develop informal protest networks using digital resources to become collective stakeholders alongside local authorities and be recognised in order for their voices to be heard. Moreover, interstitial spaces are created in old factories converted into artistic zones. Young designers, including young migrants, engage in artistic activities in these spaces, producing dissenting opinions and reclaiming social events and places. Finally, young activists engaged in an environmental struggles and who have experienced extreme precarity produce everyday resistance by advocating anti-consumerist and anti-capitalist values through alternative lifestyles.

In Chinese society, the convergence of a transition period, the widening gap of social inequality, accelerated urbanisation and the escalation of internal migration have fostered the mobilisation of active minorities. They occupy *intermediate spaces* that act as moral areas, and distance themselves from State and Market by inserting themselves in heterotopic spaces; today, intermediate spaces are on the rise where young migrants, community-based activists, young artists and ecologists gather to develop strategies for identity affirmation and set up micro-organisations on a political, economic, cultural and artistic level (Roulleau-Berger, 2010). These intermediate spaces are areas of micromobilisations organised through the temporal course of horizontal interactions, situated actions and participation that produce everyday civic spirit. Participation in collective action develops in line with political temporalities in an authoritarian government that has reinforced control and surveillance measures of

INTRODUCTION 15

spaces containing anti-establishment, dissident voices be they cultural, artistic, ecological or religious.

In China, intermediate and interstitial spaces can be defined as both spaces of social resistance and reconciliation. Resistance comes in the form of an ongoing struggle for economic, social and moral recognition and "bottom-up democracy", where individual and collective participation in society is defined. These intermediate spaces also reveal the power of active minorities: citizens who want their voices heard and to act. By building resistance, these spaces can reconcile individuals' social identities and self-identities, creating a new, mutual recognition which structures interactions. In doing so, they become spaces for reconciliation.

Compressed Individuals develop their identity in both Chinese society and in world society where they fight for social and public recognition. They try to find their place in local and international labour markets, including community-based spaces in democratic societies such as those in Europe. They develop the capacity for individual and collective action by creating professional, cultural and artistic associations to render themselves visible and make their voices heard.

In the first chapter, we address the subaltern condition of young low-skilled migrants in China by examining the forms of urban segregation, their access to only disqualifying and low-legitimated employment opportunities and the forms of social discrimination they endure. We demonstrate how these young migrants undertake floating labour in hegemonic labour regimes within the context of compressed modernity, and are forced to incorporate the norms of emotional capitalism and have their positive emotions confiscated. We describe the protests, anger and collective action initiated in factory dormitories that mobilise both 农民工 *nongmingong* (young migrant workers) and 打工妹 *dagongmei* (young female workers). Finally, drawing on the effects of collisions present in multi-compressed modernity, we investigate the different ways biographical crossroads form and the modes of differentiation between young migrants' migratory careers, i.e. exclusive, inclusive, weak and strong subalternity.

In the second chapter, we examine how a new generation of Chinese youth with diverse migratory experiences stands out from the previous one in their attempt to transition from autonomy as an aspiration to autonomy as a condition by internalising the injunction to become a hero of Chinese society. The subject of the "successful" young migrant that can become "a hero" is at the heart of multi-compressed modernity, leaving them little space and time to connect with themselves. Another face of the *Compressed Individual* therefore comes to light, marked by an *economy of arrogance* (Favereau, 2015) which produces restricted autonomy in contracted spaces and temporalities. Compressed Individuals are able to resist emotional capitalism and socialism and are adept at appropriating interstitial and intermediate spaces where they can create new individual and collective identities.

In the third chapter, we see how some young Chinese migrants produce local cosmopolitanisms in international cities in China. Here, internal and international migrations intersect, interact and coexist. The *Compressed Individual* is globalised and we begin to understand how different regimes of compressed modernity intertwine to produce multi-compressed modernity through internal (domestic) and international Chinese migrations. Through the production of covert or overt economic cosmopolitanisms, internal and international migrants mobilise to create local and global, inter-ethnic cooperative economic systems, building a society that is both local and multi-ethnic. We will observe how economies of hospitality merge with trust economies in trade hubs governed by shared economic and religious conventions and norms.

In the fourth chapter, we analyse how economic cosmopolitanisms place compressed individuals into a world society in which some of them circulate. While migrants with more resources may find their expected place at their destination society, those with less resources are assigned to ethnic enclaves and niches. Young Chinese economic elites produce global work in a *cosmopolitan spirit* (Ciccelli, 2012). Young Chinese migrants try to find a place in *bazaar economies* (Geertz, 2007) and transnational spaces and many of them will experience violent ethnic discrimination and racism.

Finally, the last chapter focuses on the moral careers of young Chinese migrants in the diverse range of migratory experiences in China and abroad. Such careers show how the *Compressed Individual* emerges on a local and global scale and within the Chinese family sphere, migrates and re-migrates and the effects of collisions in multi-compressed modernity affect biographies to varying degrees. The resulting *polygamic biographies* demonstrate how young migrants are forced to implement readjustments and identity changes. Emotional capitalism, like "emotional socialism", rapidly converts aspirations into *emodities* (Illouz, 2019) and comes in various forms for different categories of migrants. Multi-compressed modernity thus raises the question of societal inequalities manufactured around the world, and of what is decent or indecent in a world society.

CHAPTER 1

Young Chinese Migrants, Subalternity and the *Compressed Individual*

The urbanisation rate of the Chinese population increased from 18% in 1978 to 59% in 2017. From the 1980s onwards, a process of social stratification developed with the establishment of middle classes, the working class, and different economically inactive, unemployed or partially unemployed social groups. The increasing complexity of urban structures, the differentiation of social groups, the diversification of socio-economic trajectories and an unequal access to social mobility produced a social division of space. Income inequalities are becoming increasingly marked between different social classes. Li Peilin (2012), Lu Xueyi (2002), Li Qiang (2012) and other sociologists insist on the different forms of social fragmentation that are the product of an environment characterised by the concurrent process of economic transition and structural transformation. We will consider differentiated regimes of urban subalternity based on the experiences of low-skilled young migrants in the Chinese context. Introducing the subaltern condition means considering an intersectional process of spatial segregation, economic insecurity, moral disqualification and social reproduction. To live in a subaltern condition means a dynamic process of oscillations and reversibilities between strong, partial segregation and integration, between affiliative and disaffiliative spatial/professional mobility, but also means exclusions and expulsions. Finally, subalternity also means addressing the struggle for dignity through the fabric of subpolitics and collective action.

1 New Urban Boundaries and Migratory Ordeals in China

From 1949 to 1979, Chinese cities had a clear structure focused around the 单位 *danwei* (labour unit) which protected employees of state-owned companies. Cities drifted away from this model towards a more in egalitarian one layered with tensions, ordeals and apartness. Up until the mid-1980s, Chinese metropolises were characterised by its residents' low mobility due to the 户口 *hukou* system. Control of population movements resulted in very limited growth in Chinese cities. Chinese urban society has become increasingly stratified and is becoming more and more diversified in terms of the

© LAURENCE ROULLEAU-BERGER, 2021 | DOI:10.1163/9789004463080_003

composition of socio-occupational categories: upper, middle and working classes, individuals who are economically inactive, unemployed or on short-time working arrangements. This emphasises how the urban and social structures has become more complex, social groups more differentiated, residential trajectories more diverse and access to social mobility unequal. The structure of Chinese urban society has thus changed radically since the economic reforms began. After 1978, social mobility pathways started diversifying and the structural barriers to mobility were to be redefined. Li Chunling (2008) shows how economic capital played a crucial role in social mobility prior to 1949 but became a negative factor between 1949 and 1980. She also demonstrated that cultural and economic capital has come to play a decisive role in contemporary modes of constructing social mobility. The paradox of the reforms has increased opportunities for mobility and at the same time made the urban boundaries between the social groups clearer. The emergence of the middle class in an urban society in the process of modernising and moving towards the market Chinese and global economy very closely reflects the structural evolution of society. Middle classes have very rapidly become stratified as part of the general stratification process in Chinese society, and an awareness of belonging to the middle classes is developing. Professional and residential mobility is growing, creating increased inequalities and social distance, leading to conflicts and tensions. China's economy has been expanding rapidly over the last thirty years; migrant workers will remain a major driving force of this growth (Li Peilin, 2008). However, with the decline of socialist institutions, young migrant workers also experience situations of insecurity and heightened vulnerability, meaning they oscillate between urban integration, segregation and marginalisation. The less-qualified are confronted with a real deprivation of social rights leading to new forms of poverty, new injustices and new forms of marginalisation (Roulleau-Berger, 2007b).

A first line of fragmentation emerges between cities and rural areas, a second line of fragmentation between blue-collar and white-collar workers, yet more specifically between the new middle classes and blue-collar workers. A third line is visible between those with legal employment statuses in the market economy and those forced to work in informal employment situations in an illegal, or even criminal, economy. Sun Liping (2003) introduced the concept of 断裂社会 *duanlie shehui* (fractured society), emphasising the rapidity of the social polarisation process—one that has developed over the last decade. Urban society has therefore dualised—on one side the new middle classes live in gated communities—and on the other social groups live in impoverished districts. The majority are migrant workers, some of whom had previously experienced upward mobilities in urban areas, are now subject to a succession of downward mobilities.

From 1989 onwards with the decline of the socialist/Maoist structures of control and the gradual disappearance of industrial complexes and *danwei*, housing reforms foster private ownership and the rise of spatial mobility strategies on a professional and residential level. Access to the private property market is a recent phenomenon in China. City-dwellers' lifestyles are taking form, especially in the middle classes. They participate in a gentrification process and live in closed residences, modelled on gated communities. Alongside the middle classes, a "new" urban youth with average social capital is moving to the large cities. Additionally, young low-skilled migrants are arriving in growing numbers in Chinese cities and face material, social, urban and moral challenges. While the social boundaries between large cities and rural areas in China are very distinct, they are more and more striking between young migrant graduates and young low-skilled migrants in Chinese cities this last decade (Li Chunling, 2017). New socio-spatial and socio-economic divisions coupled with a hierarchical diversification of professional and residential mobilities are creating escalating inequalities, opening wider social gaps and generating tension and conflict.

Today four categories of residents can be identified in Chinese cities: the so-called "illegal" migrants, rural migrants, urban migrants and the "official" population. The segregation process dividing the urban and rural population can be observed in the construction of discriminatory behaviour towards migrants. Under the *hukou* system, temporary migrants without the urban *hukou*, even those settled for many years, are disadvantaged compared to residents or permanent migrants with an urban *hukou*. From the 1990s onwards, the urban *hukou* authority was transferred from the central government to local governments and many cities also took measures to eliminate the distinction between the rural and *hukou* in each city. Nonetheless, the most affluent classes, especially the new middle classes, can acquire an urban *hukou* more easily. Relaxing the reform of the *hukou* system narrowed the gaps between rural and urban society, yet the social boundaries that existed between cities and rural areas were reassembled in Chinese cities by creating new social distances between internal migrants and city residents. While the policy of relaxing the *hukou* system partially erased geographical boundaries and decreased inequalities between rural and urban society, it did not reduce inequalities between 外地人 *waidiren* (outsiders) and the 流动人口 *liudong renkou* (floating population). Instead, as Li Chunling (2019) aptly demonstrated, it accentuated the phenomenon in which intergenerational social inequalities are reproduced between young skilled people and the new generation of young low-skilled migrants. Today around 70% of young Chinese live in cities and are divided into groups due to the new urban and rural barriers. Students and university graduates live on one side and the new generation of migrant workers on the other. Although both groups live in the city, there are clear differences in terms of living standards, behaviours and values and many hurdles impede the upward social mobility of youth from rural areas (Li Peilin, 2019a). The restrictions imposed on the new generation of migrant workers and their lack of professional qualifications prevent any prospect of social mobility and access to the status of Chinese citizen. These young migrant workers share a collective sense of frustration and social, moral and economic injustice. Unlike the previous generation of migrants, they are aware of their subaltern condition; they fight for social rights and demand social recognition. Workplace conflicts are multiplying and tensions between young skilled people and young migrants are intensifying in the urban space. The struggle to find a place in society and the class struggle are superimposed on the internal borders of Chinese cities.

Young less-qualified migrants are subjects to stigmatisation by the host population when arriving in large Chinese cities. They are labelled and treated as outsiders, are overlooked and have access to an inferior status and salary compared with residents. Urban authorities actively participate in promoting discrimination against migrants by labelling them a homogenous social group comprised of poor and rootless individuals. In other words, they are portrayed as individuals without any historical footing and considered ineligible to be members of Chinese society (Li Zhang, 2002). Migrants are compared with dangerous classes and are viewed as a threat to public order. Some residents see them as their direct competitors in accessing public services such as water, electricity, public transport, and food. The hostility and inhospitality of Chinese cities towards migrants, especially the most underprivileged, have escalated in recent years. Urban living conditions for members of the working class and lower middle-class segments have degenerated and unemployment has soared. These residents strongly remonstrate the Chinese government accountable in their eyes for not implementing policies to reduce social inequalities and improve public services. Consequently, residents exclude migrant workers they blame for trying to take the social and economic resources they have lost (Liu Jian Kun, Xu Hong Zhi, 2019). This feeling of loss of self transforms into a desire to reject the migrants seen as undesirables. The background of these workers strongly highlights the processes of social disqualification they suffer which they qualify as unjust in view of the presence of young migrant workers in the city. Situations involving competition, conflict and urban violence are a frequent occurrence in the public spaces of large Chinese cities. Social and moral boundaries are increasingly marked between migrant workers and the local residents 本体人 *benti ren* who participate in their exclusion from the City.

As a result, young low-skilled migrant workers develop intracontinental multi-mobilities, i.e. successive mobilities from rural to urban labour markets and vice-versa. Nevertheless, a significant number of these migrants find themselves in "illegal" situations because they have no temporary residence permit. They are thus exposed to acute social and economic vulnerability and live in impoverished areas. Forced to pursue multiple geographical mobilities, they develop many increasingly diverse and complex professional pathways in line with their social, economic and symbolic resources, including family and social networks. A hierarchy for finding employment and housing governs the organisational structure of the fragmented and disparate Chinese city. Young low-skilled migrants with a limited repertoire of roles struggle to acquire positions of social recognition. The lifestyles of young migrants in Chinese cities oscillate between integrations and nonlinear, reversible segregations. They are voiceless, placeless, deprived of positive recognition and forced to be themselves against and in the face of domination. They are assigned invisible roles and marginalised in spaces of no-rights. In consequence, young migrants and the least qualified migrants from the new 基层阶级 *jiceng jieqi* (urban underclass)in Chinese metropolises.

2   Young Migrants and Urban Segregation

Some young migrant workers still live in 城中村 *chengzhongcun* (urban villages)today. In the 2000's the "urban village", with its own urban characteristics unique to Chinese cities, first appeared in Guangzhou, Beijing, Shanghai, Shenzhen and Xian. These are villages that have been absorbed by the urbanisation process and turned into urban enclaves. They retain a degree of autonomy in matters of local and economic governance and are home to farmers who lost their lands and protections stemming from their rural inscriptions (Li Peilin, 2008). This phenomenon reflects the inherent paradoxes in the growing complexity of Chinese urban society. These urban villages are shared by former peasants turned urban landowners and new low-skilled migrants looking for affordable housing. Young migrants labelled "illegals" and rural migrants also live in these urban zones. Populations that settle in urban villages may have had their lands seized or move to find temporary work, i.e. to start a small business. Urban villages have emerged in Chinese cities as distinct urban forms and zones of survival for migrants who establish local markets amongst themselves (Li Peilin, 2019b).

These 蚁族 *yizu* (ant tribes)—to use the term coined by Lian Si (2009)—emerge in different areas on the periphery of Chinese metropolises like Beijing, leading to new phenomena of urban distancing where soaring unemployment rates and economic precarity become more visible."Youth came from all over China to make their dreams come true in Beijing, yet the majority did not expect to be forced to live in a disorganised village in the suburbs north-east of the city." Lian Si (2009) notes that "[...] they closely resemble intelligent and gregarious ants [...]", describing urban villages as "ant tribes". These villages are situated in transition zones between rural areas and the city, appearing through a process of accelerated urbanisation and called home by migrants, rural dwellers and even young graduates in precarity. For example, one of the largest and most famous "ant tribes" was the village of Tangjialing 20km North of Beijing. In 2014, an estimated 20,000 low-income university graduates lived there. The village was made up of narrow streets: small shops, restaurants, street vendors and a hall with various stores selling spices, meat, vegetables and noodles crowded the main street. Chinese youth lived in two or three-story buildings; several roommates shared a single room in unsanitary conditions. Half of these 八零后 *balinghou*, or Chinese youth born after 1980, came from a rural area. In Lian Si's survey (2009) in Tangjialing,61.5% worked unpaid overtime, 32.2% had no employment contract and 36.4% had no social security (sick leave, unemployment and retirement benefits). Of the total,58.5% had been unemployed for a month and 98.6% had never received unemployment benefits. The "ant tribe districts" revealed new processes of urban marginalisation in the city and *mingongisation* (proletarianisation) (Liu Ziqin, 2014).

Urban villages, situated in areas of urban transition between cities and rural areas, have emerged in a process of accelerated urbanisation where an increasing number of young migrant workers, especially youths, are arriving. These urban villages are akin to *slums*, where poor city dwellers live while working in informal sectors. We note that the plural and diverse forms of urban villages result in unique differences between those established in Beijing, Shanghai and Guangzhou. Wu Fulong (2016) conducted a study of 60 urban villages in these three Chinese cities. He found that regulatory practices were implemented differently in urban villages in Guangzhou as the local government was quite flexible in a growing rental market. In Shanghai, the housing market relies on expanding construction spaces. In Beijing, students with few resources, especially those migrating from different provinces, flock to urban villages for cheap housing. Most residents do not have an urban *hukou*. In fact, migratory movements have been increasing at a steady pace since 1985 and the weakening of *hukou* system has led to widespread open mobilities. In Guangzhou for example, only 12.5% of residents have a Guangzhou *hukou*. On average, 30% of the population have the educational equivalent to the general baccalaureate diploma. Urban villages can first be defined as informal settlements structured around an illegal housing market (no official leases). How can the question of informality be addressed? For Wu Fulong (2013), informality results from economic policies based on the development and management of informal regulations, and even more so from overlapping social, political and economic dimensions in the context of urban growth and a dual rural-urban land market. The diversity of urban villages reflects the variations of informality in different cities and differentiated configurations of relationships between State, market, land and city dwellers. Informality translates into sales and lease contracts and practices of an informal nature that define a construction of unregulated housing. Informality also means a high population density, poor housing and sanitary conditions:

> I used to live in a dormitory, but after my marriage, my husband came here so we both preferred to move and rent a house. It's more practical [...] the dormitory is good when you're young, it's easy to sleep at night even if it's noisy [...] it's more suited to single people! Before, we all lived in the dormitory, 8–10 people per room, now I see that a lot of girls leaving the dormitory to rent rooms for more peace and quiet at home [...] but the pressure is very strong [...] rental prices here cost a fortune, and still here in Sanxiang it's cheaper than elsewhere. But when you see that in Yajule (the city centre) an apartment on average costs 1,000–1,500 yuan and you earn 3,000 yuan, you tell yourself that you have no choice, that you can't [...] the pressure is strong for us [...] and buying here is simply impossible. It is too expensive, often there is no kitchen, so most people eat dinner at the factory. My husband and I have a small room with a bed, boxes with clothes and basins for washing. Opposite, there is an electric stove with pots and pans, it's very small, but we have no choice [...] rent is too expensive in the city and we're just across the street from the factory here, so we don't lose time in transport and we don't have any transport costs either. This is the job life 打工 *dagong* (looking for a job). It won't be like this forever, one day we'll have our own house with my brother, we're building our house in 老家 *laojia* (hometown), where your two children are staying with my parents!
>
> JUAN, woman, 25 years old, Guizhou origin, interview conducted in 2016

Urban villages were called 'ant tribes', such as Tangjialing in Beijing, the informal housing blocks in and the vertical urban village in Guangzhou. Young migrants continue to flock to these villages for the low rental prices. These urban enclaves reveal new processes of marginalisation and social segregation within Chinese cities. They are linked to forms of unemployment, emerging precarity and systems of structural disqualification which target young Chinese, especially young migrants.

In parallel with the process of hyper-urbanisation, the demolition of illegal dwellings and urban villages is on the rise. The central and local governments still want to put in place forms of top-down political management, offset the lack of infrastructure and address sanitation in these urban enclaves, all without considering the practices, uses and needs of urban village residents. In 2008, the Ministry of Housing called on local governments to mobilise the residents for urban renovations, to improve their lifestyle and living conditions, to redraft land use conditions and to resolve migrant workers' housing issues. These urban policies disregarded the "voiceless" and resulted in the eviction of young migrant workers from cities. Within the framework of urban policies, demolitions are envisaged as spatial reconfigurations radically changing the ecological structure of cities, denying residents' relationships with their communities, their social ties, to violently impose removals upon them. After the time needed to rebuild these urban villages, the least affluent migrants cannot access the new housing, whose rent is very high, nor access social rental housing. This top-down and one-way urban governance logic not only meet the current strict control policy of migrants, but also strengthen the institutional social exclusion of migrants, it means ruptures and fragmentation in their social life (Zhao Yeqin, 2018). They are then subject to expulsion from Chinese cities. Above all, the demolition of urban villages signifies the destruction of neighbourly relations and social networks. Furthermore, outside urban villages, strong property development and real estate pressure paves the way to demolish homes deemed 'dilapidated' and evict their owners. In 2011, the newspaper *Nangfang Dushibao* reported the suicide of a villager in Changsha, Hunan province, following the refusal of her claim for housing compensation. Property rights only last 70 years in China, expropriation is common, and suicides are multiplying. In the public space since the 1990s, besides the mobilisation of homeowners because of the housing reform, other forms of protests linked to housing have emerged: protests against the destructions of entire neighbourhoods and the violent eviction of their residents; the creation of homeowners' committees as intermediate actors in neighbourhood communities (Merle, 2014). Evictions, especially those of the private ownership apartment tenants—that is to say long-term tenants and migrants—have set off strong mobilisations which rely on the claim for a right to the city (Gransow, 2014) in the sense of Henri Lefebvre, which is the right to indemnification, to maintaining one's social insertion in neighbourhood networks and a neighbourhood identity endowed with a history and a memory.

Clan-based organisational life in urban villages facilitate small-scale urban production in the interstices of society. They emerge as a result of enduring socialist institutions and the government's gradual withdrawal. Young migrants participate in limited economic activities such as illegal selling, rubbish collection and drinking water delivery. They also run small shops and work as street vendors, create microenterprises and develop simple urban occupations; it means a new category of small entrepreneurs has emerged. A "culture of the poor" blossoms in urban villages around the ability to tinker, salvage, and trade goods and services by employing major and minor social practices. This showcases young migrants that are both dominated yet capable of invention, *the art of making do* and tactics of the *weakest* against the *strongest* (de Certeau, 1980). In urban villages, macro and micro-economies are constantly embedded and disembedded in an all-pervading Chinese sui generis capitalism. These imbrications, alternating between continuous and discontinuous, highlight the hard segmentarities (Deleuze, 1980) inherited from an authoritarian government, and soft or rhizomatic segmentarities that form in a market economy environment. In essence, this intertwined process of globalisation, megalopolisation, and rhizomatic segmentarities appears to invigorate the Chinese market economy.

3 Labour and Subalternity

Shen Yuan (2011) showed how China had become a museum of productive systems wherein small-scale production systems—namely the handicrafts sector and family workshops (Guiheux, 2012), state-owned companies stemming from the legacy of the planned economy, and economic labour organisations linked to a globalised, monopoly capitalism—coexisted with companies from developed countries that moved offshore and foreign companies that occupied an important place in the manufacturing, construction, real estate and service sectors. While from 2005 there was a resurgence of the public sector, in 2010 the government retained ownership of only the most strategic companies [...] In this context, Chinese labour markets will strongly segment with the arrival of low-skilled migrant workers. China's megalopolises, structured by *archipelago economies* (Veltz, 2008) foster conjunctions and disjunctions between distinct segments of labour markets. Labour markets are emerging that cannot be reduced to primary markets or secondary markets, where precarious populations would be relegated. Indeed, urban labour markets in

Chinese megalopolises have become increasingly segmented with the rise of economic niches in which young low-skilled migrants are concentrated (Li Chunling, 2008; Roulleau-Berger, Shi Lu, 2004a).

According to a major national survey conducted in 2001 by the Institute of Sociology of the Chinese Academy of Social Sciences (Li Chunling, 2005) from a sample of 6,193 individuals aged 16 to 70 across 73 cities and 12 provinces, migrant populations had the following characteristics: 51% male and 49% female, 57.4% aged 16 to 30, 35.3% aged 31 to 50. Of the total, 88.2% had a rural *hukou*, 68.1% married, 77.4% employed and 22.6% unemployed. In terms of education, 25.4% had a primary school level, 46.5% had a secondary school level, and 19.1% had a high school level. Turning to employment, 28.2% were self-employed, 30.2% worked in the service sector and 18% in the industry sector. Of the total, 56.3% considered their work situation unstable and 90.3% received no social security benefits. Most of the migrants were young, poorly qualified and poorly educated in situations of precarity, and self-employed or employed in low-legitimised sectors. The outcome of a second major national survey conducted by the Chinese Academy of Social Sciences revealed similar statistics (Li Chunling, 2008).

Until 2008, most migrant workers had no employment contract and were considered supernumeraries in China's labour markets. For example, in 2007 we met a young 32-year-old worker from Hebei who had finished middle school in a rural area. After his studies, he worked in the fields. When there was not enough work in the fields, he sold rice at the market with his older brother. He earned some money and decided to leave his native region. In 1995, he moved to Beijing to join his great uncle who offered him a job in a brick factory. He worked there as a brick transporter. In this state-owned company, he had no employment contract or insurance cover, it was a temporary job. He was paid per cubic metre of bricks and earned 1.4 yuan. He received no bonus, had no fixed schedule and worked 10-hour days. He had no time off; he could only take a break when it rained. The working conditions were very poor and very hard.

Based on data from the survey questionnaire on migrant workers in the Pearl River Delta from 2006 to 2010 and recent field surveys (Sun Zhong Wei, Liu Ming Wei, Jia Hai long, 2018), it was found that the enactment of the Labour Law led to more employment contracts being signed and an increase in permanent employment contracts. This encouraged companies to develop new forms of social governance and draw up human resources management and social security policies for their employees. Although China's Labour Contract Law improved migrant workers' collective rights to a certain extent, the institutionalisation of the employment contract fostered an individuation process in labour relations. The introduction of employment contracts prompted migrant workers to defend their rights collectively. They no longer feared dismissal knowing that they would be eligible for compensation. Moreover, the institutionalisation of employment contracts has reduced the sources of workplace conflict, by relying on the norms of injunction to flexibility and mobility which further encouraged young migrants to cooperate at in the workplace in a context of personalised relationships.

In 2010, 44.7% of migrant workers in Shanghai were employed in the production and transport sectors, 64% of workers lived in Shanghai in the Pudong New Area, Minghang, Songjiang, Jiading and Baoshan districts (see Figure 1). Young migrant workers are acquiring more and more technical qualifications. A sharp rise in the number of qualified migrant workers can be observed in recent times. According to data from the 2015 1% National Population Sample Survey, young migrant workers account for 60% of jobs: 25.6% of young migrants aged 16–30 work in the manufacturing industry, 20.3% in wholesale and retail trade, 13.9% in hotels and restaurants. Nonetheless, 34.6% of migrant workers are employed without a contract.

Young migrants moved to Shanghai from Anhui, Jiangsu, Henan, Yunnan, Gansu and sometimes northern China. Today, the technical qualification level of low-skilled young migrants without a Shanghai *hukou* has increased, yet more than half are restricted to low-skilled sectors of activity.

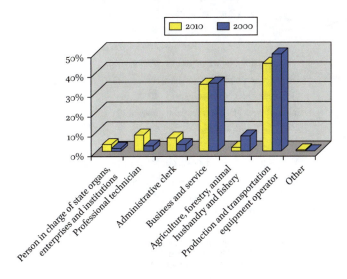

FIGURE 1   Evolution of migrant worker occupations with a Shanghai hukou in 2000 and 2010
SOURCE: CHINA LABOUR BULLETIN

China's labour markets are today facing a new reality, in particular with the young migrant workers situation. The education system has significantly improved by allowing the rural population to enrol, and wages are steadily climbing. Despite this, migrant workers are still being marginalised in Chinese cities. Analysis of migrant worker groups conducted by the Chinese Academy of Social Sciences from 2006 to 2015 revealed a trend of downward mobility for their social trajectories and an increased feeling of social disqualification (Tian Feng, 2017). Despite a rise in young migrant workers' educational level, wages have made no real progress. Many young migrants are prepared to give up the possibility of higher education, leading to a new roadblock in access to social mobility in rural areas. The ongoing deterioration young migrant workers' social condition can still be observed.

In 2017 in Shanghai, 24.6% of young migrants aged 18–30 with no *hukou* worked in the production sector, 10.41% in the catering industry, 7.44% in construction, 5.84% in the transport and equipment sectors and 9.04% in wholesale and retail trade. Of the total, 57% of young migrants worked in low-skilled sectors, and 10.76% in the information sector and computer

FIGURE 2   Occupations of migrants aged 18–30 years without a Shanghai hukou 2017 (%)
SOURCE: SHANGHAI URBAN NEIGHBOURHOOD SURVEY (SUNS) (N=874)

services (see Figure 2). Despite improved educational levels, the chances of upward social mobility are clearly low. Irregular employment has been developed in emerging industries over the last decade. More and more young low-skilled migrants work on digital platforms for e-commerce, express delivery, group-purchase, food delivery and taxi-hailing services, which have grown rapidly in recent years. According to China Labour Bulletin, it is estimated that these industries employed around 70 million people in 2017. Young migrants, both male and female, join micro-work platforms without the relevant employment status associated for the work activity and become "click-slaves" (Casilli, 2019), performing unskilled tasks at home for poverty wages.

As we can see with Chen, young migrant women interviewed in 2018, can thus reconcile precarious economic lives with their family lives. Here a young migrant woman with a low level of education, after working as a worker in an electronics company, becomes a cosmetics sales rep and then enters the e-commerce world to escape from manual, low-skilled labour.

Chen, 35 years old, was born in the countryside in Guangdong, near Meizhou. She has two sisters and a little brother. One of her sisters was adopted by her childless aunt. She grew up in a poor village to peasant parents and did not have the chance to study. At the age of 16, she moved to Shenzhen to join a friend. She initially worked in an electronics factory, earning 700/800 RMB per month. She worked 10 hours per day, living in a dormitory with 15 people per room furnished with bunk beds. Six months later, she changed factories to work shorter days. She was hired in another electronics factory, taking evening computer classes for three years because she wanted to improve. She was 20 years old: "I didn't want to go back to my 老家 *laojia* (native region), what for? I wanted to find a good job, maybe work in an office." She worked as a cosmetics sales representative for 8 hours a day, earning 2,000 RMB a month. Her rent was very expensive. Her parents insisted that she marry. She met her husband through a client, who worked in Taipei at the hospital. He was seven years older than her, a university graduate and a Catholic. Her friends had got married to Taiwanese men or had Taiwanese friends. Her future husband came to China and he started visiting her two to three times a year. They got married after two years, but her parents were unhappy. Her husband was hired by a company in Dongguan. She gave birth in Taiwan so that her child could have Taiwanese nationality, and they would perhaps move to Taiwan for his schooling. But for the moment her child is going to the nursery and they don't need to move. They also bought a house in Dongguan. She stopped working after marriage, but she buys in代购 *daigou* (bulk purchasing) every time they go to

Taiwan and brings back products to resell in China. Additionally, her friends also send products from Taiwan every Monday.

Today Chen is a member of a WeChat group of young Chinese migrants married to Taiwanese men and live in Dongguan. They meet from time to time for activities. For Chen, e-commerce is

> a good way to earn money without having to break my back in the factory [...] I can take care of deliveries, and shipments at night while my child sleeps, or even during the day [...] the products that I import from Taiwan are good quality, they are difficult to find here or very expensive [...] My sister who married with a Hong Kong man is sending me a lot of cosmetics from Hong Kong which I am reselling [...] the payment on WeChat is practical and I avoid that problems with Hong Kong and Taiwanese customs. I can order powder milk, face masks, lipstick [...] even very good quality or inexpensive baby products [...] take pictures of my friends in Taiwan and I mail them on my WeChat, I tell them the price [...] the mothers here or my friends contact me, I tell them the price, they tell me what the quantity they want. They pay me via the 红包 *hukou* (red envelope). As soon as I receive the money, I go to the post office and send a parcel or see if someone can bring back the goods [...] For example, my neighbour had to go to Meizhou, near my village, so I gave her cakes from Taiwan and cosmetic products to give to my cousin's wife."
>
> Interview conducted in April 2018

The fact that forms of nineteenth-century piecework are re-emerging through micro-working platforms reflects the clashes between pre-modernity, modernity and post-modernity inherent in multi-compressed modernity. Microtask crowdsourcing was launched by the American web giant Amazon and is now practiced by the Chinese giant Alibaba Group. Underpaid workers are now drawing attention their difficulties: their time is exploited, the time needed to perform task is underestimated, unpaid tasks and technical work technical and the non-compliance with the minimum wage (Barraud de Lagerie, Sigalo Santos, 2019). In China, the number of young migrant workers on these platforms has risen sharply. While in European countries such as France, workers'activity on the platforms is not their sole occupation; this is not the case in China due to the low levels of professionalisation of low-skilled migrant workers, such as Uber workers. In China, in platform capitalism, the organisation of labour and tasks is fragmented. Additionally, work autonomy, the control mechanisms for work performed and working hours have been discreetly and effectively reinforced. Workers are classified, evaluated and rated by consumers, and encouraged to "always work more" to participate in this platform capitalism (Wu Qing Jun, Li Zhen, 2018). While disputes involving crowdworking platforms receive little media coverage in China, China Labour Bulletin's Strike Map recorded 11 protests and strikes in the food delivery business in 2017.

4   Employment and Social Discrimination

Labour market segmentation and discrimination need to be examined together to understand how economic niches form, occupied largely by young migrants. Liu Shiding (2012) considered that discrimination against migrants in the labour markets is at the same time institutional, social and legal:

– *institutional discrimination*: in certain provinces, local governments attempt to control the mass arrival of migrant workers. They set employment caps on migrant workers from another province and order every city to comply with the fixed quotas. All employers must register the number of migrant workers they plan on hiring with the local authorities. Nonetheless, local authorities rarely check the numbers because they know that companies do not always comply with their discriminatory policies targeting migrant workers. Employers prefer to hire more productive migrant workers they can pay less. These discriminatory policies play a major role in the regulation and segmentation of labour markets and are strengthened by the fact that most migrant workers are not holders of an urban *hukou*, which is the key to accessing occupational accident insurance, healthcare and retirement benefits.

– *Social discrimination*: competition with the "autochthonous" workers creates barriers for high-skilled migrant workers entering the local labour markets and legitimises employers' discriminatory choices. In a 2002 study on temporary residents from rural areas conducted in collaboration between the National Bureau of Statistics of China and the Economic Research Institute of the Chinese Academy of Social Sciences, Li Chunling (2008) noted that just 7.2% of rural workers were employed in the public sector, 5.5%worked in urban socially-owned companies, 0.6% worked in mixed capital companies and 86.7% worked for independent companies.

– *Legal discrimination*: the non-compliance of Chinese employers with the Labour Law results in legal discrimination. Before 2008, workplace relations often had no contractual basis or were based on short renewable contracts or one-year contracts in Chinese companies as can be seen in this interview with a young migrant worker in 2008:

"We had initially agreed on a bonus, but at the end of the year, the construction site didn't pay it to me. In addition, the salary was supposed to be 45 RMB a day, but in the end, they only paid me 40 RMB a day. I was angry. In fact, they were taking advantage of me, since there was no written contract, so they did whatever they wanted. He explained to me that they deducted 5 RMB for meals, but they had initially promised me free board and lodging. That was why I didn't want to work for them anymore, so I quit. I found another construction company in Beijing. At this new construction site, the safety equipment was very poor. I worked there for several months, but on June 11, 1997, there was a very serious accident. Part of the site collapsed. A friend who was working just a few metres beside me was pierced by steel rods and died a few hours later. I was very scared. Some workers were seriously injured. I therefore resigned immediately the same day."

Workers in both state and private-owned companies had no written employment contracts and workplace health and safety regulations were not met.

The majority of migrants had temporary employment, had a short-term contract or were self-employed compared to local urban workers who had stable or long-term employment. According to a 2005 study by the Institute of Population and Labour Economics of the Chinese Academy of Social Sciences, the leading sociologist indicated that 52.3% of urban labourers had basic health insurance compared to just 6.8% of migrants.

Despite the introduction of the 2008 Labour Contract Law, young low-skilled migrants today still frequently work in unstable employment conditions with low wages and no prospect of upward professional mobility. In the same way, social security benefits are still not completely guaranteed, and some workers are still paid on a piece-rate basis. In some private companies, the length of a normal work day can stretch to 14 hours. The following practices are commonplace: no meal breaks, sleep deprivation for night workers and unpaid overtime at the current rate. In some sectors, in particular the construction sector, young migrant workers are only paid annually. However, since they have no employment contract, they cannot appeal in case their salary or bonus is not paid to them. Furthermore, when young migrant workers are paid by month or by season, they usually receive part of their salary up front and the rest either upon completion of the project or at Chinese New Year. Young migrants complain of poor working conditions; they are aware of the non-compliance with health and safety standards and feel like they are performing *dirty work*.

Many factors have triggered an overexploitation of labourers comprised of low-skilled migrant workers, including the closing of many state-owned enterprises, the intensification of work, new quality criteria and integration into the global economy.

Li Zhengang and Zhang Jianbao (2020) analyzed the scale of rural migrant workers with different employment models and their risks of in-work poverty, as well as the mechanism and constraints of in-work poverty based on the National Migrant Population Health and Family Planning Dynamic Monitoring Survey Data of 2017. In a study in eight Chinese cities, found that informal employment is the main mode and means of employment for migrant workers in big cities, the result shows that 81% of the migrant workers are employed in the non-standard employment model, while only 19% in the standard employment model. The incidence of poverty among formally employed rural migrant workers is 9,9%, compared to 15% among migrant workers in informal employment and 12% per cent among migrant workers in self-employment. Low hourly wages, rather than underemployment, are the main labour market mechanism leading to working poverty over a short time. Of course, underemployment and part-time work also have a significant impact on poverty. However, the majority of migrant workers work overtime rather than underemployment. Therefore, regulating working hours and reducing the number of hours worked by migrant workers are issues that need to be addressed simultaneously. The higher the level of educational attainment, the lower the risk of falling into poverty.

In the service sector, young migrants are relegated to bonded working the emerging personal services sector in China, comprised of many low-skilled female migrant workers. Care work consists of many activities which traditionally belong to the domestic sphere. Low-skilled rural migrants generally work as domestic help and are assigned tasks such as childcare, elderly care and housework. With the rapid onset of social stratification in Chinese society, middle-class women hire less qualified women to take care of their children. This is a new phenomenon in China that, before the reforms, would have been impossible. Care work reflects the process of social stratification where in women are forced into work situations with no social recognition. Migrants employed as housekeepers see this work as shameful and keep their true occupation a secret from their villages, claiming instead to be labourers or supermarket employees. These women are also subject to contempt by housekeepers in large Chinese cities with whom they find themselves in competition on the care market.

Very young migrants generally work as domestic help and are assigned tasks such as childcare, elderly care and housework. They also work in massage salons, karaoke bars and become "hostesses" in hotels, and find themselves forced into sex work. Donguan and Zhongshan, cities in the Guangdong province, are popular sex tourism destinations recommended by various websites. For example, Taiwanese tourists enjoy 光华街 *guanghuajie* (lit. buying the street flower), where they choose their favourite girl out of one hundred (Chen Mei Hua, 2013). The number of young female migrants turning to sex work after arriving in the city is on the rise.

Furthermore, the presence of male migrants in company dormitories leads to a sex industry being established in urban areas, due to the combined effect of globalising Chinese labour markets and violence targeting impoverished female migrants. Unable to endure the conditions of extreme violence in Chinese workplaces where they can find employment, these young women turn to the sex industry to acquire financial resources essential for their families' survival (Liu Linping, Li Chaohai, 2009). The sex industry is becoming less stigmatised in Chinese cities as city-dwellers are aware of the factors causing extreme poverty among migrants. Sex workers internalise the legitimacy of forced sex work by creating an "unspeakable identity" (Pollak, 1993), one which is never revealed to their families in their home villages. They remain decent women in their villages and sex workers in Chinese cities. Sex work is emerging as a very opaque segment of the urban labour market, resulting in limited flexibility which is violently imposed on young female migrants. The care work industry demonstrates how material, emotional and corporal resources (Ehrenreich, Hoschschild, 2004) circulate in the *invisible* Chinese city. Sex work explicitly reflects a new form of the commodification of young female migrants in the context of the economic fragility of certain social categories.

Young low-skilled migrants circulate from one economic niche to another, and from one megalopolis by way of deterritorialisation. They create continuities in economic networks—be they short, long, covert or overt—and if we accept that the economy is also moral, this succession of economic inscriptions engenders situations of moral insecurity which generate social contempt. We can see then how these forms of contempt contain compressed conflicts of social verticality, referring to the struggle between the employers and subaltern groups, and conflicts of social horizontality referring to the struggle to find a place.

5   *Floating Labour,* Hegemonic Labour Regimes and Emotions

While the wage society remains one of the paradigms of privileged society in modern economies, entailing full-time work, an employee's status with an optimal protection system (social security, labour legislation and an employee benefits agreement) and guarantees a path to social integration, different production methods intermingle in the Chinese economy and characterise multicompressed modernity. Young low-skilled migrants constantly oscillate from one job and one space to another without finding a sustainable social, economic or relational foundation. Multi-compressed modernity over mobilises populations of young low-skilled migrants in areas of production and renders them invisible due their intense circulation in a plurality of spaces and temporalities where they are denied citizen status. Floating labour revolves around interconnected economic spaces in a system of *high-order compressed modernity* in which the bodies of young migrant workers are mobilised, disciplined and exploited instead of valued. They face difficulties finding a sustainable footing in the labour markets and thus fall into *low integrative mobilities.*

While the old socialist order extolled a vertical division of work, new global capitalism introduced new hierarchies in multi-compressed modernity. The decline of socialist institutions led to decentralisation and individuation, depriving numerous workers, including rural workers, of their economic, legal and social rights. Floating labour became the dominant norm to ensure the regulation of the labour market and keep underqualified migrants underemployed. The development of temporary work among young migrants demonstrates the extent to which the generations born in the 1990s and 2000s (Roulleau-Berger, 2009; Shen Yuan, 2013) are constrained to endure a succession of spatial and professional mobilities. In practice, this sets them on a path to horizontal social mobility. In the past, Chinese migrants were able to rely on local order which acted as a system social recognition, but now various situations of floating labour force Chinese migrants to continuously circulate, resettle and refer to new normative orders. Floating labour arranges spatially dispersed work situations and reveals local contexts of domination.

Urban labour markets may be defined as institutions of injustice subjecting low-skilled migrants to disregard and anonymity more often than eroding recognition. Given that the experience of injustice, according to Renault (2004), can take the form of a violation of explicitly formulated principles, implicit principles of justice, including situations that are compatible with these two principles of justice, very clear in imposing maximum flexibility. The Chinese urban labour markets as institutions of injustice employ young migrants that emerge as the new supernumeraries in Chinese society; they are either unemployed or employed in a precarious, temporary manner. The young low-skilled migrant figures for the most part as a dominated individual, prevented from maintaining positive self-esteem as a result of the rejection of recognition that altered his or her identity. This rejection should be labelled as contempt given that these institutions of injustice generate different forms of contempt (Honneth, 2000) in a regime of "disorganized despotism" (Lee, 1999) and "disciplinary labour" (Chan and Zhu Xiaoyang, 2003) including violence, humiliation and physical abuse in the workplace.

As can be seen through the eyes of Bao who completely internalised his condition of subalternity.

In 2018, Bao is 31 years old and comes from Sichuan, she has one brother. He didn't finish middle school and moved to Guangzhou. He felt free and far from his family. He worked in a building site as a mason and every evening he cried because his hands hurt. He worked from 7 a.m. to 7 p.m., earning 30 RMB a day. He stayed there for a few months, and then he went North to Heilongjiang with 老乡 *laoxiang* (people from the same hometown) to work on building sites. He stayed there for six months. "The living conditions are terrible, this is what we had to do in order to survive". However, life at the construction site felt freer to him than at the factory. When he was exhausted by construction work, he returned to Guangzhou and worked in a children's toy factory in a very unsanitary environment. His working days were shorter than at the building sites in Northern China. He stayed there for three years and rented a small house in the migrants' neighbourhood not far from the building sites (100 RMB per month). The first time at the factory, he received his salary after three months because of the deposit. In 2012, he married to a young woman from the same village and who works in the same factory as him. His child lives in the countryside with the grandparents, Bao and his wife cannot take care of their child. He bought a house in *laojia*: "we are 打工 *dagong* (workers), not 高层 *gaoceng* (bourgeois), we cannot live in the city, it is not a question of will, but a condition, a state of affairs". The day he can return to laojia, to the village, depends on money: "Dagong life is unstable, you can't have everything".

Hangzhong's experience shows that the *jiulinghou* (90s generation) young migrants today, faced with the deprivation of employment and social security rights, develop strategies of resistance and mobilisation to obtain their wages. They first protest at the 劳动局 *laodongju* (employment bureau, party body) and next at the local government, successfully reclaiming their rights. Workplace conflicts are currently escalating in relation to non-compliance with social rights, and young migrants no longer accept workplace abuse and mobilise to reject their subaltern condition.

In 2018, Hangzhong is 25 years old, and he was born in Sichuan to peasant parents. He also has a little sister. He finished middle school and, due to economic difficulties (he also wanted to send his little sister to school), he went to work in building sites in Beijing and Tianjing). He was very apprehensive of this extremely tiring work. It was very hot in summer and very cold in winter. He worked 11 hours a day, earning roughly 1,000 RMB a day, then the salary gradually increased. He lived in a dormitory with bunk beds, 7–8 people per room. He had no insurance, so if he got sick, it was up to him to pay. Instead of being paid monthly, he received his salary at end of the year just before the new year. Every month the 老板 *laoban* (boss) gave him about 500 RMB. "If you needed money, you asked others to lend you money or you ask the laoban for it. Sometimes I needed money to buy clothes or money to send home for my sister and my parents». The first year he earned about 19,000 RMB, when his boss should have given him 27,000 RMB. "It's an unequal system, the boss didn't have much money and he didn't give me what I was owed. We were a large group of masons, so he couldn't pay everyone. I spoke with my colleagues, we complained». So, he ended up changing *laoban*, who gave him more money when he needed it. But at some point, the employer stopped paying the masons (and now he still owes him 5000 RMB). Together with about 100 fellow brick-layers, they went to the employment office/party body to explain the situation and protest. He said that initially he was not aware of what this institution was and of his rights, but gradually, by talking with colleagues, he became aware of it. The *laodongju* was afraid that the workers would be physically violently with the boss, so they assured them that they would be paid. The money was low to arrive, so the workers went back to the *laodongju* again and then they went to the local government to protest. The government advanced them the money, fearing demonstrations and conflicts. After getting partial compensation of the money he was owed, Hangzhong went back to his native village to build a house.

On the basis of a 2006–2010 survey (Wei Wan Qing, Gao Wei, 2019) with migrant workers in the Pearl River Delta region, it was found that the enactment of the "Employment Contracts Act" had promoted the signing of employment contracts and their extension as part of the implementation of a policy to protect the rights of migrant workers and individualise labour relations in order to reduce the risk of conflicts at work.

Young low-skilled migrants experience everyday verbal abuse, the late or non-payment of wages and non-compliance with workplace health and safety regulations.In the transition from traditional work cultures to cultures produced by multi-compressed modernity—which vary between workplaces—some young migrants become anesthetised by the effects of a contrasted work environment and the obligation to submit to crushing production rates; they are quickly alienated. The "fear of sinking" is exacerbated in the context of a multi-compressed modernity in hegemonic labour regimes and the product of authoritarian structures. Notwithstanding the fact that young migrants rotate from one workplace to another, they experience situations where they are voiceless, as described by Zhuiyi, interviewed in 2017.

Zhuiyi, a native of Guizhou, is 28 years old. He has one brother and he grew up with his grandparents because his parents worked in a factory in the city. When he finished middle school, his family had no money. He also wanted to leave the village to be more independent and earn his own money. With a friend, they left for Guangdong, in Yangjiang, to do factory work. Initially, he worked in a handbag factory, earning 600/700 RMB a month (8 years ago), and he stayed there for two years. "We worked 11 hours a day, despite the working conditions, the workers were all *dagong* and we had to accept everything". He then left in search of a better job. He found work in a factory packing fruit. It was exhausting work, both day and night. He had to walk for 20 minutes to the canteen, even though he only had a one-hour break. He worked 10-hour days, earning 800/900 RMB a month. "I was young, I was not afraid being tired, I came from the countryside and I didn't understand much". He then moved to Dongguan because he had friends there and wanted a change of scene. He worked in an electronics factory that employed around 1,000 people, from 8 a.m. to 8 p.m. + overtime, for roughly 1,800 RMB a month. In the dormitory, there were many cockroaches which used to bite him, so he rented a small house in the migrants' quarter next to the factory with a friend for 200 RMB total. He sent 700–800 RMB a month to his family. Now he says he feels old, and has no money and no girlfriend. It stresses him out. In the Dongguan factory, a new superior arrived and insulted him, so he decided to leave. He spent several weeks visiting factories and then he found a children's toy factory. The work was very tiring, he couldn't take breaks on the assembly line. He stayed there for three months, working 11 hours a day non-stop for 2,000 RMB a month. He rented a room for 200 RMB because the dormitory was too dirty. He then found a job at a steel factory, where he worked 12-hour days for 2,400 RMB a month (not bad). Despite this, the working environment was dirty. If the workers were tired, they had to sit on the floor because there were no chairs. He stayed there for two years and then left. His job criteria are: fairness, which for him means working, so he can improve and specialise, the physical effort involved, the salary and the environment. Afterwards, he worked in a food factory with quite a high salary—3,500 RMB a month. However, there were no young women, so he decided to change after a year. He worked at S. for a year, but he was dissatisfied because he found the work too tiring and he had no time to think about the future. So, he thinks he will change in the new year. If he can't find a good job, he will stay in the city, otherwise he will go back to the village. For the moment, he's not thinking about it. The city is better than the countryside, "but life is not easy. If you don't have a house, you can't send your children to school. Houses are very expensive and I'm just a dagong worker, I can't afford it. Maybe in 20 years' time I'll be able to buy one, but it's hard dagong life is a simple life; if you have a job you can live".

Low-skilled migrants were born into a traditional culture, grew up during a time of modernisation/industrialisation and now must survive in a postmodern/ post-industrial era. For these youth, living in a context of multi-compressed modernity results in the hyper commodification of emotions in hegemonic labour regimes created by authoritarian structures and associated to *emotional capitalism* (Illouz, 2006). Young low-skilled Chinese migrants are forced into emotional labour which, in an authoritarian context and in hegemonic labour regimes, means accepting or rejecting the confiscation of their positive emotions and enjoyment in the workplace. This emotional confiscation comes about through the implementation of labour division systems which dispossess the subaltern of any form of reflexivity on their work and deprive the many possibility of self-fulfilment and freedom in the workplace. This emotional labour may trigger strong internalisation due to the false consent to forced silence or the refusal of forced silence. In both cases, multi-compressed modernity gives rise to the hyper commodification of emotions in hegemonic labour regimes and corporal commodification at work, for example with the instrumentalisation of *guanxi*.

Before the 2008 Labour Law was implemented, personal support networks and interconnected networks of family, friends and acquaintances ensured the circulation of economic, social and symbolic resources, granting access to differentiated niches in the labour markets. Employment opportunities came via systems of trading, gifts, counter gifts, influence and information based on social mobility and "circulatory skills" (Tarrius, 2000) linked to spatial capital held by migrants. The first generation of migrants born in the 80s tended to group together by provincial affiliations.

> At that time, a construction site in Dongbei asked the Zhejiang company to find them a worker. The manager appreciated my technical level, so he sent me. This time I earned 17 RMB a day. It was much better than in Zhejiang, so I worked there for a year and went back to my village for the Spring festival. Then I got a job at a construction site in Yangzhou. I oversaw of a group of workers, I worked as the Supervisor. I could read the blueprints and tell the workers how to carry out their, because they didn't understand the project. Moreover, I had to explain the best work

practices to them. In fact, I was a bit like their leader, although I still had to work with them. I didn't have a contract with the building site, I didn't have a contract with my workers. I worked in this construction site for three years until 1994. The building site paid me all the workers' salaries, and then I paid them, keeping a percentage for myself. For three years, I earned an average of 6,000 RMB a year, because I had also to pay expenses. In 1994, there was a reform in the company, I couldn't find work, so I went to Shanghai and took some of the workers with me. A friend introduced me to a building site, but when I arrived, the salary was only 26 RMB a day. It was less than what we had agreed on. In addition, there were no bonuses, so I decided to leave. Then the company in Zhejiang phoned me because they had a construction site at the Three Gorges (Yangzi River). They asked me to find workers, so I recruited 80 people. The company paid them 5 RMB a day in advance while we waited for the green light to leave. But, in the end, the company lost the site and the workers left. Then I recruited a few people, we were working in small construction sites in our region until the end of 1995. These workers followed me everywhere, so we had a very good relationship. I also had very good rapport with the companies. Then a construction company in our city (Yangzhou) got a building site in Beijing, so they asked me to go there with my group. I was the workers' supervisor responsible for construction (quality). The company paid me 45 RMB a day.

> NING, man, 23 years old, Zhejiang origin, interview conducted in Shanghai in 2007

Prior to 2008, professional relationship networks developed in situations where workers had no access to social rights and were organised by institutional arrangements. The strength of *guanxi* 关系 (social networks) alleviated fear in the workplace and did not so violently impose emotional confiscation. Uncertain loyalties and institutional arrangements helped to understand the inability of migrant workers to claim their rights without integrating the role of the *guanxi* tied to the old organisational system of traditional kinship relationships and geographic affiliations. The strength of migrants' *guanxi* in Chinese labour markets revealed networks built around the transfer and trade of economic, symbolic and market resources. This exchange of resources was built on group loyalties and trust relationships in interconnected networks of family, friends and acquaintances that played a fundamental role in gaining access to Chinese labour markets. All the same, the *guanxi* did not encourage solidarity to resist situations of domination in the labour market. In fact, *guanxi* could create a relation of dependence and even captivity with the employer and fore-man, effectively preventing any collective action and fracturing solidarity.

A group of researchers (Shen Yuan, Guo Yuhua, Lu Huilin, Fang Yi, 2010) from Peking University and Tsinghua University carried out a study involving a hundred young migrants working in Shenzhen. These migrant workers used pneumatic drills and contracted lung cancer due to the lack of sanitary pro-tection. Three elements were identified to analyse these work situations. The workers had no work permits and therefore no healthcare insurance and had to pay hospital fees. In addition, a fragile trust relationship between the 农民工 *nonmingong* (rural migrant workers), and the entrepreneurs hiring them through the *guanxi* left them completely dependent on their supervisors and open to exploitation. Finally, there was complicity between the local govern-ments and employers to not comply with work health and safety regulations. If *nongmingong* from a village refuse to keep working, fearing for their lives, workers from another village take over with full knowledge of the situation. The researchers call it the "fatal relay race". They thus use notions of hegemony and despotism to analyse professional relationships in Chinese labour markets, particularly between employers and *nongmingong*. They reflect a situation of ever-increasing flexibility which triggers situations of social disqualification through forms of control and extreme violence in labour markets. It is evident that *guanxi* are today used to balance work control and discipline systems in hegemonic regimes (Wei Weng Jing, 2019) and that emotional capitalism in a compressed modernity does influence the *guanxi*.

The extraction of work exceeds the psychological limits of these young work-ers considered as "deportable" supernumeraries (Bastide, 2015; Sassen 2014). Emotional confiscation fosters a type of fear in the workplace, workers worry about the risks, being abused or losing their jobs. In 2016, Hangzhong wanted a change of scene and a new job, so he followed the advice of his fellow villagers and moved to Dongguan in Guangdong. He spent a few days there looking for a job, but he didn't like the city because he found it to be very dirty and dan-gerous. As a result, he moved to Zhongshan because his uncle worked there at S. Initially, he didn't know how to work on an assembly line, he had never done it before and felt trapped, subject to orders from superiors and restricted by a stressful work pace. "You do the same thing, repeat it all day long, you're worried about messing up, you stress yourself out, you're worried about failing. And if you do your work badly, the superior insults you and you have to start from scratch, so you're also afraid of being fired". He has been working in this factory for two years. From the outset, he earned 3,000 RMB per month and now receives 4,000 RMB. He didn't want to sleep in the dormitory because it's dirty, noisy and houses a lot of people. He therefore rented a 5 m² room in the urban village for 200 RMB a month. He doesn't have hot water, so he has to buy it in a shop down the street. "Being a *dagong* is an ugly, hard and very unstable life. I would like to start a business. I don't feel free here because I work 11 hours a day. In this factory, the work is relatively stable, but I would like to change".

In China, the subject of fear at work is coupled with political fear. Working in a hegemonic regime in China means being forced to experience emotions at work which alter the individuals' selves. Emotional confiscation creates breaches of trust in Chinese youth, already vulnerable and detached from themselves, their colleagues, and their families and attempts to enforce their isolation and disconnection of self. Yet while the majority of the *balinghou* generation low-skilled young migrants did not protest so much, the *jiulinghou* and *linglinghou* generation is less tolerant of situations of moral captivity and is quick to express their indignation, anger and solidarity. These generations appear to be developing a form of emotional labour in an authoritarian context in which they can express social emancipation readable in the awareness of a gap between the experienced emotions and those imposed by an economic order linked to multi-compressed modernity. Emotional labour also becomes visible through anger and the refusal to be humiliated or mistreated when young oppressed migrants cannot express their protest at work.

Nevertheless, where emotional confiscation has played a role in the primary socialisation of children raised in rural areas, especially girls, this paradoxically promotes an ability to adapt to hegemonic labour regimes and is widely used in an emotional capitalism that is encouraged and embodied by Chinese company directors. In a recent survey Wang Ou (2019) found that "world factories" preferred to hire young female low-skilled migrants, children raised in rural areas. Why? These young girls are perceived as being harder working, more disciplined and more compliant at work than their young male low-skilled migrant counterparts. These young girls received a unique primary socialisation—their parents migrated to the big cities to find employment while they remained in their region and village of origin and were required to carry out all the everyday tasks and look after their brothers, sisters and grandparents. These girls were obliged from a very young age to take up their mother's role of family reproduction, an area in which young boys played no part and therefore had time for fun activities. The patriarchal structures in rural China have actively participated in creating gender inequality between children raised in rural areas. Since these girls have internalised the problems of balancing production and reproduction activities in their primary socialisation, once they start work this creates unconscious abilities of hyper adaptation to hegemonic labour regimes and emotional labour they have previously experienced. They are deprived from an early age of any possibility to express anger or protest at what was forced on them in their youth. The gender division in labour between children raised in rural areas is apparent once they start work. This reinforces gendered differentiation during the search for employment in Chinese labour markets. Wang Ou (2019) also showed that rural young female migrants were preferred by recruiters over young female migrants brought up in the city with their parents. The latter had not been raised with the obligation to balance production and reproduction activities, and therefore did not develop the same hyperadaptation capacity to hegemonic labour regimes. Young male migrants manifest resistance to the labour markets' norms of flexibility and are more often made redundant. Consequently, they must develop mobility skills in order to find new employment.

In a context of structural disqualification, work biopolitics has developed, based on the hypercommodification of young migrant workers' emotions to generate extreme productivity in high-order compressed modernity regime. This same biopolitics is producing injunctions to be oneself, to a false sense of autonomy and very strong investment in work (Zhuang Jiachi, 2018).

6   Social Conflicts, Collective Action and Dormitory Regimes

Since 2000, there have been an increasing number of workplace conflicts in China. Protests organised by young migrant workers and structured social movements are on the rise. The migrant working population in the Pearl River Delta is a major actor in these movements. Pun Ngai (2016) found that migrant collective actions are undergoing a process of radicalisation, leading to strikes, street action and demonstrations. In the construction sector, young migrant workers who experience indecent working conditions frequently gather to protest. Certain forms of complaint used to exist in the collective visitation mode at the time of the warring States, and have been resurgently recurrent in the political history of China. Over the last seventy years, this space of complaint has been transformed through the construction of individual and collective actors who publicise the ordeals of injustice with which they are confronted and who express demands for recognition to instituted powers (Thireau, Hua Linshan, 2010).

Hao is thirty-two years old and comes from Anhui province. He currently lives and works in the southern city of Zhongshan. In 2016, he was employed in an electronics factory owned by a Chinese entrepreneur. The working environment and dormitory living area were insanitary, and the salary was low. However, Hao was satisfied with the working hours and therefore put up with the work conditions. However, from March 2016 onwards, workers like Hao stopped receiving wages. Due to the company's economic strife, the boss could not pay his workers. For him, it was not only a matter of "respecting the agreement and the regulations". It was also essential for his family's survival as he converted the bulk of his salary into remittances to send to his wife and children in Anhui province. Therefore, Hao banded together with twenty other workers to protest. The workers could not even rely on the factory trade union, but together they could organise collective action:

> I needed my salary, it was the duty of the boss to pay us! I also needed money for my parents and my wife [...] I had two children at home and one of them was a baby [...] taking care of little children always requires lots of money! [...] We didn't have a choice [...] Nobody thought about the consequences [...] what consequences? We had to be paid! [...] In months previous, we had seen many workers in the street protesting, and we followed suit. Mostly, they were employed in the construction sites, and they protested in the middle of the street. In the morning, we blocked the entrance to the factory. We just set up in front of the main gate and didn't allow anyone to enter [...] and the night workers already inside gradually joined us. Then, we blocked the street. We waited in front of the factory. Then we moved to where the traffic flowed and blocked the cars [...] The police came quickly and few of us immediately went to the city employment office. A few hours later, our boss was called there too. When all of them left, we were promised our wages. We got our money. However, a few weeks later we lost our jobs because the factory had to close.
>
> HAO, man, 32 years old, Anhui origin, interview conducted in Zhongshan in 2018

Late payments or unpaid wages are often the main reasons which drive workers to organise and protest. Qian narrates her experience which mirrors that of Hao:

> After the third month we should have been paid, but we did not get any money [...] Young people started leaving the company, but we stayed [...] We went on strike; we decided not to work. The boss had no choice. Like me, there were other women who did not want to look for another job, since we thought that this was a stable job and we didn't want to leave. We wanted to be paid since it was our right. When we knew we weren't going to be paid, we reduced our working hours, decreasing them incrementally. The boss said that we had to work, but we said that we weren't

going to work for free. Gradually, the whole sector stopped working for about seven days [...] in the end, the boss called us. We stayed at the dormitory and refused to go work. The boss closed the canteen and said we wouldn't get any food. We said we could eat elsewhere. He threatened to kick us out of the dormitory, we said we could go elsewhere. He said he would pay us and gave us some of the money. We went back to work and at the end of the month, we received our wages. We had won the battle.

QIAN, girl, Guanxi native, 27 years old, interview conducted in 2016

New forms of workers' collective action are being invented to face the privatisation of public companies which engenders political and economic conflicts of interest. If workers had integrated the idea of strong mutual ties between them, the company and the State, the Reform broke this unwritten agreement and the workers felt betrayed and left to face inequalities and injustices (Tong Xin, 2008). Shared socialist culture and class consciousness have shaped the struggle of a subjugated underclass in these post-reform workers' mobilisations. Collective action from traditional state sector workers is specific to China, especially the demands concerning property regimes. Class consciousness also rose amongst migrant workers to fight for workers' rights and against

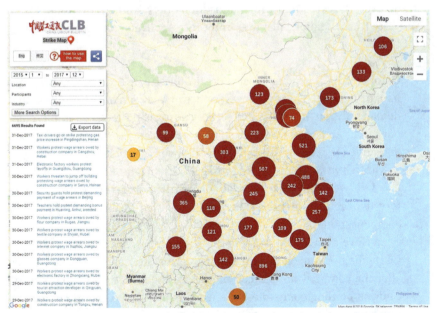

MAP 2   Collective protests recorded on CLB's Strike Map from January 2015 to December 2017
SOURCE: MAPS.CLB.ORG.HK

foreign capitalistic takeovers. These migrants combat local government and global capital. Since the beginning of the 1990s, strikes, protests and revolts repeatedly occur amongst migrant workers, especially in Southern China. The more China becomes involved in the global production system, the more it must face protests. A formerly socialist context merges with current political events to produce new working-class cultures, based on solidarities and relations built in individuals' local communities. A growing number of export-focused companies have closed and their workers, mostly migrants, have been laid off. Migrants have protested and faced the police in the Pearl and Yangtse delta cities, such as Shenzhen, Dongguan, and Huizhou. Now, riots and urban social movements occur in all Chinese provinces.

Young migrant workers demand respect and recognition, a decent working conditions and social justice, namely their wages, social security and severance pay. In December 2015, the Chinese authorities launched a sustained and coordinated attack on civil society labour organisations in the southern province of Guangdong. The report by the China Labour Bulletin "The workers Movement in China 2015–2017" mentioned 6,694 cases of workers protests in different sectors concentrated in Pearl and Yangtze River Deltas: 39% in construction, 26% in manufacturing, 11% in transport, 11% in services, 4% in mining, 3% in retail, 3% in education, and 3% miscellaneous. Several activists were arrested and the organisations they worked for were closed. From 2015 to 2017, labour disputes and protest movements soared throughout China.

> October 2015. Fuchang Electronics in Shenzhen suddenly announced bankruptcy and closure. Over 3,000 workers gathered to protest and demanded that management settle wage arrears and economic compensation issues. The workers surrounded local government offices and demanded that authorities step in and solve the problems.
>
> 5 March 2016. Around 2,000 workers at Changying Electric (Shenzhen) Co., Ltd. went on strike after management began the process of factory relocation to nearby Huizhou but refused to discuss the issue of compensation.
>
> 21 November 2016. Workers at three Coca-Cola bottling plants in Chongqing, Changchun and Chengdu launched a coordinated strike after the company announced the sale of the facilities to two domestic Chinese bottling companies. The workers demanded lay-off compensation based on their length of employment.
>
> SOURCE: CHINA LABOUR BULLETIN, "The Workers Movement in China 2015–2017"

In 2017, we interviewed an employee in the employment office in Zhongshan city who explained that:

> in most cases, companies do not comply with the law and workers request assistance from the employment office when labour conflicts arise. This governmental office is responsible for protecting workers and professional relations, managing employer-employee relations and resolving conflicts through mediation or judiciary remedies in court. The government encourages the trade union to control the workers, but the union does not. Workers should take action against their boss via mediation at the labour office, because in court the boss can hire a good lawyer and the worker cannot [...] Workers don't know the law, they block roads because they don't know how to have their rights respected. The police cannot stop the protests either.

In China, labour regulations appear to be incomplete and fragmented. These legal loopholes provide the company owners and managers with a vast degree of latitude. On this subject, Wenjing, a 28-year-old from Yunnan, works for a company in Sanxiang, explains her worries about the effectiveness of the employment office in case of conflict with her employer:

> The 劳动局 *laodongju* (employment office) is not really transparent, it is corrupt,formally, it is responsible to protect workers, but the reality is that boss always wins at Court because they have their own *guanxi*. The government doesn't want any problems, everything needs to remain stable and orderly [...] that is why for me going to the labour office is not useful at all. It happened to me once, I had an accident at work. The first time I went there alone, but now, I bring a few colleagues with me. Last year, the working conditions in the factory where I worked were not good. Bits of the roof would come loose and fall on our heads. After complaining to the boss for a while, he repaired the roof. However, the repair was poorly done, and several workers went taken to hospital because of the falling stones. We therefore went to the *laodongju*. But in the end, after complaining and explaining the situation, things didn't change. They couldn't do much there, so we decided to leave.

The *balinghou, jiulinghou* and the *linglinghou* generations endure the same suffering and humiliation as their parents. And while they are outraged, they have developed a set of skills to resist and fight oppression and injustice. They are also increasingly conscious of their social rights and their level of aspirations is rising (Cai He, Liu Linping, Wang Xiangdong, 2009). Qin Cong (2013) describes peasants fighting with rationality and legality for rights by engaging in protection activities and resistance in daily life. This resistance has its roots in rural culture and stems from the tension which arises from the central government's authority and local governments' appetite for economic growth.

Workers, often from the same villages or cities, are lodged in factory dormitories. This allows them to set up collective actions to fight for their rights and express strong resentment against the involvement of foreign capital. The *dormitory labour regime* has been defined by Pun Ngai (2005) as a form of spatial labour politics, characterised by the reconfiguration of daily production and reproduction space within a factory space in which work and housing are highly concentrated in the same place. Three forms of dormitory arrangements have been identified:

– companies rent dormitories from the local government or residents for their workers
– companies own dormitories
– workers rent dormitories from the residents in the industrial town.

For Pun Ngai (2016), the dormitory is a hidden facsimile of the slums, and gender is central to understanding the specificity of the Chinese dormitory labour regime and the formation of the new Chinese underclass. The dormitory labour regime reveals how young migrant workers must face to a double injunction to be able to share a collective life and to be considered individual workers by management. The case of young female migrant workers shows how urban factory dormitories are performatively transformed into spaces where new social ties, affinities and affections can be produced. Additionally, practices of solidarity and mutual help (Zani 2019; Pun Ngai, 2007) create tactics of practical and moral resistance against the biopolitical control women endure in the factory and hostility spaces, stay in "niches of survival" (Bastide, 2015). In this regard, Wenfeng's narrative illustrates the extent to which the strict contact women are subjected to within the working space of the assembly line, and the emotional space of the dormitory, can generate new social and emotional bonds.

> The dormitory was huge. There were around twelve of us in my room. We all came from different places, our home villages were far away and we all suffered from homesickness [...] We knew each other very well, and that is important when you are far from home, it helps to feel less lonely [...] Sometimes, when we came back late at night, exhausted after work, we used to eat little snacks together and to make fun of our superiors [...] I remember that there was a little Cantonese boss who was very powerful and had a big ass, and we laughed a lot together about that [...] My co-workers became my family; we helped each other when we needed something. I knew I

could rely on them. I liked making new friends and socialising. Time passes quicker if you have good colleagues. You can easily forget how tired you are, how much you hate your job and how awful the assembly line is [...].

WENFENG, girl, 33 years old, Chongqing native, Interview conducted in Shanghai in 2017

Physical and emotional closeness sustain the collectivisation of labour experiences. In the factory of inside the crowded dormitories rooms where they reside, young women gather together to both individually and collectively organise new socialisation processes, based on reciprocity and support. Consequently, they quietly make fun of their superiors during their evening chats before sleeping, buy food or medicines for colleagues in need, bring hot water to banish the cold from the rooms, or borrow money. In this way, by claiming that her colleagues became her family, Wenfeng shows how *guanxi* (social networks) produced and performed by migrant workers during their mobility paths, can be individually and collectively translated and transformed by women who share spaces of daily life and work and face a similar condition of subalternity (Zani 2018). The way women talk about 姐妹 *jiemei* (sisters), in terms of friendship, attachment, affinities and closeness, suggests strong emotional investment. It demonstrates an awareness of sharing a similar working-class condition and the ability to resist and protest. Xiang, twenty-seven years old, worked in an electronics factory for several years. Afterwards, she found employment in Zhongshan where the workers, mainly young women, were paid their wages at the end of the month:

By that time, we had not been paid for a couple of months. I didn't know what to do and felt worried because I had no money [...] I complained to my 姐妹 *jiemei* (sisters), but we didn't know what to do [...] Progressively, more and more workers started complaining [...] We could not say this to the superior [...] it was pointless. When we complained to the *laoban*, she used to answer that we would be paid by the end of the month, but that was a lie. In the evening, with few *jiemei* we had a discussion before sleeping. We were all worried about money. We had to send money back to our parents in the village, but we had no money. We were all frustrated and sad. How miserable! I cried, and my *jiemei* cried with me [...] after few weeks, we got an idea [...] We formulated a plan while queueing for the showers [...] We decided to find the boss the following morning and ask for an explanation [...] We got organised. During lunch break, instead of going to the canteen, we went our bosses' office. He was there [...] Six of us entered the room. We said we wanted our wages! It was his duty. He said he would pay [...] We said we wanted money immediately. He said he had no money. But it was not true. All bosses have money [...] So we locked the door and we said that we wanted money now. We told the boss that he would not leave until we had been paid [...] We locked him inside for six hours, until we got our salary.

XIANG, girl, 27 years old, Guizhou native, interview conducted in Zhongshan in 2016

Young migrants are developing new working-class cultures of resistance based on ties and solidarities brought from home communities. As a result, class consciousness is being developed and new creative skills are being forged in actions and struggles in the workplace. A specific process of proletarianisation amongst migrant workers has led to these labour revolts. But when regimes of fear intensify in the factories where young migrants work, phenomena of emotional contagion manifest, triggering riots and forms of mass suicide such as the case of Foxconn. Although life in shared dormitories promotes the circulation of negative emotions and the process of disconnection of self, it also facilitates reconnection with others through different channels, such as gender solidarity. Management through fear in an authoritarian context is responsible in part for producing multi-compressed modernity.

Shen Yuan (2014) shows that we have entered into a period of rights and that Chinese citizens are defining their relationship with the State and the Market by developing the ability to act and mobilise in the public space. Individuals' reflexive capacity is deemed to be engaged in interactive situations (Shi Yunqing, 2014) in everyday forms of resistance, and covert discourse and practices (hidden transcripts) which identify ways to counter situations of contempt, humiliation and discredit (Scott, 1990). Following the example of Burawoy, Shen Yuan (2014) put forward the concepts of an "active society" and "civil society" to analyse the production of Chinese society. Inspired by Antonio Gramsci, he asserted that in between the State and the Market, different popular associations, movements and mass organisations emerge.

7 Multi-Compressed Modernity and Mobility

In China, mobility skills facilitate the fleeting escape from systems which appropriate individuals' bodies. It open new horizons of connecting with the self in an environment which is the catalyst for a process of colonisation of individuals' experience and weak social groups. These skills also lay the foundations for "aspirational capacities" (in terms of power, dignity and material resources) (Appadurai, 2013) and geographical and professional mobilities express a form of resistance to wage subordination experienced by young migrant workers—a refusal to submit to forced labour (Roulleau-Berger, 2015). Migratory flows allow young Chinese workers to, in part, momentarily reappropriate some personal time held hostage by hegemonic labour regimes. Resisting wage subordination by developing mobility skills also signifies rejecting the confiscation of positive emotions in an environment characterised by authoritarian governance structures in the labour markets and facilitated by the State and the Market. Mobility skills develop in societal, temporal and spatial gaps, spaces where young low-skilled migrants can temporarily escape from oppressive, predatory and demeaning treatment. These dispositions may stem from the internalisation of strong mobility systems in China, the reason why young Chinese workers do not always live in precarity, even though wage stability standards are still in play and many of them internalise uncertainty as a professional norm.

In a multi-compressed modernity, strong aspirational capacities do not necessarily lead to strong mobility skills. Weak aspirational capacities may entail strong mobility skills in a plurality of economic activities areas. The combination of aspirational capacities and mobility skills can be defined as a local or Chinese singularity. If, as Arjun Appadurai (2013) suggests, the map of aspirations for the poorest consists of a smaller number of aspirational nodes and a limited capacity to navigate its pathways, it develops on a scale of widespread and open migratory pathways in China, standardised by different economic norms and the nature of the areas where young skilled migrants circulate (Roulleau-Berger, 2010).

Most of young low-skilled migrants experienced a traditional way of life in rural areas or in small Chinese cities, finding employment in local Chinese markets established between the main supply markets and the local workshops. Rural family businesses maintained their organisation via tight-knit social networks in an environment of strong competition characterised by commercial spaces. Consequently, young migrants worked in industrial groups of small and medium enterprises, a phenomenon resulting from the industrialisation process of rural zones initiated by local farmers founding businesses with their own capital (Qiu Zeqi, 2014). These economic spaces are the result of the convergence of industrial technology distribution, the effects of the industrial agglomeration and social networks linked to rural communities. Accordingly, young migrants in the traditional regime worked in an economic organisation connected with the local history and Chinese productive worlds.

In multi-compressed modernity, the intensity and violence of productive and urban temporalities continuously inform migratory careers by constantly creating biographical crossroads (Bessin, Bidart, Grossetti, 2010; Roulleau-Berger, 2018). Biographical bifurcations are at work at these junctions, potentially becoming turning-points where the changes occur during a period characterised by a new regime. Biographical crossroads emerge as breaking points between differentiated work experiences. These bifurcations are defined by double geographical and professional mobilities which are weakly correlated to upward social mobility.

Migratory careers are shaped from steps and sequences that develop in the context of multi-compressed modernity. They are based on young migrants' repertoire of social, educational and economic resources, the diversity of their experiences, work situations and *hukou*-related policies. This series of bifurcations reflects the pace of productivity in labour markets and gives rise to professional mobilities, causing a diminishing number of opportunities for social mobility today. Bifurcations form with the convergence of professional mobilities and geographical mobilities and their proliferation varies according to academic qualifications, employment opportunities and social and economic resources.

As we saw through this worker's experience first interviewed in 2006, the construction of multi-compressed modernity at each biographical crossroad and the unpredictability and uncertainty inherent in the construction of compressed modernity were already manifesting. This combined with the effects of the societal context and situation, and the objective and subjective careers of young migrants:

> I'm 38 years old and from Jiangsu. I started working in the factory at 17. I got married at 25 and had my first child at 27. I worked at the factory from 17 to 27 years old. I went everywhere, to Henan, Jilin, and so on. The wages in my home province are very low, they are higher in other provinces. I learned the trade for a year in Huaiyin, Jiangsu and then returned to Zhuyong where I worked for a year. Afterwards, I went to Henan for a year to a private factory where someone introduced me. I stayed there for a year and then I went to Anyang for a few months. He wasn't a good boss though; he didn't pay us. Later, I went back home to a rural company, a branch factory in Shanghai where I worked for a year. I went to Jilin again for a year, then I came back and worked for three years in Wuxi, and for six months in Jiangsu. Afterwards, I went back to the village and worked again in this rural factory. A Shanghai man came to open a factory, he asked my husband to be the supervisor and teach the workers. I worked there for two years. Then in A., where we lived, they opened a shoe factory. They asked my husband to go there, it was very hard. I followed my

husband, we worked together because he made the shoe soles and I made the uppers, we each had our own speciality. I didn't want to move, I was earning 1,000 RMB in my rural factory. In the end, they insisted that I move there, so we did. In the factory, they didn't have certain shoe models, so my husband had to make new ones. We stayed for about a year. My husband didn't do the manufacturing, so we brought someone from the rural factory in our village to sell. The business was going very well for one year. But the boss wanted to keep everything for himself, so we went to Jiangxi where we rented a department in a shop to sell the shoes. It didn't work out well, so we came back six months later. The Shanghai man who had set up his factory in A. knew my husband and told him, "Set up your own factory". So, we opened it in 1985. After three years, we went bankrupt and left. In 1989, we went to work in a factory in the countryside back home, my husband earned 1,500 RMB a month. As we had hundreds of thousands of RMB to repay, we moved to Shanghai.

LIN, man, 38 years old, Jiangsu, interview conducted in Shanghai in 2006

Identity resources are mobilised in a continuous or discontinuous way in the diverse range of careers practiced by low-skilled young migrants. Mobilities can be both a resource and a constraint. The economic, political and societal context influences the processes involved in entering an increasingly differentiated and hierarchised labour market. Migratory careers give an insight into the social reproduction process of inequalities, accentuated in an environment of multi-compressed modernity. Li Lulu (2008) demonstrated how internal policies in the market and educational system breed inequalities and social differentiation; he was already formulating the concept of dual social reproduction based on the hypothesis of determining social heritage through restructuring social relationships, the development of the market economy and the decline of the State through the construction of redistribution systems. He explained how the process of maintaining acquired social privileges and positions operated via strategies of hidden reconversions that contain forms of manifold domination.

8 Compressed Mobilities and Subalternity

For young low-skilled Chinese migrants, biographical pathways are organised around spatial mobilities that may or may not lead to professional mobilities, i.e. the transfer from one branch of activity, professional status or social mobility to another. The pathways of young low-skilled Chinese workers thus wind

54   CHAPTER 1

TABLE 1   Three types of pathways for *balinghou, jiulinghou* and *linglinghou* young migrants

		Principles of construction		
Pathways of young Chinese migrants		Different sectors of activity	Social mobility	Professional mobility
	Weak subalternity	-	-	+
	Integrative subalternity	+	+	+
	Strong subalternity	+	-	-

through a series of professional experiences in small-scale production work-shops and in state-owned or private enterprises, either Chinese or joint ventures in the service or trade sectors. The frequency of bifurcations in the pathways of Chinese migrants is a principle of social differentiation that reflects discontinuity in employment experiences. The quick succession of bifurcation situations results in discontinuity between work experiences in very different sectors. Indeed, their short compulsory presence, in formal or informal employment, does not leave time to find a place and acquire new social and symbolic resources, often restricting them to a horizontal mobility made up of a series of "invisible" yet ongoing experiences. These close bifurcations arise through professional and spatial discontinuities and manufacture migratory careers that operate in spaces of weak economic legitimacy that may compel migrants to return to their home region.

There are three types of pathways for *balinghou, jiulinghou* and *linglinghou* young migrants, see Table 1.

8.1   *Strong Subalternity*

In strong subalternity, pathways are organised around activities across different sectors without professional and social mobility, there is therefore no social mobility. Young migrants move cities to find employment in unrelated branches of activity and thus remain in a position of subalternity on labour markets. The double spatial and professional discontinuities arise through their horizontal movements in differentiated segments of the labour market in low-level positions, meaning that young migrants perform many different jobs without progressing in the social space. Migratory careers are not structured around a rationale of gaining resources, but rather losing them, as if each time, a new work situation erases the previous one. The quick succession of bifurcation situations results in discontinuity between work experiences in very different sectors. Indeed, their short compulsory presence in formal or unemployment employment does not leave time to acquire new social and symbolic resources and order them to reconstruct individual repertoires in each new professional situation.

Therefore, a societal paradox linked to multi-compressed modernity emerges. On the one hand, young low-skilled migrants are subject to injunctions to live in multiple spaces and temporalities, on the other, they are forced to remain static in social space. This very paradox creates the conditions for the reproduction of an inegalitarian society. It excludes the most fragile and vulnerable individuals, deprived of all social, economic and emotional resources.

8.2 *Integrative Subalternity*

In integrative subalternity, pathways are organised around activity across different sectors with professional and social mobility. Young migrants move cities to find employment in different branches of activity and are integrated on labour markets. The double spatial and professional mobilities mean that young migrants perform many different jobs in progressing in the social space. Migratory careers are structured around a rationale of gaining resources. The succession of bifurcation situations results in continuity between work experiences in very different sectors. This is illustrated in Xiao's experience, 33 years old, whom we met in Shanghai in 2017:

> Xiao is from Chongqing and was born in 1994. In 1990, Xiao's parents came to Shanghai and started working in the auto parts factory. He also has a brother who is 7 years older than him. Before his first birthday, his parents were selling some seafood at the market. When he entered kindergarten, his parents started a crayfish business. His parents' work is very busy. They often got home at 11 p.m. and had no time to take care of him. After kindergarten, Xiao went to the food market to help his parents. From the first grade to the fifth grade, Xiao went to an elementary school in Baoshan and his parents were working in Jiading. His parents rented a room for him in Baoshan, where he lived alone.
>
> After studying in the fifth grade of primary school, Xiao returned to his hometown to attend the sixth grade. In the same year, Xiao's parents opened a restaurant in Jiading, Shanghai, and the business started very well. His parents bought two apartments, a car in their hometown, and Xiao lived a prosperous life. He was in junior high school in Shanghai, the so-called 贵族学校 *gui zu xue xiao* (elites schools). He stayed at the school, and the annual tuition fee was nearly 80,000 RMB. At the beginning of junior high school, his father's restaurant started losing money. The father sold the car and two houses in his hometown, struggling to

maintain the restaurant's operations. The family was unable to pay Xiao's expensive tuition. After studying in elite school for two years, he was transferred to a migrant school. In this school, he felt very lost, then he entered a vocational high school near Shanghai University and studied logistics. After almost two years, he decided to leave school and look for work. When Xiao stopped his studies, he had just turned 16 years old. He found his first job at a computer assembly factory in Songjiang. He conducted quality inspections of Apple computers, with a starting salary of 900 RMB per month. He worked 16 hours a day.

In Jiading, Xiao found a job of a sales representative in an IT company. With his job in the IT company, he earned 500,000 RMB. He gave most of the money to his parents, keeping just a small part to start a crayfish business. After that, Xiao participated in the food festival in Zhenjiang in Jiangsu. However, the management of the food festival was chaotic, and Xiao lost a lot of money. After the food festival, he found a partner and invested 300,000 RMB to open a 100 m^2 store. Xiao didn't make any money. "That year was the darkest year of my life." After a year, he bought an apartment in Shanghai. During this period, Xiao's parents' crayfish business greatly improved, he then helped them with the business. They signed a supply contract with a large restaurant chain in Shanghai. Xiao's father had worked in the seafood industry in Shanghai for more than 20 years, so suppliers trusted him.

8.3   *Weak Subalternity*

In weak subalternity pathways are organised around professional mobility without a change in sectors and no social mobility. Young migrants move and continue working in the same branch of activity, the construction industry for example, and remain in the same subaltern position. Double spatial and professional discontinuities arise as a result of their lateral movements in differentiated segments of the labour market, meaning that young migrants work in many different workplaces without progressing in the social space because most of them have not *hukou*. Over the past decade, opportunities for upward social mobility have been declining for low-skilled young Chinese migrants. Still, a minority of them resist their subaltern condition by starting small businesses, this is the case of this young migrant who founded a transport company.

Niu was born in rural Henan, he is 27 years old. We met him in 2016 in Shanghai. His two uncles and aunt are all teachers. His father used to be a soldier and has learnt to drive a truck. When Niu was a child, his parents moved from their hometown to Shanghai. His father started as a rubbish truck driver in Pudong and later founded his own transportation company. Niu grew up with his grandparents. When Niu was 10 years old, his father's business was stable, so he joined his father in Shanghai. Niu started studying in the second half of the fifth grade of primary school. After that, he went to a football school in Jiading for three and a half years. However, he was not selected as a professional player. Niu's parents then sent him to a school in Zhengzhou (Henan) for three years of secondary school and two years of university, as part of a vocational cycle. During this time, his father and mother worked in Shanghai. Niu could only go to Shanghai for summer and winter holidays to see his parents. During the Spring Festival, the family returned to their hometown in Henan for the New Year. Niu's university diploma did not help him find a job. After graduating from University, he worked as a stockbroker for four months and then worked in a freight forwarding company as a salesman. After four years, Niu knew more about the container industry. At the same time, he felt that there was no future in the company, so he started a transport company. He helped the freight forwarding company to find trucks to earn money on the side. At present, all his family members are working in his transport company. His younger sister is 3 years younger than him and has similar academic experience (primary school in Shanghai, junior high school in her hometown, high school and University in Shanghai). After graduating from a junior university, she joined his company and was responsible for finance. Niu was in charge of contacting customers and maintaining customers relationships. Niu's father is 56 years old. He stopped working as a driver and was instead was responsible for liaising with the company's truck drivers. Niu's home is also the office of the transportation company. Niu is used to living in Shanghai, but in daily life he often senses social disharmony and inequality between people. He does not have a Shanghai hukou. He regrets not buying a house when housing prices were low in Shanghai. If he had bought a house at that time, his family would now have a Shanghai *hukou* with public medical insurance and living in Shanghai would be much more convenient. His biggest concern is now the question of his child's education.

Biographical crossroads develop in line with situations of unpredictability and economic uncertainty embedded in multi-compressed modernity. These situations suppress any hopes and aspirations on the horizon for these young migrants; they choose one bifurcation over another without knowing why.

The discontinuity in the work experiences of Chinese migrants reveals a certain face of multi-compressed modernity: the inequality of social, educational and emotional resources and the bleak horizons for young migrants anxious about the need to find employment. Primary socialisations and acquired dispositions influence the effects of biographical discontinuity. Social inequalities are revealed in the ordering of repertoires of resources—the more ordered the repertoires of economic, social and symbolic resources are—the better individuals can mitigate the effects of biographical discontinuity. One of the characteristics of the subaltern condition in migration stems from the individual's inability to mitigate the effects of biographical discontinuity. Here too a paradox of multi-compressed modernity rears its head, producing concurrent spatial hyper mobility and professional and/or social immobility.

CHAPTER 2

The Fabric of "Heroes" and Emotional Capitalism

Since 1979, the internal migration of young graduates in China has been a key phenomenon in understanding the transformation of Chinese society in all its forms, especially in megalopolises (Li Chunling, 2012, 2013). The young generation with a higher-education diploma are a reserve force for the new middle class. The working conditions for young graduates today continue to deteriorate, particularly for young skilled migrants. In this chapter, we will describe their migratory careers, both objective and subjective. We will analyse how the young skilled migrant—as *Compressed Individual*—is redefining his/her social identity in the face of an "economy of arrogance" (Favereau, 2015) and restricted autonomy. Finally, we will identify how socialist heritage and compressed modernity influences socialisation at work and produces resistance to emotional capitalism.[1]

1 Young Migrant Graduates and Employment

Until the late 1990s, young graduates were considered the society elites and had access to stable employment in State enterprises and public institutions. This is no longer the case. Young diploma-holders have to accept informal employment or unemployment. In 2010, Li Chunling and Wang Boqing (2010) conducted and published a survey of 445,000 young diploma-holders who graduated in 2007 from 2,113 high schools and universities in 31 provinces, six months after obtaining their diploma. This study found the following: 12% were seeking employment; 55.1% had a job related to their training: 28.6% had a job unrelated to their training; and 1.2% had created their own employment. The authors showed that access to both stable and precarious employment was more and more difficult, and that the number of young job-seekers had increased.

---

1 This chapter uses some data from *Young skilled Chinese migrants and work in Lyon and Shanghai* CMIRA Program led by L. Roulleau-Berger, financed by the Rhône-Alpes Region (2012–2015) in cooperation with Zhen Zhihong and Yan Jun, School of Political Science and Sociology, Shanghai University. Some parts written by L. Roulleau-Berger in L. Roulleau-Berger, Yan Jun, *Travail et migration. Jeunesses chinoises à Shanghai et Paris*, La Tour d'Aigues, Editions de l'Aube, 2017, are revised and published in this chapter.

© LAURENCE ROULLEAU-BERGER, 2021 | DOI:10.1163/9789004463080_004

60 CHAPTER 2

In Shanghai, the migrant population increased by 221.1% between 2000 and 2015, from 3,057,400 to 9,816,500 individuals. Migrants aged 20 to 44 years represented 69.09% of the total migrant population. In 2010, of the migrants residing in Shanghai, 55.2% were junior secondary school graduates, 30.4% had the equivalent of the General Baccalaureate diploma (of which 14.1% had received tertiary education). Young migrants today are better educated than the previous generation. They hail from thirty different provinces, of which 29% from Anhui, 16.7% from Jiangsu and 8.7% from Henan. For the first time in 2015, the migrant population in Shanghai decreased by 104,100 individuals compared to the previous year.

The 2011 *Chinese Social Survey* revealed that "informal employment" has risen by 20% per annum, representing 60.4% of employment, and that temporary work has become widespread and only 41.1% of young workers—particularly migrant workers—have signed a fixed-term contract and 13.8% an open-ended contract. The transition from informal to formal employment is difficult. In China, job insecurity and flexibility are increasingly gaining ground. Many urban jobs are informal, held without a contract or on a short-term basis only, such as seasonal work or piecework activity. Such "informal employment" occurs in both the private and public sector, even though the latter was traditionally a provider of formal employment.

According to a 2013 study (Zhong Yunhua, 2015) in three universities in Changsha (a University of Excellence, part of the 985 programme, a medium-sized university, and a professional institute), of the young graduates entering the labour market in the last five years (classes of 2004, 2005, 2006, 2007, 2008 and 2009), 40% found initial employment that did not meet their expectations. Another 2011 study of 10,000 graduates found that 70% of those surveyed had changed jobs five years after finishing university. Half of graduates surveyed had engaged in professional mobility at least once during the five previous years (172 of 340, 50.58% mobility rate). The more socially privilege (gender, parents' social positions, rural or urban residence) graduates enjoy, the higher their chance is for upward social mobility. The wider the gap between graduates' expectations and their employment opportunities, the higher the chance is for spatial mobility. However, upward social mobility is far more likely for young graduates with employment that matches their interests and motivations.

Young graduate migrants find skilled employment in Chinese megalopolises as technicians or managers in public or privately-owned Chinese companies, as well as in international firms. However, most of them retain their migrant status and face insecure employment situations. Some young graduate migrants call themselves 北漂 *beipiao* which can be translated as Beijing vagabonds. Most of these young migrants do not have an urban *hukou* and are exposed to discrimination in their workplace by local authorities as a result. For example, a young graduate will struggle to find a job with a rural *hukou*. The loss of job security affecting these young graduates could be a result of the maladjustment of the training system with the employment system, the discrimination in the modes of accessing employment via the *hukou* and the transformation of urban policies.

High-order compressed modernity quickly leads to social and economic, disqualification, exclusion and discrimination. The least educated young migrants run the risk of not accessing a place in Chinese society while the most educated often only access spaces of employment in which the content of professional socialisation is poor. In China, the last five years have been marked by increased competition, the devaluation of academic achievement, a decreased return on academic investment and a simultaneous and continual rise in youth's social aspirations. This phenomenon of *structural disqualification* (Bourdieu, 1978) impacts low-skilled migrants in China above all. The *widespread and systemic downward social mobility* (Chauvel, 2016) has affected the young middle-class, while also leading to increased fragility among young people of peasant or working-class origins, particularly young low-skilled migrants in China.

Before 1979 in China, young recent university graduates had automatic access to reserved jobs. This significant phenomenon is telling of the economic transition and the rise of temporary and informal jobs. It has created collective disillusionment springing from the structural divide between the positions accessible by the education level and those offered on the foreign and Chinese labour markets. Young Chinese migrants face mounting competition for academic qualifications, which in turn widens the structural gap between their aspirations and their ability to enter the labour market. The social differentiation inherent in the process of social stratification will become increasingly pronounced with the phenomenon of educational inflation. For all young skilled Chinese migrants, the overall distortion of the relationship between the academic and employment markets results in a growing division between the nominal value of educational qualifications and their measured value in real transactions in the employment market. The gap between young migrants' social aspirations and tangible opportunities in the labour market rouses a feeling of social disqualification, injustice and protest in the workplace for young migrants in China. Those who have faced discrimination and exclusion in the workplace—whether directly or indirectly—hope to find real autonomy in their work. They refuse to have their autonomy restricted and successfully create their own employment:

I would like to have a better life, earning money is secondary. But you can't do anything without money, so the ideal is to have a balance of both. Everyone comes to Shanghai to study and work. We all have an ideal, we want to reach a certain standard of living, but this isn't something you can necessarily measure with money. I would like to start my own business later and contribute to the country's development. You should always have your own ideal and not say to yourself "this year I'll earn this much, so next year I need to earn this much [...]." It's better to have your own business and dealings, so you can say "I'm going to work the way I want". Starting a business is not necessarily just about earning money. On the one hand, it can be a way to prove to yourself that you have the ability to do something. On the other hand, once your business has reached a level of satisfactory development, you will perhaps be more at ease and able to enjoy life a bit more. Enjoying life doesn't mean staying trapped in a city. It's about having the time to take more holidays, travel, not stress about work all the time and be happy.

CAI, man, 28 years old, interview conducted in Shanghai in 2016

Young graduates employed in the public sector as temporary workers—deprived of any opportunities for internal mobility—feel strongly subjected to a denial of recognition. The results of the MyCOS survey conducted in 2010 noted that 49% of baccalaureate + 4 years' higher education (Bac+4) and 55% of baccalaureate + 3 years' higher education (Bac+3) graduates were not satisfied with their salaries, 23% wanted to change jobs or try a new line of work, 14% found the company management inadequate, 13% cited a lack of job security and 12% complained about stress at work. According to the Mycos Institute's 2019 Blue Book of Employment, in 2018, 85% of the licensed workers in Beijing are skilled migrants who do not have the local *hukou*. This proportion is 80% for the city of Shanghai.

In 2017, the majority of young migrants graduates in Shanghai work in the information, computer services and software sectors (21.23%), in the finance sector (13.21%) and in the production and construction industry sectors (18.87%). A minority (5.66%) work in leasing and business services, or in the public sector and administration (2.1%) (see Figure 3).

Discrimination in terms of access to employment emerges by the presence of jobs reserved for young migrants and also in employer/employee relationships, noting that most company managers in Shanghai are locals. In addition, whether or not the employee speaks Shanghainese may be used as part of distancing strategies in everyday work life. For example, Wang worked for a Japanese company and her colleagues refused to speak to her in Mandarin,

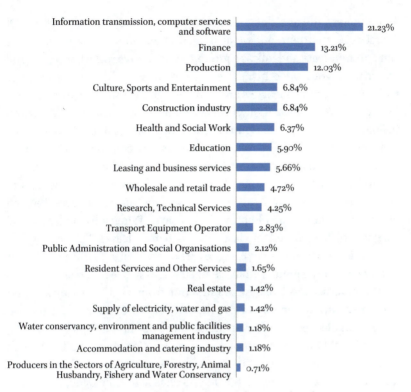

FIGURE 3   Economic sectors of young migrant graduates in Shanghai
SOURCE: SHANGHAI URBAN NEIGHBOURHOOD SURVEY (SUNS) 2017 (N=424)

addressing her instead in Shanghainese. Experiencing this situation as exclusive and violent, she resigned. These situations are clearly experienced in a doubly negative way: firstly, they are subject to covert exclusion by the work community which they belong to and secondly, in China, professional socialisation is highly important for individuals. These forms of covert yet active discrimination create identity issues among young Chinese and cause them to doubt their adaptive, relational and professional skills.

Young overqualified migrants feel that they are overlooked, and their professional skills are not recognised. They fight for recognition in the workplace. They vocalise the lack of regard by Shanghai natives for others in labour markets. Highly individualistic attitudes develop in the workplace and migrants are often viewed with contempt (Zhao Yeqin, 2012). Consider the example of this acupuncturist who explains that her Shanghainese colleagues do not treat her as a professional equal, and that tensions arise in her doctor-patient relationships because she is a not from Shanghai.

To be honest, life as a doctor is really tiring. Money isn't everything. Of course, it's important, but we also need others to look out for us. If we can communicate and talk as a group, we can derive some happiness and life at work goes smoothly. If we're happy at work, if the relationships with our boss and colleagues are trouble-free, we'll still stay even if we're underpaid. These days though social relationships have lost all warmth in Shanghai. The main reason is because the Shanghainese have inflated egos and are too proud to show foreigners any consideration. Another reason is, that in a practice, employees come from different parts of the country, and they move about all the time. One day we're colleagues and we're sharing a room, and the next they've gone, and we'll never see each other again. There is an old proverb that says, "When a friend leaves, the tea goes cold". No friendship lasts when a person leaves. This means that the relationships with our colleagues are superficial, and this has a major influence. In my opinion, what we need today is love and respect. That's what I think, it's how I analyse the situation from what I see. I am a doctor and I treat patients and try to give them relief, which makes the situation more bearable. People also respect me more because they need my help. But I think that the most important thing is dialogue and really listening to others. Some patients that we see are depressed, and what they are missing is love and people to talk to and engage in a dialogue.

JU, woman, 30 years old, interview conducted in Shanghai

The example of this young doctor reveals her emotional involvement in her work by bringing to light the tensions between Shanghainese doctors and doctors from other Chinese provinces, as well as between Shanghainese patients and non-local doctors. While the ways of coping with emotions varies depending on the occupation and professional field, young skilled migrants are forced to emotionally reintegrate into each new work experience.

Furthermore, the feminisation of salaried employment also has reinforced a gender-based division of jobs, with reinforced gender discrimination in the access to higher positions within the hierarchy and inequalities in salary reflecting gender inequalities. This can be illustrated by an analysis proposed by Tong Xin (2014) based upon a comparison of the careers of female company bosses and their male counterparts in China focusing on the vertical mobility of women in the context of the market economy and the particular mental dispositions of these women in a masculine world. The "glass ceiling" is a concentration of the ideas of visible and invisible barriers for women engaged in projects of vertical professional mobility. Although, in both situations, the distribution of employment, the type of business, the sector and the position

THE FABRIC OF "HEROES" AND EMOTIONAL CAPITALISM   65

held, the type of employment (full-time or part-time) as well as the career itinerary contribute to the construction of invisible barriers for women, in China, membership of the Communist Party plays an important role in overcoming these obstacles.

In China, the vertical division of labour and the system of professional relationships conforming to the socialist order is being progressively concealed by new hierarchies linked to a globalised capitalist order. With the decline of socialist institutions, there is a process of de-collectivisation and individuation which is depriving certain categories of workers—including young peasant-workers—of social, legal and economic rights. The systems of professional relationships produce situations of discrimination and domination in labour markets analysed as resulting from a conflict or shock between different regimes of compressed modernity. In the extension of communism and within a process of transformation, capital, power and control linked to compressed modernity combine according to a specific mode. Flexibility appears as a dominant norm in the regulation of the labour market in which poorly skilled migrants genuinely occupy a position as supernumeraries.

2   Compressed Modernities and Migratory Careers

Against the backdrop of widespread and systemic downward social mobility and structural disqualification, biographical bifurcations emerge along young Chinese' pathways. These appear through the convergence of largely unregulated and multi-scalar labour markets, multiple geographical mobilities and their experiences and social mobility skills. Most young Chinese migrants from the 80s, 90s and 00s generation do not have siblings. As only children, they alone receive all parental investment and are the sole custodians of their families' social, economic and emotional capital. Due to their parents' overinvestment, these youths have extremely high-level aspirations, and many believe that they are entitled to a high-level job. They believe that society owes them and quickly find themselves in situations of conflict with their hierarchical superiors. An only child will struggle to find a job in the employment market where they will receive the same level of investment as within their family. Being an only child can thus cause conflict in professional relationships and consequently encourages mobility processes. The latter occurs when these young people are unable to attain their desired status as the gap between educational level and social aspirations continues to widen. They have high social ambitions, causing them to resign when confronted with a lack of recognition in the workplace, even if this means being inactive at home with their parents for a while. The status of an only child reinforces the individualisation process which many young Chinese are experiencing and leads to a broadened range of professional experiences.

As discussed in chapter one, the professional pathways of young low-skilled migrants are formed by means of biographical bifurcations, or in other words, turning points between different work experiences. For young skilled migrants, these bifurcations result in strong professional mobilities founded on experiences of varied work content and geographical mobility with opportunities for professional development. These pathways are structured around spatial discontinuities that do not necessarily lead to professional discontinuities; migrants may move cities to find work in the same field of activity and acquire a position of equal status. Young Chinese migrants pursue career paths made up of a wide array of professional experiences in state-owned or privately-held companies, including Chinese firms, joint ventures, and even business start-ups. For example, in Shanghai they work in the transport, information technology, pharmaceutical, media, sports, public management, educational and cultural sectors, among others.

This series of bifurcations is a result of the competitive nature of labour markets and gives rise to professional mobilities that may or may not lead to social mobility. These bifurcations also demonstrate the young migrants' capacity in terms of action and reflexivity: when they can no longer tolerate their employment situation, they resign and look for another job. Bifurcations form through the intersection of professional and geographical mobility, yet their proliferation varies according to academic qualifications, employment opportunities and social and economic resources. Primary socialisations and acquired aptitudes influence the effects of biographical discontinuity. Social inequalities are revealed in the ordering of repertoires of resources—the more ordered the repertoires of economic, social and symbolic resources are—the better individuals can mitigate the effects of biographical discontinuity. Today, social inequality is increasing against this backdrop of intensifying migratory flows and the development of flexible capitalism.

Young skilled Chinese migrants move and circulate to improve their qualifications and education levels and develop pathways to upward social mobility. Our study carried out from 2012 to 2015 in collaboration with Shanghai University revealed that of the reasons that motivated young skilled migrants to move to Shanghai, over ½ of those surveyed hoped to develop pathways to upward social mobility.1/3 of young people hope to find stable employment. When asked at what stage these young Chinese quit their jobs, ½ of respondents left when faced with very hard work conditions, 1/5 left when they found no self-fulfilment in their job, and 1/10 left when they were not offered further training. The common thread amongst respondents was that they had developed mobility skills across different regions of China. We have drawn on the notion of the *habitus* of mobility which allows us to understand the ability to change jobs. An example of this is the case of a young 25-year-old man, having graduated with a Bachelor of Forestry Science, he began work as a real estate agent; he later joined an IT firm where he sold software, before becoming the supervisor of a fresh and frozen fish department in a large retailer.

Of the skilled migrants, the least skilled are subject to double-bind situations in terms of geographic and professional mobilities and their pathways are structured around multiple turning points. These young people resign due to low wages, overly intense work patterns and unpaid overtime. Additionally, they may choose to set up their own businesses. The career paths of the most skilled migrants, on the other hand, are characterised by fewer bifurcations. These may multiply, given that workers in the private sector often do not have employment contracts and can therefore circulate in labour markets. Professional mobilities often lead to higher wages. The careers paths of the highly skilled migrants are more likely to experience vertical mobility.

The spatial discontinuities of skilled young migrants' career pathways are punctuated by family temporalities, particularly for women. These paths feature sequences of temporary or definitive return home as, in keeping with tradition, families want their daughters close to them. An example of this is the case of a young Chinese woman who completed her Masters in Telecommunications and found a job as an engineer in a company in Beijing. She later returned to her home region and accepted a job her parents had found for her as a purchasing agent in a Malaysian company. They wanted her to live close to them.

Chinese families go to great lengths to find jobs for their daughters so that they can play their traditional role. Young migrant women's aspirations are often stymied by their parents upon their return to their home region. For example, a young woman, after having been employed as a factory worker in Tianjin, returned home to her small village to become an aesthetician on the advice of her aunt. Her father opposed the move, so she was forced to accept a job as a cement worker in a nearby village.

The sexuation of social relationships has a direct impact on the structural modes of spatial and professional discontinuities, exacerbating them during sequences of temporary or definitive return home to native provinces. The weight of family traditions does not promote a path to female emancipation for those lacking the psychological resources, strong self-affirmation and capacities to resist. Gendered inequality, spatial and professional discontinuities and family traditions subjugate Chinese migrant women, exposing them

68 CHAPTER 2

to instances of social disqualification through a process of commodification of social relationships.

We will make a distinction between three career paths young skilled Chinese migrants:
– careers with disaffiliative mobility
– careers with affiliative mobility
– careers with alternative mobility

These different forms of mobility produce weak or strong economic affiliations, differentiated vocational and social integration, and may also be linked to economic resistance in the context of compressed modernity.

2.1 *Disaffiliative Mobility and Weak Integration*

Of the group of skilled workers, the least qualified are subject to geographic and professional mobilities and their pathways are often defined by a high number of close bifurcations. In China, these close bifurcations arise through professional and spatial discontinuities and produce careers with mobility that take place in low-skilled spaces. Take the example of Ming, a young female migrant born in 1981 in Heilongjiang. She graduated from Harbin University with a Bachelor of Management and Tourism:

> After I quit my job in Shenzhen, I realised that I wanted to learn how to grow flowers. I decided to go to Kunming in winter. I stayed with a friend for a month; it was very cold and there was no heating. I told my friends that I wanted to grow flowers. They were surprised because it had nothing to do with my previous professional experience. I felt like I didn't know how to work with people, so I thought that trying with plants would be a good idea. Neither my friends nor the industry professionals supported my choice, they either thought I was too old to learn or they didn't trust me. They thought I was being lazy. I really wanted to start this job, but in the end a friend offered me a job in her business which manufactured PVC pipes. I accepted because I already had experience at U. I didn't know what else to do. They told me that the boss was going on a work trip to Europe and would only return in the new year, so I went to my parent's house in the North I am an only child, so I don't have a choice. I have to go home to see my parents in Harbin, in the North.
>
> After the new year, I went to live in the city of Lanzhou because a good friend of mine from university lived there. I discovered that if you knew someone there, it was easy to find a job in a travel agency. The only problem was that I had no professional connections in this little town. My friend told me to look for a job in Qingdao, the province's capital.

I decided to leave, even though I was hesitant since I didn't know anyone there either. I lived in a university dormitory for three months; I found a student who gave me his spot. I looked for work in tourism. I applied for a job in a travel agency that operated out of a hotel and they hired me. We worked with other companies and organised activities for them. We went to Laoshan every week to the islands to go hiking and see the sights. I worked there for two months, I was happy and loved working there. After two months, it started getting extremely hot in Qingdao in July, so we couldn't do anymore outdoor activities. As a result, my boss asked me to do sales, to take calls and talk to clients. I would spend all day on the phone trying to find new clients by canvassing companies to offer them our services. It felt like I was doing advertising for our company. I didn't enjoy these new tasks and I still wasn't sure what I wanted to do, maybe I was too young at 26 years of age. So, I decided to quit and travel to the Liaoning region to Lingyuan, which is the flower capital of Northern China. I still hadn't given up on the idea of growing flowers! Each time I failed at communicating with men, I told myself that it might be easier with plants. I discovered that with flowers and vegetables it's the same routine, you cut them with a machete and then head to the market to try and sell the harvest. It's mind-numbing and wasn't what I had imagined.

One day someone told me that because I spoke Russian, it might be better to go back to the north of China close to the border with Russia, to Harbin, the city where I did my studies [...]. I worked for six months in a company that conducted international trade, in particular with Russia. I liaised with factories that manufactured in China and sold products in Russia. That's when I met my first boyfriend. It was in 2008 and I was already 27. I was old and needed to start thinking about marriage, my parents were pressuring me. Our company opened an office in Shenzhen in March 2008, so we moved there. We stayed in Shenzhen for just three to four months and I found work in a hotel as a secretary for three months. My salary was 4,000 yuan, which isn't bad. I quit and then my boyfriend and I moved back to the Heilongjiang province. Instead of going to Harbin, we decided to go to Suifenhe, which is not far from Vladivostok. We thought that we could find jobs in international trade there.

MING, woman, 33 years old, Heilongjiang origin, interview conducted in Beijing in 2014

The career path of this young female migrant, a Bachelor of Management and Tourism graduate—who lived in different Chinese cities over a period of nine years—is a perfect example that underscores the high mobility skills of young

Chinese migrants. They assert strong personal identities and appear to have freed themselves from Chinese family values. They constantly cycle through different jobs and training; a cycle that reflects both the economic uncertainties in a China undergoing a major transition, and the issues surrounding career orientation in labour markets that facilitate neither stable employment, nor the development of professional expertise in a speciality field. The series of jobs held by this young woman appear disjointed from each other and her training as a florist underlines the young migrants' vague horizon of expectations. The succession and diversity of spatial and professional mobilities do not give rise to social, economic or mobility capital. After nine years, Ming still had not found a place in Chinese society.

Careers with disaffiliative mobility are defined by a high frequency of spatial discontinuities linked to low-skilled employment. Professional pathways are structured around employment experiences in unrelated sectors. With each step along the migratory pathway, young migrants develop weak capacities to organise and hierarchise the knowledge and expertise acquired in their previous professional experiences. Social and spatial capital, aspirational capacities and mobility skills combine negatively to produce economic disaffiliation in compressed modernity.

2.2 *Affiliative Mobility and Strong Integration*

The most qualified have more control over their geographic and professional mobilities, and their pathways are often built around distant bifurcations.

> At that time, I wanted to find a job in the large private Chinese companies in the city of Hangzhou. I had applied for a job online and two months later I found full-time, ongoing employment with a large retailer. I learnt the ropes very quickly and followed a training course for the first few months. I worked as a checkout assistant and then joined the financial management department. In the second year, I became client relations manager for the State Taxation Administration. I was fortunate because my old classmates worked as civil servants in the State Taxation Administration, which was helpful. In 2007, my fiancée (an old university classmate) went on to study a PhD in Singapore and in 2009, she went to France on exchange. I visited her in Singapore in 2008. When I returned to China, I spent one year preparing to go to work in Singapore. I sat an English test and also obtained an internationally recognised certificate in accounting. I moved to Singapore in February 2009 and lived there for two years. I looked for work every day for two months and finally found a job as an accountant in a small firm. I moved to Singapore on temporary

visa granted to graduates of the five major Chinese universities, which included mine. After finding a job, I acquired a work permit that had to be renewed every year. I had a one-year renewable work contract. Since I was a foreigner, I didn't have access to public services or social security in Singapore. Many of my old classmates and Chinese friends had finished their PhDs there and were able to acquire permanent residency permits easily. Without this status, it's difficult to find employment in Singaporean companies. When you have a temporary work permit, the company must pay a tax to hire you. That's the reason why SMEs prefer to hire locals.

> LI, man, 29 years old, interview conducted in Shanghai in 2015

Careers with affiliative mobility are structured around a low frequency of spatial discontinuities and skilled employment with opportunities for professional development. Professional pathways are structured around employment experiences in related sectors. With each step along the migratory pathway, young migrants develop strong skills to organise and hierarchise the knowledge and expertise they acquire in their previous professional experiences. They bring their previously acquired skills to the new market segment. Social and spatial capital, aspirational capacities and mobility skills combine positively to produce economic affiliation in compressed modernity.

They experience repeated employment situations that overlap and are strikingly similar in content. They are able to hold long-term positions in various positions and can therefore establish themselves and generate continuity across their professional experiences.

2.3 *"Alternative" Mobility and the Distancing of Compressed Modernity*
A group of young Chinese migrants take up a stance of resistance to the norm of the cult of excellence, which is the beating heart of compressed modernity. They reject employment situations that feature strong injunctions to flexibility and productivity in order to best adapt their professional expertise and aspirations to their chosen job. For example, Yalin, an only child born in a rural zone in the Anhui province, studied finance in a business school, although he was only marginally interested in this field. He then found a job in a company based in Kunshan as a sales representative and had to contact prospective clients on a daily basis and persuade them to buy the company's products. After two months, he found this job increasingly monotonous and decided to join his father in Beijing where he worked in a real estate agency for fifteen days before returning to his university for his graduation ceremony. He then moved to Hefei, the capital of the Anhui province, and worked there for two months as

a professional gamer. After the 2013 Chinese New Year, Yalin went to Shanghai to work as a waiter in a café. Despite not being satisfied with the salary, he was more and more willing to accept mobility. He planned to continue his studies in design and want to find a job in Suzhou with his girlfriend.

This approach of creating distance with compressed modernity prompts young Chinese migrants to start their own microenterprise or become self-employed in industries such as the arts, craftsmanship and sports. Careers with alternative mobility are structured around employment experiences across a variety of fields of activity. Social and spatial capital, aspirational capacities and mobility skills combine through distancing from flexible work. Young migrants develop skills to organise and hierarchise the expertise when they position themselves with a positive relationship in the workplace. They refuse to bring previously acquired skills from different professional experiences when faced with work situations perceived as having no future prospect for professional development.

Finally, there is a category of young graduates who develop careers of alternative mobility in taking distance with compressed modernity and undertaking social work as moral entrepreneurs (Becker, 1963). Migrant labour had been the subject of significant political investment since the early 1990s, and in the 2000 saw a growing mobilisation of various social actors such as members of NGO s, intellectuals, journalists, artists, etc. (Froissart, 2011). In 2001, the Ministry of Education put forward the "Two Mainlines" policy, suggesting that the local government and the public schools of host cities play key roles in the education of migrant children (Xiong Yihan, 2015). Over the past decade, many social organisations and non-profit foundations have set up educational programmes for these 流动儿童 *liudong er tong* (migrant children). For example, Shanghai is among the six areas in China with the highest percentages of internal migrants, there are 970,000 migrant children who account for 41.51% of all children in the city (Xiong Yihan, Li Miao, 2017; Yiu Lisa, Yun Luo, 2017). Today, young qualified migrants who want to adopt standards of social justice for migrant workers, especially by safeguarding their rights, have become moral entrepreneurs by investing in social work in NGO s. They deal with situations of social injustice and discrimination of young workers, including the marginalisation and social abandonment of *liudong er tong*. Young people have been heavily involved in NGO s to promote citizenship education in China, as in the case of Weiwei, a 38-year-old teacher in Shanghai we met in 2017.

> I arrived in 2009 in S. and have been working there for 8 years. I was born in the countryside and was educated in rural areas until the age of 18. I obtained a good score in the 高考 *gaokao* (college entrance

examination) and was admitted to the Social Work Department of Fudan University. My classmates from primary and secondary schools, those who couldn't enter university, found employment instead. At university, I worked for 4 years on week-ends as a volunteer in schools for migrant children, very poor children who had no hope for the future. I wanted to volunteer because of my rural background. Before 2006, these children and their parents had poor living conditions, they could not go to public school, and their only option was to attend a private school. They felt inferior to others. They had no hope or confidence in themselves or in the future. This situation affected me. Children their age in Shanghai are very energetic at first glance and are very optimistic, but these migrant children are very desperate, especially those in middle school who drop out of school. This is the most important experience of my life outside of school.

These young moral entrepreneurs attempt to develop citizenship education and multidimensional citizenship by producing social recognition and respect for young migrants' skills with the view to "build citizens". For example, the aim of Changban's New Citizen Plan is to provide migrant children with an educational philosophy by recognising them as autonomous, responsible and socially competent citizens, capable of building their own social identity in belonging to urban and rural areas (Xiong, Li, 2017). They have developed policies of recognition based on individuation and the promotion of young migrants' self-esteem. Upon graduating, some migrant students in the NGO can choose to work as full-time social workers.

This category of young migrants who become social workers manufacture spaces of social restructuring between the State and the so-called "vulnerable" populations. They build bridges between different Chinese worlds, the urban and rural worlds, and participate in the production of forms of ordinary citizenship in an authoritarian context.

3 Moral Economies and the *Compressed Individual*

Young migrants' careers paths cannot be considered from a purely objective angle. In fact, subjectivities are constantly at work on the structural modes of career sequences and vice-versa. The migratory experience contains situations of self-redefinition characterised by a strong social distortion in which a considerable gap opens up between individuals' subjective feelings about themselves and their real identities (Goffman, 1963), as well as between self-identities and attributed identities (Dubar, 1992). Self-identities contain the "actual self", the "ideal self" and the "ought self" (Higgins, 1987). The migratory experience creates gaps in self-identities, attributed identities and conflicts between the dimensions of self, in other words:

- between the actual self and the ideal self: young migrants rarely succeed in finding their dream job;
- between the actual self and the ought self: young migrants feel that society owes them a debt.

These gaps and identity-based conflicts that young Chinese migrants must manage alter their self-ownership, which can in turn gradually give way to loss of self (Castel, Haroche, 2001). They are often denied their expected place in Chinese society and face uncertain employment. Nevertheless, they strive to reach their ideal of social success and maintain ownership of themselves. The idea that the individual has innate value is challenged with each change in their employment situation. Self-ownership emerges as a possession linked both to self-worth and the power to influence others. It is also dependent on young people's family, educational, economic, social and cultural resources as well as the social interactions in which they are used and transformed. The nature of the types of employment and status to which young Chinese migrants have access influences the way in which self-ownership grows stronger or weaker. The more social recognition is eroded in Chinese labour markets, the wider the identity gaps grow, self-conflict intensifies, and self-ownership is further altered.

While the feeling of social competency develops in part during the process of primary socialisation, it constantly redefines itself during migratory cycles. We will address the question of how the migratory experience can generate a feeling of social incompetence across different modes through:

- weak or strong family and peer networks
- weak social, moral and legal recognition
- difficulty accessing the labour markets

In *disaffiliative mobility and weak integration,* close bifurcations do not foster the recognition of skills in social spaces of weak legitimacy. These young migrants endure social contempt present in the brutal restriction of personal autonomy and the corresponding feeling of being denied the status of fully interactive partners experienced by the Subject, having the same moral rights as their peers. This privation and rejection can cause psychological breaks. Young Chinese migrants may be overwhelmed by the loss of self, and the relationships in their network of peers and friends are affected (Castel, 1995). In this case, young Chinese migrants may be deemed to have lost self-ownership since they have no social or symbolic goods. Shame sets in where the migratory experience becomes an ordeal, where they can no longer endure the symbolic violence caused by the ever-widening gulf between their aspirations and what they are offered (Roulleau-Berger, 1999).

In *affiliative mobility and strong integration, distant* bifurcations foster the recognition of skills in social spaces of strong legitimacy. A succession of skilled employment situations with opportunities for professional development result in a feeling of competence and social standing and equally affects their family and peer network. Young migrants who receive recognition from their peers and loved ones come into ownership of social, economic and symbolic goods, and may be defined as having self-ownership in Chinese society.

In *alternative mobility and the distancing of compressed modernity*, in which young migrants reject injunctions to flexibility and productivity, a succession of mobilities could lead to troubled socialisations and confused identities. They can lead to limited social recognition through atypical forms of employment and peer networks. These careers foster social standing, ensuring the predominance of self-worth over self-loathing through the development of different social roles. Young Chinese migrants retain self-ownership in situations of economic affiliation linked to social spaces with unequal legitimacy.

We can therefore say that there are different forms of loss and self-ownership according to young Chinese migrants' resilience and ability to adapt. Nevertheless, self-ownership can rapidly transform into self-loathing, and conversely, shame can develop into self-worth. When young migrants enter employment situations with opportunities for professional development after a succession of jobs where they are none, the individual's self-worth is strengthened in the eyes of society. The opposite is also true in situations of degrading work; shame suffocates self-worth. Self-worth and shame appear to be aspects of self-identity that are reversible and dynamic. However, young Chinese migrants can reach a saturation point where they lose their reflexive ability amid the host of precarious situations they face. The phenomena of repetition and intensification of situations degrades their status and generates the irreversibility of the feeling of loss of self in some young migrants.

In compressed modernity, *forms of relational self-identities* draw on the reflexive self, and the forms of biographical self-identity, referring to the self-narrative (Dubar, 1992, 2001), intersect and overlap through processes of identity conversion (Strauss, 1959) and even alternation (Berger, Luckmann, 1986). These processes are permanently imposed on the individual who experiences great difficulty adapting to the different selves across a plethora of spaces and constrained temporalities. Here we witness the emergence of the *Compressed Individual.*

76 CHAPTER 2

4 "Being a Hero" and Restricted Autonomy

In *compressed modernity*, flexibility and mobility emerge as the principal norms of action in the construction of an enrichment economy (Boltanski, Esquerre, 2017) which contributes to the advent of global capitalism divided into different branches in an anarchic way. We can therefore speak of the *arrogance of the* economy and the *economy of arrogance* (Favereau, 2015) which is based on violent forms of modern management designed to stir the spirit of competition, the journey of self-discovery and the taste for adventure (Linhart, 2015). Within a context of compressed modernity which generates accelerations and illimitability in a diversity of spaces and temporalities, we are witnessing the rise of the Chinese middle-class and the process of professional exclusion of young skilled people. These young skilled migrants, some of whom are graduates in precarious situations, are partially aware of their social position due to the injunctions to be oneself. They face an intense "dyssocialisation, or a violent contradiction between the values, representations and identities transferred from the previous generation and the conditions and situations experienced by the emerging generation." (Chauvel, 2016, p. 170).

The organisation of the labour system in the information technology sector is a clear illustration of an economy of arrogance. Tong Xin (2015) demonstrates that in this Internet age, global share capital resulted in an image of wealth among the technical elite. On the one hand, this image has a strong cultural and symbolic significance. On the other, it enforces a work regime in which young people work the maximum amount of overtime in a segment of the highly skilled labour market. Many youth work in Internet subcontracting firms in which employees have access to profit-sharing schemes. The symbolic value of this type of immaterial labour and the enrichment myth masks the changes in employer-employee relationships based on the instability, high productivity and fragmentation of work.

The young technical elite always seek to further their intellectual and innovative expertise by adhering to a work ethic based on self-discipline, which perpetuates the myth of enrichment and heroic work. There are three types of workers in Internet firms: core staff, a large number of temporary workers, and managers. The latter play a central role in management, technology and sales and have full-time contracts and company shares. Professional relationships in the Internet sector have undergone widespread change and clearly reflect what is occurring in other sectors of the Chinese labour market. The intellectual and technical elite currently play an important part in the production of global share capital by perpetuating the enrichment myth accepted by many Chinese youth. In this economy of enrichment and arrogance, the control of technical symbols becomes an issue of major importance. The Chinese intellectual elite are very active in Internet firms, where becoming a hero is possible when young migrants in precarious work conditions are silenced.

In an environment of collective anxiety (Li Chunling, 2019), young Chinese migrants fight for themselves (Yan Jun, 2014). They do this through a process of contradictory socialisation structured around exhausting identity work and managing double-bind situations between injunctions to take their place in the city and difficulties accessing spaces of strong urban legitimacy. Social and moral systems that capture selves result in new forms of alienation and forced servitude to the regime of compressed modernity. This highlights the widespread transformation of forms of arrogance gives rise to Subjects under constant evaluation by others, victims of the tyrannies of the overexposure of self. As noted by Claudine Haroche (2015) these evaluation schemes contribute to making the formation of subjectivity a Market object that fragments individuals' identities. One question remains: what strategies of self-maintenance are available to young skilled Chinese migrants when confronted with situations of restricted autonomy in an environment of arrogance and economic and moral uncertainty?

The *Compressed Individual* is restricted to individual self-realisation and mandatory autonomy. For young graduates in China, the rise of autonomy and responsibility comes at the cost of the abrupt loss of protections they previously enjoyed. The Compressed Individual is both more restricted and more autonomous in an economy of arrogance where "becoming a hero" ensures access to a social position and public recognition. However, young Chinese migrant graduates are increasingly implicated in a multi-compressed modernity in that they are born in a traditional culture and have transitioned into a modernising/industrialising era and have to survive in a post-modern/post-industrial era (Chang Kyung Sup, 2017). Consequently, they must continually juggle with new forms of restricted autonomy which force them to acquire strong adaptability skills and creates a sense of fatigue regarding being oneself.

Against a background of compressed modernity, restricted autonomy can be understood as a dramaturgy that brings order and progress into conflict (Ehrenberg, 2010), it can also be understood as a dramaturgy linked to the political evolution in China and a desire to escape from a form of political authoritarianism. While autonomy entails independence in a democratic context, it cannot take on the same meaning in an authoritarian environment. The construction of social and moral autonomy in China must be understood through the history of the Chinese civilisation and the policies of the Chinese society. Although the transition from autonomy as an aspiration to autonomy as a condition or restriction seems to be a movement characteristic of neo-liberal societies, this transformation occurred very rapidly in Chinese society at the apogee of the "cult of excellence". Just as autonomy became a condition for competition at the same time the Welfare State entered a crisis period in Europe, it also became a condition for competition in China during the development of its market economy.

At the same moment autonomy emerges as a strong aspiration amongst young people at odds with a socialist heritage, it almost immediately becomes a condition. This almost instantaneous change weakens family, community and social ties, unravels solidarity networks, exacerbates competition between young people and breeds individual and collective fears. Above all, young Chinese migrants may face the ordeal of loss: the loss of employment, loss of family networks due to the distance from their home region, loss of peers due to repeated mobilities in different places and loss of self. These personal ordeals seem almost contradictory and effectively inhibit aspirations of autonomy and place individuals in situations where they are forced to "be themselves". The ordeal of loss becomes more acute in a context of the growing instability in the lives of young Chinese migrants, resulting in inequalities and exposure to objective and subjective risks faced with flexibility and the injunction to achieve "social success".

As a result, fears arise out of the impossibility of "being a hero", being unable to use their social, family and cultural heritage to become themselves in the future, and being unable to take advantage of networks forged in their previous socialisations. These fears feed feelings of failure, disappointment and disillusionment which are subsequently internalised. The ordeal of loss can quickly anaesthetise young Chinese migrants whose strong capacities to act and mobilise must first be used in social and economic competition.

The quest for recognition and happiness at work become a key element in the production of emotional capitalism; young graduates respond "positively" to these injunctions. Young Chinese migrant graduates with ambitions to "succeed" are blind to the fact that their aspirations to become "heroes" in Chinese society are commodified. The sphere of capitalist consumption is far-reaching in China and transforms and commodifies their feelings and emotional states into "emodities": they are overexposed in the workplace and "actively appropriate the offered stimuli by transforming their own emotions into commodities" (Illouz, 2019). On the one hand, they do this to conform to a heroic role, and, on the other, to participate in consumerist culture.

The pathways of young migrant graduates are a flagrant example of how rationality and emotionality strongly underpin Chinese capitalism. If, according to Axel Honneth, self-realisation became an institutional requirement during the second half of the 20th century in Western societies, in China it abruptly

THE FABRIC OF "HEROES" AND EMOTIONAL CAPITALISM   79

became a requirement in a context of compressed modernity founded on the incompleteness of self. In an authoritarian environment, some young migrants participate in the "industry of happiness". It shapes an individual according to their emotional rationality: their ability to keep their feelings under control to better suit the standards of compressed modernity; to employ reflexive and strategic choices; and to master their emotions in order to access their inner selves (Cabanas, 2019). It is evident that compressed modernity generates beliefs around the possibility of creating self-made men who will never achieve self-fulfilment.

Nonetheless, young migrant graduates do not all place themselves in compressed modernity in the same way and do not internalise the injunction to succeed and be a hero in Chinese society to the same extent, an injunction that impacts both their personal and professional sphere.

In *affiliative mobility*, young migrants perform emotional labour to conform to social expectations and may overexert themselves out as a result of internalising norms of competition, flexibility and productivity. The wide range of work situations slightly alters their relationship to work founded on overinvestment and the quest for excellence and self-realisation.

In *disaffiliative mobility* young migrants develop weak social and emotional capacities, drawing on repertoires of social, economic resources which can lead to situations of "failure" in relation to their aspirations to become "heroes" in compressed modernity.

In *alternative mobility*, young migrants distance themselves from work and criticise the injunction to internalise the norms of success and excellence, seen as impeding self-realisation. These young people criticise the disrespect of human dignity at work intensely in a society which, in their eyes, places too much importance on the pursuit of money. In addition, they distance themselves from "heroes" who act out of over affirmation of self and the contempt of others.

These skilled young migrants develop social lives in spatial and temporal accelerations and illimitability in an unbridled struggle to gain access to themselves. This struggle creates moral and physical fatigue that may provoke physical and mental illnesses. The modes of social differentiation between young Chinese migrants are defined by social, economic and moral abilities to "be oneself". This lack of limitations upsets young migrants' interactions with their environment and identities, challenged in a plurality of spaces and temporalities in China and on a global scale. Migratory flows, experiences and careers illustrate how young Chinese migrants can lose awareness of spatial and temporal limits in a context of great economic uncertainty and acceleration. They show how these youths enter an endless struggle for self that makes

80 CHAPTER 2

them forget the tangible, available resources they have on hand to make their aspirations and life goals a reality. The conquest of self seems linked to accelerations and the overlapping social and economic temporalities reinforced by high-compressed modernity.

5 *Guanxi* and Professional Relationships

It is impossible to consider professional relationships and work life in China without taking *guanxi* (interpersonal relationships) into account. Yang Yiyin (2008, 2009) defined two forms of *guanxi*: the *guanxi* passed down from the previous generation and a second form born out of affective relationships built on trust and obligation. *Guanxi* here set out a type of relationship and coordination in the workplace which abides by implicit and hidden criteria which are more or less visible, rendering professional relationships particularly complex and above all, maintaining them.

Luo Jarde and Yeh.K. (2012) demonstrated the Chinese are both collectivists and individualists as reflected by their circles with different types of trust related to the differential modes of association in terms of family, familiar, and acquaintance ties (Luo Jarde, Yeh. K., 2008). If *guanxi* is not a unified concept in Chinese sociology, flexibility and trust play a central role in *guanxi* circles: a circle is an ego-centric network, it had a structure of what Fei Xiaotong (1992) called a 差序格局 *chaxu geju* (differential mode of association), the boundary of a circle is not closed, and outsiders may be included in the circle. The concept of trust is related with the Chinese concept of 伦 *lun* (or moral codes in family relationships); the norm of *lun* requires collectivist behaviour in the sphere of family ties, trust in family ties is mainly the type of personalised trustfulness as trust-as-choice. Familiar ties also means strong ties, a mixture of instrumental and expressive ties. Finally, guanxi means both instrumental exchanges and emotional involvement (Chen Qi, Wu Qi, 2014).

Chinese sociologists talk of institutional arrangements subtended by *guanxi*. It is indeed difficult to understand the inability of migrant workers to claim their rights without integrating the function of the *guanxi* linked to the old system of organising traditional relationships of family and geographical identity. However, the strength of the *guanxi* of migrants within Chinese labour markets reveals networks which are constructed from the transfer or exchange of economic, symbolic and commercial resources. These exchanges of resources are constructed upon the basis of loyalties arising out of group membership and relationships of trust within the framework of inter-acquaintance and family networks which play a fundamental role in accessing Chinese labour markets. Nevertheless, the strength of these *guanxi* does not favour solidarities for resisting situations of domination in the employment world. These *guanxi* can create a relationship of dependence, even captivity between the worker and the employer or foreman, a relationship which prevents collective action and shatters solidarities (Shen Yuan, 2011). *Guanxi* are a real means of regulating organisational structures and give rise to forms of professional integration, coordination and collective action within companies. In the socialist tradition, interpersonal relationships in the *danwei* (work unit) were founded on personal and professional relationships.

Since the end of the *danwei* regime, despite the diversification of the labour market, the separation between professional and interpersonal relationships defines the lives of young Chinese in the workplace today. The *danwei* regime was characterised by the expression of emotions and feelings and a certain level of intimacy in professional relationships. However, the systems of professional relationships in Chinese companies are established through strong competition that governs interactions between different categories of workers to improve work efficiency, and through the restriction of promotions and bonuses (Du Hui, Lu Yini, Li Ding, 2013; Yan Jun, 2014). In the past, *guanxi* paved the way to interpersonal relationships and personal feelings, but now a focus on competition and performance between employees underpin working life in companies.

Compressed modernities, the change of labour regimes, the growing importance of economic competition and the escalation of geographic mobilities structure young migrants' interpersonal relationships in the professional space. Today using *guanxi* without the required professional skills can lead to forms of marginalisation: "if you find a job through your *guanxi*, your colleagues may dislike you. They know you have no skills and that you'll never be entrusted with important tasks" (Man, 28 years old, interviewed in 2016 in Shanghai). Young people with limited *guanxi* can assert their personal success and work engagement by excluding individuals with extensive *guanxi*. Local norms, the norms of compressed modernity and norms linked to global capitalism are constantly overlapping in a process of economic transformation on Chinese labour markets.

For example, Wang moved to Shanghai with five classmates and they all found a job in a telemarketing company. One of Wang's classmates found the training too hard, so he quit early on. The job involved writing a long list of phone numbers; it was very boring work. Moreover, they experienced extreme levels of competition with their co-workers and felt immense pressure. Two months later, Wang and all his friends resigned. He then felt into a depressive state, launching into a series of geographic mobilities which altered his network of personal acquaintances every time. Some of his co-workers became his friends and they developed collaborative relationships outside of work.

When the Labour Law is applied and professional roles are well defined, employers' personal authority is limited to a certain extent due to the stability of the work roles. As a result, it is no longer useful for employees to establish personal working relationships with their employers as this no longer provides any benefits. Additionally, directors also want to avoid any intimate relationships in order to steer clear of potential issues. Where previously personal relationships helped contain conflicts, today mobilities play an active part in differentiating between professional and interpersonal relationships. In the *danwei*, employees worked and lived in the same place, developing intimate relationships with their colleagues in an emotionally-charged work space. In today's environment of increased commodification, however, young migrants forced into mobility and unbridled competition disproportionately invest in multiple work spaces. In compressed modernities, working relationships are made, unmade and remade in a succession of biographical bifurcations and changing identities that create indifference in each new work situation. Young migrants must adapt to emotional sub-cultures specific to different professional segments and employ different social and symbolic resources.

6   Socialist Heritage, Compressed Modernities and Work

By virtue of the long-standing historical tradition and socialist heritage, the job of civil servant in China has taken on a particular meaning. From the 1990s onwards, young Chinese have expressed collective refusal to work as a civil servant. They see this role as being too closely connected to their parents' lives, captives of a work regime that they reject. Refusing the position of civil servant did and still does unlock new horizons of opportunities and self-realisation in a context of economic and political transition.

> My classmates who worked as civil servants decided to quit to launch into the business world! Because, when you're a civil servant, it takes time to get a promotion. Unless you want nothing out of life, I think that wasting time reading the newspaper and drinking tea all day is throwing away your youth. Is there really any meaning to it? It's impossible to stay in this type of job for long, it's deadly boring. Of course, work as a civil servant is a stable job, but this stability consists of doing nothing at all. If you are young and have dreams, there is no point locking yourself in an office to

THE FABRIC OF "HEROES" AND EMOTIONAL CAPITALISM   83

play cards and read the newspaper. If you start with nothing, you'll finish
with nothing and have spent your life sitting idly in a chair.

JIE, man, 28 years old, interview conducted in 2016 in Shanghai

After this initial movement of young Chinese flatly refusing the position of
civil servant in the 90s, some of them took up the job in the end when faced
with situations of intense economic uncertainty. While this role does not meet
their social aspirations, they long to have a status which guarantees real job
security. However, young migrants also do not want to commit themselves to a
job that is founded on denying the meaning of performance, social distinction
and individual differentiation.

> I didn't like it, I already had a range of work experiences and thought
> about going back to university, but the thought of studying again didn't
> sit well with me. I didn't want to live in a dormitory again. After living
> there for one week I couldn't put up with it anymore, so I decided to
> return to our danwei 单位 *danwei* (work unit) and start working again.
> I worked in the administration department and handled policy regu-
> lation. I was responsible for taxation for a few months. I had to sign
> documents every day and check that the documents had been stamped
> correctly. If they weren't, I would take care of it and sign the document.
> That's all I did, stamping, signing, nothing else. I had to get my boss to
> sign the documents, but I could never find him. I therefore forged his
> signature, everyone did the same. This is what I did from my first to my
> last day when I resigned; I couldn't stand it anymore. I remember that
> when we left school to attend the training course, the director for the
> province came to see us. He told us he hoped everything was going well
> and that we didn't feel too alone. Being a civil servant in China means
> losing your personality and killing off your individuality. They don't like
> originality and difference. If you're different, the other will quickly see
> you as a threat.

CHAN, woman, 26 years old, interview conducted in Shanghai in 2016

The status of civil servant is therefore still a valid option for some young
Chinese migrants. In China, this status symbolises their parents' forced labour.
It is viewed as a repetitive, methodical job lacking in creativity, but one that
offers promotion opportunities and internal mobility. In today's uncertain
times, some young migrants choose a stable job in the public sector where
employment contracts are generally signed for four years.

My father was employed in a work unit equivalent to the marine police. Prior to that, he was a salesman in the construction industry. He's retired now. People of his generation found work at a very young age and didn't change jobs for more than twenty years. I think travelling overseas is important, but because I'm an only child, I can't leave." After graduating with a Master's degree, Gang found an administration job online that involved helping students in a research centre: "My primary responsibility is the daily management of Master's students at the J campus (Shanghai district). There are five of us in my department. We take care of everything, from students' recruitment and training to their graduation. Because I'm young, I didn't have many responsibilities at the start. I was an assistant for the most part [...]. Yes, my work is repetitive, but I'm very satisfied with my current job. I'm happy that it's not in line with studies I finished in the environmental field, because studies in this area condemn you to an exhausting and boring job. I don't want to change jobs. I want to buy a house and start a family.

GANG, man, 26 years old, interview conducted in Shanghai in 2016

Young migrants resign from state-owned companies to find jobs in other companies with the idea of quickly developing internal mobility pathways, especially in foreign companies. In the following example, the transition from the public to the private sector is evidently complex. It required this individual to accept social marginalisation and build strong geographic and professional mobility capacities.

Yiyin started her first job in 2008 in a public company, staying in the same role until 2010 where she was head of sales. The salary was not particularly high, but it guaranteed a certain degree of job stability. She liked the fact that her boss was young and dynamic. Nevertheless, she faced a serious problem: there was a language barrier as most of her colleagues were Shanghainese. She felt excluded and went to great lengths to integrate. After two years, she changed jobs and worked for another company, where she was given more responsibilities. She moved from sales to management, moving further away from her initial qualification. However, the company's share capital was held by an American national of Chinese heritage living overseas, triggering conflict between the regulations for foreign-owned companies and those of the Chinese labour market. Yiyin had difficult relationships with her colleagues, and gradually realised that the job suited her less and less. In 2012, she found a new job that failed to meet her expectations: "I want to try my hand in start-ups, even just to feel like I'm gaining experience. Also, the salary in a public company compared to a private one is not the same. My salary in the first company was 80% of what I earned in the second company." With a prospect of upward social mobility, Yiyin started a new job in a video game start-up, she secured a managers's position. We met her in 2016, she was 28 years old.

The 90s and 00s generation have criticised the phenomena of corruption and underhanded tactics in the public and private sectors. They assert a work ethic that is critical of the norms of circulation in labour markets.Some of the most skilled migrants aspire to a working life that allows them more time off to enjoy recreational activities that are currently developing in China. Being a public servant today in China looks paradoxical for young people. The status is both appealing due to the inherent job security, and unappealing owing to its repetitive nature, including the lack of creativity and the dearth of future possibilities. This paradox reflects the tension between a socialist heritage and compressed modernity.

Since the end of the 1990s, the workplace has been increasingly viewed as a place of disappointment and disillusionment for young skilled Chinese migrants. They experienced a widening gap between their aspirations and opportunities on the job market. This disillusionment had varying subjective and objective impacts for each category of migrant, and this phenomenon gradually affected the more skilled young migrants. This disillusionment reflected a sense of shared injustice and shame. The rejection of all types of "dirty work" effectively leads to the growing divide between these young migrants' aspirations and the opportunities afforded them on the job market. They felt exploited, excluded and increasingly worried about the prospect of a future with insecure employment with no opportunities for professional development with no social mobility. Nevertheless, young skilled migrants are fully engaged in their work providing it fulfils the conditions for their aspirations, moral autonomy and social creativity. They all place importance on having engaging tasks and responsibilities, the prospect of social independence and a company incentive scheme.

The phenomenon of structural disqualification also plays a role in inhibiting the aspirations of young skilled Chinese migrants. Geographical and professional mobilities generate multiple and paradoxical socialisations that give rise to double-bind situations between the injunction to work and the impossibility of working under the expected modes. Different types of double-bind situations arise in the young migrants' different career types. In alternative and mobility and the distancing of compressed modernity, they number of double-bind situations are reduced, while they increase in segregative mobility and adaptive mobility. In careers of integrative and alternative mobility, young Chinese migrants are generally able to plan and fulfil their careers prospects. A type of agreement governs the organisation of the selves and maintains the harmony between the social, instrumental and symbolic dimensions in the workplace. In careers of segregated and alternative mobility, ever-changing work situations have the effect of fragmenting dimensions in the workplace, meaning that the instrumental, social and symbolic dimensions come into conflict.

The question of young Chinese migrants' commitment to work is therefore acutely raised in the multifaceted usages of employment status—all the more since it seems to be reversible, protean and fluctuating—depending on the time, situation, and place, in China or Europe. The different double-bind situations in the relationship to work underline a plurality of possible meanings and significations attached to employment and business in China, as the following example illustrates:

> Most of my university classmates had found a good job; many had chosen to work with international accounting firms or in banks as civil servants. I didn't like this type of job; you have to work hard in an international accounting firm. I can't adapt to the atmosphere in a government organisation. There is a lot of underhanded behaviour with this type of work. My father was a civil servant, so I know what it's like. Also, with regards to banks, I have family members that worked in a bank and it's very boring. Now, with a bit of hindsight, I will perhaps look for a job in a national bank. Recently, I have been looking for employment in large private Chinese companies in the city of Hangzhou. I applied online. Two months later, I found a job in a large retailer.
>
> Man, 29 years old, interview conducted in Shanghai in 2015

Today's generation has adopted different work models to prior generations. While the previous generation followed a work model linked to a planned economy, the current generation tends to adhere to a work model based on an enrichment economy. Today the young Chinese migrants in the Chinese labour market are very distinct from their parent's generation. The latter lived out their professional lives in the same workplace and the same job. Although work prior to the reforms was structured and viewed as an obligation and duty to society, its instrumental value is still valid today, but now it is organised around the injunction to be oneself and self-development. Listen to a young man, 28 years old, product planner in a multinational we have met in 2016 in Shanghai:

> After my graduation, I notice that most people only cared about their income. After all, when you start working life, you need to survive. You

THE FABRIC OF "HEROES" AND EMOTIONAL CAPITALISM 87

hope to have a good life and a good income, especially if your parents live elsewhere. In my case, I prioritised my interest in the job, although I have to admit that my income isn't bad. If I compare my salary with what I could earn in other companies, I know it's not great, but my job is engaging and that's important for me. There's a good atmosphere at work, so the salary takes second place.

A category of young migrants in China clearly state that the job security their parents sought after and enjoyed is not what they are looking for. However, some young men that have experienced situations of exclusion seek a stable and settled life. Today's generation adopted a different work model to those prior. The previous generation followed a work model linked to a planned economy, whereas the current generation focuses on flexible work and the injunction to be oneself. When the pressure becomes unbearable, young migrants riposte by quitting their jobs, unsurprising given the short-term employment contracts. Their parents who have spent all their live working for the State do not understand how these young people bear the pace, pressure and cadence of foreign companies.

It was at a time when my father was sick. My mother really wanted me to get married because I was already 26 years old. They thought I should start living a stable life. So, I thought since my boyfriend was alright, why not with him? He came from a family from the Red Army, so my family that it was a good idea to be with him. He worked in the technology industry. Maybe it was because of the environment, those close to me or family pressure. I didn't really know what to think, so I finally decided to get married. My grandfather believed that stability was essential. My boy-friend suggested that we get married and then start a business. I figured that if I chose to marry him, there would be less financial pressure. The fact that my father was sick was always in the back of my mind, and that all his hospital costs had to be paid for. I liked the fact that my boyfriend went to a lot of effort to convince me. I felt confident in our business plan which would help me join the middle class, now I am business director.

JIAO, woman, 30 years old, interview conducted in Shanghai in 2016

Youth who distance themselves from the myth of heroes in compressed modernity often leave their jobs because they struggle to satisfy their desire for recognition and creativity. Young migrants that have strongly internalised the cult of excellence express their demands for recognition, creativity, participation and self-realisation. Some young people will resign if these demands are not met. Above all, they aspire to join the middle class.

In the history of work in socialist China, the establishment of the ethos of self-realisation in the workplace competed with the ethos of duty which dominated prior to the 1979 Reform. Some young skilled migrants spend all their wages by the end of the month. They differentiate themselves from their parents who in general followed the injunction to save during the economic transition. The idea here is not to engage in excessive consumption but to make up for the fatigue of being oneself in the workplace and reject the capitalist society.

> I am graphic designer. I was barely able to survive on my wage. Once I had paid rent and bought food, I had spent everything I had earned. On the weekend, I like going to a restaurant with friends, doing some shopping and going to the cinema. I said to myself that it's important to enjoy life once in a while, to forget the tiredness and be happy. There is an enormous amount of pressure on me right now. I want to stay positive; I don't want to give up. I part of the moonlight clan, that is to say I am part of a group of young people who have a different conception of money compared to their parents who tended to save a lot of what they earned. We prefer to eat when we are hungry and go out with friends instead of saving by any means necessary.
>
> BI, woman, 22 years old, interview conducted in Shanghai in 2016

Confronted with identity conflicts, reassessments and readjustments, young Chinese migrants find it increasingly difficult to adjust to their different "selves". Social exclusion and discrimination, family pressure, double-bind situations, work stress and events that exclude the possibility of social mobility lead to resignations and biographical bifurcations that create hurdles in their moral careers and working relationships.

7 Compressed Modernity and Resistance to Emotional Capitalism

Today a group of young migrant graduates resist the economy of arrogance. They are aware that the economic and political injunctions to become heroes in Chinese society are commodified and that emotional capitalism transforms and commodifies their feelings and emotional states to become *emodities* (Illouz, 2019). These young migrants distance themselves from work and criticise the injunction to interiorise the norms of success and excellence. They

THE FABRIC OF "HEROES" AND EMOTIONAL CAPITALISM   89

no longer wish to prioritise their professional interests over their emotional lives in order to succeed, nor do they want to be overexposed in the work environment and participate in a consumerist culture. In an authoritarian environment, some young migrants choose not to participate in the "industry of happiness", which produces self-made men characterised by their emotional rationality, i.e. their ability to employ reflexive and strategic choices and to develop on a personal level (Cabanas, 2019).

Consequently, some young skilled migrants develop resistance strategies to counter compressed modernity by refusing the injunction to be heroes in emotional capitalism. Young skilled migrants are violently subjected to inter-individual relationships based on competition and performance in order to gain access the "government of self" (Foucault, 1975). These active minorities move to heterotopic spaces in cities and rural areas which act as moral regions that experience a widening divide with those of compressed modernity. Today, minorities comprised of young migrants, community-based activists, young artists and ecologists gather to develop strategies for identity affirmation and set up micro-organisations on a political, economic, cultural and artistic level in *intermediate spaces;* these spaces come to occupy places next to spaces created to produce discreet, liminal socialisations that are built in non-institutional worlds, where meanings are built related to situations of economic and political fragility, and political skills related to the affirmation of democratic values (Roulleau-Berger, 1999, 2011). Young migrants gather here to produce "alternative" material and symbolic economies and draw the borders of spaces in which forms of mutual recognition develop.

It can be noted here that young people develop local resistance strategies in intermediate spaces that contain discreet and even invisible social forms, as well as dispersed creativity which reveals resistance strategies in the context of negotiated authoritarianism. These spaces reveal the power of active minorities to act; minorities who demand societal and social capacities in order to build themselves as individual and collective actors and reappropriate their subjectivities. The intermediate space helps us understand the progress Chinese society has made outside of the establishment in an authoritarian context. For example, collaborative spaces are flourishing in Shanghai, offering services that allow young people to access websites censured on the Chinese internet, exchange information and implement projects. Another example are the small groups of young people developing informal protest networks using digital resources to become collective stakeholders alongside local authorities and to be recognised in order for their voices to be heard.

In the same perspective Marie Bellot (2019) has shown that discreet practices in youth spaces reveal how young migrant graduates build their identity in Chinese context, and how collective actors attempt to generate forms of everyday civism in increasingly intermediate spaces. The purpose of these spaces is for skilled young people to make their voices heard in a context of "constrained politicisation" in places appropriated by young people. Against a backdrop of negotiated authoritarianism, forms of everyday civism can only be intermittent, temporary and fragmented, a product of skilled youth's ability to compartmentalise. These include militant individuals that forge their identity through subtle games between constrained politicisation and biographical turning points, committed individuals that explore the scope of actions around public issues, and the temporary individuals of everyday civism.

Moreover, intermediate spaces are created in old factories converted into artistic zones in Shanghai, in which young migrants engage in artistic activities to produce dissenting opinions and reclaim social events and places. Young activists engaged in the environmental struggle and who have experienced great hardship produce everyday resistance by advocating anti-neo-conservative and anti-capitalist values through the practice of alternative lifestyles. For example, Chun, met in 2016, a 24-year-old Sichuan-born woman, was raised by her grandparents in a rural area and her parents are food traders in Chengdu. After failing her Master's degree and following a few work experiences, she found a job in an environmental NGO and then volunteered, gradually questioning her own life choices (Botazzi, 2016).

> I spent my childhood in the country and then lived in Chengdu for four years to complete my studies. In the country, I would help my grandparents and my sister do agricultural work every day. My parents come from the country as well, but they lived in Chengdu and sold rice there. Then when I went to secondary school, they changed the business and started selling more food, including chicken and dried fruits. My parents had a primary school level education. The first time I went to Chengdu, I found it so noisy and very difficult to get from one place to another. My parents didn't have much money, and so neither did I [...] it was hard to buy things. I worked a few casual jobs in my spare time selling televisions and washing machines. I didn't like these jobs; I felt out of place and didn't enjoy the work. When I failed my exams in my Master's degree of non-profit management, I went for a trial in an environmental NGO. They focused on a natural lifestyle or a new lifestyle. The work consisted of helping people to change. I therefore learnt a lot in two years, and I thought to myself, maybe I should make some changes in my own life. I decided to leave. I quit my job one and a half years later. I don't want to have a job, I just want to live the life I want in a very simple house in my

home region with my family, plant trees and feed the animals. I want to go to look for a natural setting to visit with my friends and parents, or a place to get healthy food. I'm set on this lifestyle now and I everything I do is in line with this path. I'll never spend my life amassing money. For me, a simple lifestyle is a good lifestyle. I can live a happy life alone, doing everything myself. So, I think having a place in the country is a good choice; a place I could cultivate the land and satisfy my basic needs without anyone's help. I may need money as well, but if I live a healthy and happy life, the things I do could help others too. That's why I think that could generate the small amount of money I might need. I wouldn't be much, just what I need. When I first told my parents that I had discovered a new lifestyle, they thought I was crazy and that I was making a mistake. It's a concept they were not familiar with. They told me to find a new job and to find someone to marry. I responded simply with a "no". I have always said what I think and that year they started to understand me. Two or three weeks ago, they called me and told me they wanted to go home, plant trees and live with me in the country in their home region. They had always worked in Chengdu, but they didn't feel comfortable with the people there and had also noticed that it was increasingly difficult to earn money. Yes, harder and harder. The financial pressure, the pressures of life and the costs are steadily rising. Before they used to think that a happy life was having enough money, buying a large house in Chengdu and having a stable income. They changed their mind. They understood that they could make new choices and take action. In China, we think that people are successful if they have lots of money! You must have a good job, a big house, and so on. As a result, everyone wants to be "a successful person", they say to themselves "I want all these things and then I will be happy." The one thing that worries me is everyone's lifestyle. It's everyday life that causes so many environmental problems, such as excess consumption and electricity use. They buy more products, use them briefly and then throw them out! No, we're not recycling our waste, everything is piled together and then burned or covered up [...] like a big mountain of rubbish. I've seen two sites which pollute the soil and water table. If the rubbish is burned it creates air pollution and the vicious cycle goes from bad to worse. Nevertheless, individuals are realising that they can take action on a small scale, and now more and more people are perhaps doing things differently. Big changes start with small ones. If people make one change in their lifestyle, perhaps they will change two or three things. Nowadays in China, I know many people who are making different life choices such as not buying too many things, repairing broken products or finding a new use for them. I think that more and more people are going to realise that if their environment becomes contaminated, it will affect everyone. At first, they don't know how to act, but solutions such as permaculture or natural agriculture will arise; they will know what they can do to make a difference, and maybe then change will come.

CHUN, woman, 24 years old, Sichuan origin, interview conducted in Yunnan in 2015

As Jean Tassin (2020) shows, in movements promoting peasant agriculture, 返乡青年 *fanxiang qingnian* (young people who have returned to the land) engage in small-scale organic farming after periods of urban life, often as students or unqualified workers. As ethical consumption entrepreneurs, these young people call themselves 新农人 *xin nongren* (neo-farmers), who are producers, retailers, experts and promoters of quality food. They redefine "peasant agriculture" as an ethical and entrepreneurial choice. They are contributing to the renewal of production practices—notably according to ecological or permaculture principles and distribution methods—giving a predominant place to e-commerce short supply chaines. The young returnees highlight family farming as an opportunity to respond to the crisis of trust in institutions by inventing new transaction networks in a green economy.

In China, intermediate spaces can be defined as resistance spaces against compressed modernity in rural and urban worlds. Resistance in the sense that struggles for economic, social and moral recognition and new societal projects are being formed and structured in which individual and collective societal commitments are redefined by creating distancing with what "makes compressed modernity". These intermediate spaces also reveal the power of active minorities to act, and youth who claim a right to the city in both social and societal capacities. They can promote reconciliations between social identities and self-identities of individuals, create new arrangements between different vulnerable social groups and.

CHAPTER 3

Young Chinese Migrants, Economic Cosmopolitanism and Globalisation

At the same time as internal migration brings to light the internal borders of Chinese society, borders which give rise to distancing processes of the most vulnerable migrants, certain Chinese cities are seeing the production of *local cosmopolitanism* (Tarrius, Missaoui, 2000). These are created through economic negotiations, exchanges and dealings between young Chinese migrants and international entrepreneurs. The rise of new information technologies has triggered the intensification of transnational and transregional dynamics via intracontinental and transnational movements across interconnected Chinese cities. These networks also link other cities in the Asia region such as Taipei, Seoul, Tokyo and Singapore, stretching to cities in the Middle-East, Africa and Europe including Paris, Milan, Naples, Barcelona and Lisbon, to name a few.

1   Young Chinese Migrants and Local Cosmopolitanisms

As per Xu Tao (2013) since China's reform and globalisation's process, more and more multinational companies have established enterprises in China. With the rapid development of Sino-African trade over in 90's a large number of African businessmen have arrived in Chinese coastal cities such as Guangzhou and have made mutual adjustement and cooperation, but also conflicts in the business relationship with Chinese businessmen, but they followed the instrumental interests principle.

Then in the late 1990s, Iranian, Iraqi, Syrian, Lebanese, Saudi, African and Indian retail traders began settling in Guangzhou, Shenzhen, Keqiao and Yiwu, and opening stores, restaurants and cafes. Yiwu has become the largest market in the world with 92,000 stores. While new internal borders and differentiated alterity regimes emerge in international Chinese cities, other economic borders are disappearing in the internationalisation process. This facilitates the flow between spaces of transnational exchange and other international cities. We can therefore speak of local cosmopolitanism with the emergence of young traders and both Chinese and foreign entrepreneurs settling in China and "conducting business" together.

© LAURENCE ROULLEAU-BERGER, 2021 | DOI:10.1163/9789004463080_005

I was in business; I've always been in business. I most often worked in the Sétif province in Algeria in a market called Dubai. I sold women's accessories, jewellery, costume jewellery, scrunchies, things like that. I first came to China in 2002. I made a Chinese contact who was working in Dubai at the time and who wanted me to go to China to do business in Yiwu. I then met an Iranian was going to the Guangzhou fair. He invited me, so I went with him. We found a big market in Yiwu that no longer exists today and we carried out our business there. It was where the Fujian market is. You can find everything there: bags, suitcases, clothes, everything, absolutely everything! The prices in Yiwu are very low, the cheapest in the world. It's the world's factory; you can find anything you want in unlimited quantities. I come here, I do my business and then send it to Algeria in containers. I come for work, to order goods. I live between Algeria and Yiwu, I came for a few days each time. I had already visited Guangzhou a few times to take part in international trade fairs. I first went to Guangzhou in 2002. After the trade fair, my Chinese friend from Dubai invited me to go to Yiwu and we started working together here. At that time there weren't many foreigners in China, there weren't many of us. Now there are a lot of foreigners in China. Before, you would only see this many foreign traders at the Guangzhou trade fair. Now they're everywhere, especially in Yiwu. It's like a permanent trade fair here, the goods are ready and on display. You can come for just three days and send anything you want abroad. Another advantage over Guangzhou is that you can buy different goods. China is a safe country, people from all over the world who live together here with no problems. Here in China, you can forget your bag somewhere and it will still be there a few hours later. I was in France in the 1990s, and it wasn't like that.

AHMED, man, 38 years old, interview conducted in 2018

Chinese cities are increasingly cosmopolitan, and the development of new ethnic borders can be observed in tandem with the establishment of transnational networks. Since the 1980s, African retail traders have been forging economic networks between Dubai, Kuala Lumpur, Bangkok, Hong Kong and Guangzhou in an effort to strengthen the prominence of trade hubs in East linked to Senegal, Congo and Mali. Chinese cities illustrate how new migratory flows challenge certain former diasporic forms and give rise to others. They actively and covertly compete with economic, religious, regional and local networks. Solidarity and mutual support networks interlink Chinese cities and connect them to their European, American and African counterparts. These new urban dynamics show how local Chinese markets become globalised in a more or less visible way, becoming even transnationalised due to the flow of Chinese migrants transporting goods, products, beliefs and norms.

Yiwu, a global city in the province of Zhejiang, is one of the most important wholesale markets in the world. This is the departure point of the "new silk roads", supplying *small commodities* to a large proportion of the global market. Yiwu, a megalopolis, is home to over 4,300,000 m2 of marketplaces, with over 400,000 products offered by more than 100,000 suppliers. A small city in 1970, Yiwu gradually grew as Chinese retail traders and entrepreneurs developed internal economic networks in China with other local markets. These cities appear to play a pivotal role in covert and overt economic globalisation (Choplin, Pliez, 2018). This is indicative of the internationalisation of labour division, the spatial reorganisation of production, the restructuring of global industries and the informalisation of work. Economic activity in Yiwu demonstrates that a reshuffling of migratory flows is underway, particularly between China, the Mediterranean and Africa. Migratory routes that actively participate in shifting and redefining the borders of new productive territories are decreasing. Transnational economic networks between cities compete with local and national economies and, to a certain extent, overshadow them.

Migrant entrepreneurs operate in large trade hubs in Guangzhou, Shenzhen and Yiwu and play a key role in the global circulation of goods and products to regions such as Europe, Latin America and Africa. For example, young Chinese migrants are involved in global business; for example some of them established in the semi-precious gemstone market in Guangzhou have forged business relationships with Brazil and African countries. New local and international trade hubs are created as a result of the varied cases and entrepreneurs and retail trade figures develop their own rules, conventions and norms on local and global urban markets. They exercise their exceptional ability to develop economic and social cooperation networks that link Chinese cities and connect them to international cities. Transnational flows generated by these retail traders and entrepreneurs reveal a dynamic of dispersal and spatial centralisation. In the district of Xiaobei in Guangzhou tiny ethnic shops are selling leather goods, kaf name-brand products, bright African clothing, and electronic goods. The emergence of the transnational urban spaces occupied by Africans in Guangzhou has provided jobs to local Chinese (Li Zhigang et alii, 2013).

Local and transnational markets are developing in Chinese cities like Yiwu through the establishment of agreements, understandings and economic exchanges. These are based on inter-ethnic relations between small and large retail traders, small and large young Chinese entrepreneurships, and other traders and entrepreneurs from Arab and African countries. Consequently, multi-ethnic labour organisational systems emerge through partnerships between Chinese, Turkish, Lebanese, Syrian and Jordanian nationals, among others. The following provide a clear example:, in a Turkish restaurant, two Chinese and foreign managers run a Turkish kitchen with two Turkish chefs; a Syrian kitchen is staffed by a Turkish and a Jordanian chef; an Arab and a Chinese chef work in an Arab kitchen; a Turkish baker and his two Chinese apprentices, young migrant workers, are employed in a Chinese bakery and a Jordanian national works in a butcher's shop. Foreign entrepreneurs, thus, create jobs that attract young Chinese eager to work in an international setting.

> Since January 2018, so for the last four months, all of China has been talk-ing about us. We have had a lot of success and that's a good thing for us because some people wait years for business to kick off. We have custom-ers from all over the world, I am happy to have an international clien-tele here in China. I find it stimulating. There are many Middle-Eastern customers, which is normal because they rediscover the flavours of their country. We also have a lot of Chinese, Africans, Indians and Pakistanis. The other day an important Ugandan businessman who owns many com-panies in China came in. He gave me his business card. It was the first time I had met someone from Uganda. Russian, British, Kenyan, Kazakh and Ukrainian nationals also visit. Our clientele is very international.
>
> ARMAN, man, 29 years old, Jordanian, interview conducted in 2018

Partially denationalised economic systems are being created, organised around complex transactions based on a hierarchy of trust and loyalty on global mar-kets. These international Chinese cities are interlinked via social, economic, religious and political networks. Discreet transnational spaces emerge and become circulatory territories at certain points in time by way of economic activities conducted in local networks. The small-scale productions hubs in Chinese villages and market towns on the outskirts of Yiwu, Keqiao and other cities, are an example. They breach the borders of local labour markets and give rise to a diverse range of polycentric economic systems with internal hier-archies for the manufacture of a wide range of products and commodities. The Fujian market, for instance, has a total of 50,000 stalls and is connected to a plethora of small-scale production hubs. Each one is specialised in manufac-turing a specific product (toys, textiles, religious objects, bowls, costume jewel-lery, etc.) and employs young Yiwu locals and young Chinese migrants.

Yiwu has become an important centre of a map of new networks of inter-secting economic anchor points, connected by more or less visible routes along which young Chinese migrants circulate. These modes of multiple inscriptions in economic spaces highlight the embedding and disembedding between "formal" and "informal" economies on a local, societal, and global scale between villages, market towns and other cities in China.

2 Compressed Society, Migration and the Digital Economy

In Yiwu and other global cities, young Chinese migrants are also joining the digital economy to become ' "digital nomads", or ICT-based mobile workers, by setting up e-commerce platforms and online stores. Building on local cosmopolitanism, these migrants create virtual jobs by using ICT technology (computers, the internet, e-mail, social media) to develop new transnational economic territories. How do these young graduate migrants, usually from second-tier universities, become digital nomads? Many of them start in a foreign company established in Yiwu and move roles within the organisation. They first gain the trust of one client, followed by several international clients, before launching into the world of e-commerce.

In 2019 we met Liang, originally from Jiangxi Province, born in 1987 into a peasant family. She is the eldest daughter of three. Her father is the village mechanic. Thanks to the support of her uncle who works as a civil servant, she had a smooth transition to a secondary school in Ji'an and passed her 高考 *gaokao (college entrance examination)*. After four years studying law at a second-tier university in Shangdong, Liang obtained a qualification to work in the legal profession. In 2011, during her internship in Hangzhou, she visited a friend in Yiwu and decided to go and work there. With her skills in English, she first worked for an Iranian company as a buyer for one year with a salary of 2,000 yuan a month. She then worked as a sales manager in a diamond factory, earning 3,000 yuan a month. She was invested in this role and garnered the trust of an Indian customer who would later become her main business partner. However, she failed to obtain the recognition of her boss in Wenzhou. A friend asked her to start doing business together and at the end of 2014, she resigned from her position and joined her friend. The two young adults started selling diamantes to foreign traders, especially Indians, Pakistanis and Afghans. With no capital or company in their name, the two partners found a company that signed purchase agreements on their behalf in exchange for commission (50% of the profit). In 2015, her partner moved towards e-commerce and Liang continued the business activities. Her business took off under her own trade name and her younger sister started helping her. The business rented commercial space in the Fujian market. Her parents, uncle, aunt, big sister all began helping with her business, so she rented a large apartment across from the Futian market to house them and store the goods. She made a name for herself in India thanks to her Indian business partner and built a distribution network. She created a shell company in Hong Kong for banking transactions. In 2017, she registered a company in her name in Yiwu which took over the entire purchasing process, including shipping and zero-rating. She sends around ten containers abroad each year and has an annual turnover of around 20 million yuan. Today, she is aiming to focus on a few key products and promote her own brand.

In compressed modernity, forms of digital economy develop rapidly in a digital no man's land with legal grey areas. New types of jobs are born out of modes of collaborative production where the distinction between manufacturers and consumers, employees and colleagues are blurred. These young workers can be defined as freelancers. They are IT autodidacts that successfully join platforms by developing resourcefulness strategies through trial and error. For example, when Yang was still a college student, he repaired computers at Hangzhou Computer City. While at university, he started doing business on the Taobao platform and opened a clothing company that very quickly went bankrupt because his associates were not working. He then got his family involved, including his brother, which triggered frequent conflicts. Afterwards, he founded in Yiwu a successful company that sold basic necessities:

> The family workshop model was a sad failure, because I've spoken very little with my parents since I was a child. My brother communicates better with them. When you don't earn money, everything is fine. But as soon as money is involved, conflicts arise. My brother used to deliver goods to clients on site. He said to me: "how can you sit in front of the computer all day, while I wear myself out all day doing dirty jobs?" This was at a time when the company was making millions of yuan a year. I gave everything straight to my brother; I didn't want anything for myself. I left immediately. After I got out, I got scammed by a pyramid scheme. I only had a few hundred thousand yuan left and I invested everything in it and lost it all. So, I started again from scratch by myself. I founded a company selling basic necessities, all while studying various software applications.
>
> YANG, man, 32 years old, interview conducted in 2018

Young Chinese migrants play a crucial role in the open outsourcing of work (crowd working) and setting up online global trade hubs in which smalls goods circulate. Chinese platforms dedicated to outsourcing, as we have seen, do not always comply with commercial, data protection and consumer protection laws. Young migrants teach themselves the ins and outs of the world of e-commerce. In the following example, Lu developed an e-commerce business by selling counterfeit goods. These goods underscore the conflicts of economic norms between the habitus of local markets and that of virtual global markets.

We met Lu in 2019, he was born in 1995 in a rural village of Wenzhou, he has a brother one year younger than him. Initially, his father repaired bicycles for the villagers. When Lu was 10 years old (4th grade of primary school), his parents migrated illegally to Italy to work. They returned to China seven years later and traded in Guangxi and then Henan. Lu grew up with his grandmother. He did not perform well in primary and secondary school and so entered a vocational college for his final years of high school in his hometown. In 2013, he studied logistics management. Lu became an active member of various university associations and started his business with his classmates. The year 2013 marked the beginning of e-commerce fever in China. From 2013 to 2016, Lu successively created three online shops with different teams made up of his classmates. Lu and his co-workers started selling counterfeit toys on e-commerce platforms in October 2014 during his second year of university. These counterfeit toys were produced in Yiwu factories and bought by Lu thanks to his contacts. The university offered them storage space. The products they sold were mainly counterfeit toys of major foreign brands produced in Yiwu. The products were sold in foreign markets such as Russia and Brazil. However, once counterfeiting was reported by manufacturers or other traders, their products were taken off the shelves. Although Lu interviewed for roles at Amazon, he ultimately decided to continue his entrepreneurial adventures. From 2018, Lu taught on an e-commerce platform, which allowed him to earn 900 yuan a week. At the same time, he maintained an online store that generated a turnover of $20,000–30,000 a month with a 20% profit margin. The products he marketed were mainly bags and suitcases manufactured in factories in Yiwu.

Compressed modernity stimulates the diversification of digital economies that form due to principles of social differentiation and the production of cyber-elites and a cyber-proletariat (Huws, 2003) in different places. As Béatrice Zani (2020) aptly demonstrated, young Chinese migrant women immigrate to Taiwan to develop e-commerce platforms that offer a range of small products on new virtual marketplaces using the WeChat platform. They trade a large variety of goods such as chicken feet, milk powder, spiced meat, spices, bras, clothes, lingerie and cosmetics between their hometowns in central Chinese provinces, large Chinese coastal cities and Taiwan. This e-commerce business is run on a digital platform which becomes a place to interact, forge emotional ties and create innovative social and commercial practices.

3 Retail Traders, Entrepreneurs and Workers

Multiple migratory chains arise in an environment of globalised economic development. Some young Chinese migrants try their hand at opening shops that sell essential items (rasers, bowls, thermoses, etc) and other export products.

For example, a young woman from Wenzhou married a Catholic man and moved to Yiwu to sell religious objects to Catholic and African countries. In addition, she sold small statues of the Eiffel tower, the Arc de Triomphe and the Statue of Liberty. These goods were manufactured in a small factory in Wenzhou which employed many young temporary migrant workers. Her husband handled factory management and logistics and she took care of store management and product sales.

Another woman, after working for 15 years in the public sector in Fujian, left her job to start selling religious Catholic objects following her conversion to Catholicism. She started a small business with a work force of around twenty employees. A further example is a young woman from Anhui province who moved to Yiwu to join her parents who had set up a business selling thermoses.

Young Chinese migrants from provinces such as Fujian, Henan, Hunan, Sichuan and Guizhou move to Yiwu, Guangzhou and Keqiao, among other cities, with the goal to create a small business. Some migrants open small factories across a wide range of sectors. He Lin, who grew up in a rural family in the Jiangxi province, established his own international retail company and his own factory. These young migrants usually recruit workers and other young temporary migrant workers and pay on a piecework basis to ensure production levels.

The pathways of young retail traders and Chinese SME entrepreneurs bring to light production conditions in high compressed modernity. It elevates rural migrants, some of whom have experienced hardship and poverty, to an intermediate social position recognised in transnational networks. These migratory pathways reveal both the process of globalisation of regional economies and migrants' individual and collective practices, their capacity for action and economic mobilisation. They build their lives in uncertain economic contexts where they will invariably face unpredictable situations, such as delayed product deliveries and employee absenteeism.

In Chinese cities like Yiwu, Shanghai, Shenzhen, Guangzhou, young Chinese skilled migrants learn to conduct international trade both by improvising economic governance and the ability to organise various local and international networks. It is patently clear that in order to access transnational spaces, young migrants develop the "art of doing" through informal relations in local spaces. For example, a young skilled migrant who had no idea how to set up a company was helped by a friend of a friend who was a sock manufacturer. This individual shared his expertise on how to choose materials and set prices. The skilled migrant then contacted the managers of small-scale production networks on the outskirts of Yiwu directly to avoid slower production turnover in factories.

Jinxiao was born in 1982 in Henan Province. The eldest son of farm workers, he has a younger brother and sister. From an early age, Jinxiao participated in agricultural work, selling local produce to support his family. Confronted with poverty, he worked hard at school. He was a good student and passed the高考 *gaokao* (national college entry examination), enrolling at the Northeastern University to study international trade. In 2005, his last academic year, he came to Yiwu and completed an internship in a company that manufactured scarves. His role was dealing with foreign customers, particularly Indians and Pakistanis. He worked in the same company from 2006 to 2009 and was paid 1,200 yuan a month. During his time there, he met an American client who liked him and encouraged him to set up his own business. In 2009, he left this company and created his own import/export company. With no knowledge of the export industry and no contacts in fabrication, Jinxiao faced many difficulties starting his business. Even though he received orders from foreign customers, local suppliers did not trust him. A friend introduced him to a sock manufacturer who taught him the tricks of the trade and through whom Jinxiao met other plant managers who became his partners. He also went door-to-door in Zhuji, an industrial town 60 km from Yiwu, to look for suppliers. In 2010, he bought his first car, a Peugeot 408 for his return trips between Yiwu and Zhuji. His network of producers expanded, and he signed more and more purchase agreements. In 2012, he married a former model from Shandong and bought his first apartment in Yiwu. His son was born a year later. Today, his company exports clothing and clothing accessories to North America and Europe. The company has one employee with a turnover of between 10 and 20 million yuan per year.

Yiwu, like other global cities in China, has significant international social, economic and symbolic resources that are constantly growing with the rise in international migrations. Regimes of small, medium and large production interlink to create economic globalisation.

> We sell many different items in this store, including everything that can be used at home. We sell them very cheaply. Chinese products sold in Yiwu are cheap and of good quality. All these goods are produced in Yiwu! We make them at home. We have the machines. That's why it's cheap, because there's no middleman. It's still very hard. At night we work until 3 or 4 in the morning, and then we start again a few hours later. There are many manufacturing sites. They're in every neighbourhood. Each product can therefore be made at a different location. In Yiwu, we have many small products, especially plastic ones. Usually a specific product will come from a particular neighbourhood. In our village it's the same thing, we only produce one specific product. Everything is done at home. Everyone has two machines and that's how it is. [...] In Guangzhou, they could also follow the same economic model, even though it's not usually the case. There are also a lot of people from Guangzhou who come here, including foreigners.
>
> TANG, man, 28 years old, interview conducted in 2019

For example, young migrant workers from Henan, Hunan, Sichuan, and poorer provinces such as Guizhou, move to work in small factories or production workshops close to Yiwu. There, they manufacture toys, shirts, pearls, belts and locks, etc, destined for export to Latin America and the Arab world. These young migrants find work in factories producing marble and ceramics in Foshan, furniture in Sunde, and doors in Donggan. They are often paid piecework rates as temporary workers and form a new young Chinese underclass. Working in difficult conditions, they are exposed to loud noise and toxic odours without protective gear and sleep on-site in dilapidated lodgings for between 4,000 to 6,000 yuan a month

4   Inter-Ethnic Relations, Muslim Solidarity and Discrimination

A number of Turkish and Lebanese restaurants in Yiwu and other Chinese cities have been highly successful. In Yiwu, a Turkish restaurant opened by a group of Syrians that was hailed as a model of economic success and awarded a medal by Xi Jinping for the quality of service is one such example. Foreign entrepreneurs from Pakistan to Senegal settle in Yiwu and, along with Indians and Iranians, recruit young Chinese migrant workers. For example, a Turkish restaurant opened by an Indian entrepreneur employs 43 Xinjiang natives as kitchen staff. The chef is Chinese while the manager is Turkish. Young Chinese migrants are also employed in textile stores in the Fujian market in Yiwu, as well as in Guangzhou and Keqiao. Other more qualified migrants who speak Arabic, English and French are recruited by foreign entrepreneurs alongside low-skilled young Chinese migrants. This is true for a 32-year-old entrepreneur from Yemen who opened an electronics company. Access to employment is made possible through a network of interpersonal relationships, or through Chinese companies that specialise in services to foreign entrepreneurs.

Many young Chinese Muslims that have migrated from Yunnan, Gansu, Xinjian and other region are employed in the host of Turkish restaurants in Yiwu. This is the case for 20-year-old Nour, originally from Yunnan.

> I come from Yunnan where there are a many Muslims. My parents farm land in a village. I am the eldest. I have two little sisters and a little brother. My little brother and one of my little sisters are also here. They are 19 and 17 years old. They basically do the same work as me. My youngest sister is still living with my parents, she's at school. I'm almost 20 years old. I studied for two years, but it takes five years to graduate in our school. I have a large family, and since I didn't want to be too much of a burden on my family, I decided at the age of 16 to leave to work. I did that for two years, and then when I was 18 or 19, I thought to myself that I was a Muslim, so I also wanted to study my religion. My family are all Muslims. We always have been. There are many Muslims in Yunnan. Many people do not know this and think that Muslims are in Ningxia, or in north-west China. We are not a very good or a very bad faith, we know that we are believers. I started working at the age of 16 in a Muslim restaurant. Before I left home, I knew I was a Muslim, but I didn't pray. After arriving in Yiwu, I realised that everyone, well, all Muslims, knew things I didn't about Islam. I didn't know anything about it. I didn't know about praying, going to the mosque and listening to the imam. That has changed now, but I still need to deepen my knowledge and practice. But now I would say that it's not the same with the situation in Xinjiang. I currently work as a waitress in a Muslim restaurant. I live in the restaurant dormitory. This is one of the restaurants in Yiwu that pays the highest wage, because it's very international and is good quality; it's not a small restaurant. I work eight hours a day and the monthly salary is 3,000 yuan. In other restaurants the salary is between 2,200 and 2,600 yuan. So, it's not bad here. Although wages at the Yiwu markets can be higher, it often doesn't include food and lodging. For us it is in addition to our salary. Even so, we are always running around serving dishes. And those who work in the kitchens are very hot. I am Hui, but I am also a Muslim […]
>
> NOUR, woman, 20 years old, Yunnan origin, interviews conducted in 2018 and 2019

Economies of hospitality merge with trust economies in trade hubs that are governed by shared economic and in particular religious, conventions and norms around a Muslim cosmopolitanism. This Muslim cosmopolitanism connects Chinese cities such as Keqiao, Qingdao, Yongan, Shenzhen and Ningbo, including international cities in India and the Arab world, in countries such as Yemen and Pakistan. The migratory routes of transnational entrepreneurs and retail traders make it possible to map the pathways of these non-western economic networks in which economic, social, religious and moral resources are constantly mobilised, transformed and enlarged in each different place and country.

Interlinked "minor" Chinese cities are home to transnational entrepreneurs on connected local markets. For example, Yiwu has unprecedented level of urban multiculturalism. On its Exotic Street, Yemenis set up barbecues and sell lamb skewers after sun down while Jordanians dine next to Pakistanis and Indians smoking shisha pipes. Men from India, Pakistan, Egypt, Africa, Yemen, Algeria, Turkey, Russian women and young veiled Chinese woman from Xinjiang all occupy the local and global public space. Mandarin, Arabic, Hindi mix while and Arab, Indian and Chinese cultures creolise.

Young Muslim Chinese migrants develop relationships of solidarity and mutual support with young foreign entrepreneurs. For instance, there are many young Yemenis in Yiwu who want to start shipping and transport companies and need Arabic to Chinese translators for their business dealings between China, Yemen and Arab countries. Young Chinese Muslims also help Yemenis open Halal food stores. Further, young Yemenis protested alongside Chinese against the closure of a mosque, with the local government supporting the Yemenis visa applications in recognition of their important contribution to the local economy. Inter-ethnic solidarity between young Chinese Muslims and foreign Muslim entrepreneurs is built on ethnic and family networks that enable them to settle quickly in Yiwu. This is true for a 23-year-old Palestinian who, following brutal attack by an Israeli soldier, had no choice but to leave Tel-Aviv for China where he joined his uncle who worked in a translation agency.

Muslim entrepreneurs from countries such as Sudan, Syria, India and Pakistan describe feeling they are in an international city first and foremost, and a Chinese city second. Muslim economic cosmopolitanism facilitates inter-ethnic negotiations and exchanges between young Muslim Chinese entrepreneurs and their foreign counterparts. International companies recruit young Muslim Chinese workers, such as the young Muslim women from Xinjiang working in Turkish restaurants. Muslim solidarities in China may encourage the diversification of intermediate economic systems through trust, reputation and loyalty in local labour markets. They can also give rise to mixed marriages between young Chinese and entrepreneurs from Africa and the Middle-East. This in turn strengthens Muslim solidarities and transnational economies.

The events in the Xinjiang province and the discrimination against the Uighurs have prompted Muslim Huis to move to cities in China's south-east. Yili is a prime example of this development. She managed a restaurant in Urumqi for three years and speaks Uighur, Mandarin, Kazakh and a dialect of Hui. She then spent three months on the island of Hainan before arriving in Yiwu to start a business in 2018. After settling in cities in south-eastern China, some young Muslim woman are victims of discrimination that only escalates in the professional and family sphere.

For example, 30-year-old Fatima arrived in Yiwu in 2011 after divorcing her Muslim husband. After working odd jobs in the Yiwu market and in various stores, she took two years off to raise her son and then worked in an international trade firm for three years. Fatima went on to found her own international trade firm in 2018. Having suffered violence at the hands of her first husband who treated her like a slave and from her own family who refused to support her defiance of her step-family, Fatima then faced double discrimination based on her cultural affiliation and religion. One the one hand, as a Muslim woman, her Indian and Pakistani clients did not recognise her as an entrepreneur. On the other, American and European clients were wary of her religious identity.

Yiwu has attracted an increasing number of entrepreneurs and retail traders from Arab countries, India, Pakistan, Syria, Turkey, Egypt, Yemen, and countries in sub-Saharan Africa and the Maghreb. The Exotic Street district is the centre of a *non-Western global city* and is home to a succession of restaurants, bars, nightclubs, sports clubs and boutiques that display shop signs written in Chinese, Arabic and English. This gives rise to a multi-ethnic and Muslim urban co-presence structured around the rise of a male-dominated Muslim economic cosmopolitanism which is both a highly local and global phenomenon.

Young Chinese, Arab, African, Indian retail traders and entrepreneurs forge inter-ethnic and religious alliances in economic cosmopolitanisms with the view to develop international trade activities. Being Muslim emerges as a primary resource in the economic globalisation taking place in cities like Yiwu. Negotiation, trust and loyalty are based more on a shared religion than ethnic affiliation. For example, an Arab retail trader and a young Muslim Chinese translator jointly oversee the development of sets of bamboo fibre tableware earmarked for the Russian, the Middle-Eastern, African and South American markets.

Intracontinental migration in China and transnational migration is increasingly mixing with a sedentary Chinese population who live in these global

Chinese cities. A diverse range of "circulatory territories" (Tarrius, 2000) come to life through local cosmopolitanisms and transnational spaces linked to the Middle-East, India and Africa. Moreover, globalised "moral regions" (Park, 1926) emerge in which mutual trust, sometimes uncertain loyalty, ethnic and religious recognition and inter-ethnic and religious contacts take precedence over the norms of nation-states and international agreements.

The mobilities and movements of young Chinese, in all their complexity and diversity, shed light on local cosmopolitanisms and the hierarchised processes of globalisation "from above, from "the middle" and "from below" (Tarrius, 2000). They challenge the organisation and disjunctions between economic, moral, cultural and social orders in international, minor and non-cities between China, the Middle East, India, Pakistan, Yemen and Africa. While the home communities of the least skilled young migrants orient them towards labourer jobs, other young migrants develop inventive and creative solutions in the economic interstices by founding shops, small companies and production workshops. Covert and overt globalisations develop in globalised trade hubs, transnational spaces and "bazaar economies" (Geertz, 2007) which are spaces with internal hierarchical structures in minor and global cities that produce horizontal globalisations and define the "new limits to capital" (Harvey, 2006).

5   Transmigration and Economic Assemblages

And in the suburbs of the European cities of Milan, Barcelona and Lisbon, young Chinese migrants also are drawing the borders for new global markets via transnational flows that intersect with "bottom-up globalisation". The presence of young transmigrants in international trade, especially young Chinese, goes largely unnoticed. Nonetheless, they play a central role in the trading networks of tangible and intangible goods between local and global spheres (Sassen 2006) and facilitate exchange between the neighbourhoods of cities in their country of arrival and their point of departure from China.

We see how spatial flows are embedded in social relations specific to the society of origin, and how young Chinese migrants rely on acquired or inherited resources in their society of origin by manipulating the spatial capital that will enable them to integrate into transnational networks. The conditions for the success of forms of entrepreneurship are conditioned on instances of weak and strong solidarity that do not always guarantee economic success. These limited instances of solidarity give individuals an edge over their competition

YOUNG CHINESE MIGRANTS, ECONOMIC COSMOPOLITANISM

through access to internal trust networks, all the while limiting their solidarity obligations (Steiner, 1999). Systems of judgment and trust play a pivotal role in the local "reputation market" and the terms of agreement of migrant traders and entrepreneurs in international business activities. The success of entrepreneurial activities also rests on family networks which enable migrants to tackle forms of competition. The story of this young Chinese hairdresser—we met in 2018 in Milan—will shed light on this phenomenon.

In 2017 we met B., 23 years old. He comes from a rural village in Zhejiang. For the first six years of his life, he was an undeclared child At the age of six, his parents, migrant workers, brought him to the city with them where they worked in a factory. B. suffered in life as a 外地人 *waidiren* (outsider). He tells of discrimination at school and poverty. Without an urban *hukou*, he returned to the countryside with his grandmother and brother to continue his studies at primary and secondary school. He discovered that his parents had left China for Italy and that he would soon join them with his brother. At the age of 15, he travelled to Mantova, Italy, on a family reunion visa (B.'s parents had been undocumented in Italy for a long time, but had obtained their first residence permit by that time). His parents were working there in a Chinese textile factory. "I arrived and I felt lost. Everything was very different, and I missed China [...] I was happy to leave, but I was a little scared too [...] I had been told about Italy before, but I didn't really know what it was like." He lived with his brother and parents in the factory dormitory and had to start school. The educational experience was painful for Beibei mainly because of the language and his parent's financial difficulties. Nonetheless, he met teachers who helped with his schoolwork. He helped his parents at work by doing overtime in the evenings after school. He says he had difficulty entering Italian society because the factory dormitory where he lived was far from school, his parents only socialised with Chinese and he had difficulty with the Italian language. Shortly afterwards, he dropped out of school and joined his uncles in Turin, they had opened a hair salon there. In Turin, he lived with his uncle and family and started working off the books in a Chinese homeware store. He then worked as an apprentice (almost unpaid) in his uncle's hair salon for two years. Meanwhile, the small family business went bankrupt, so he had to support his parents financially who then decided to open a new small factory. B. worked part-time at Aumai's and with his parents until when he decided to buy a license for a Chinese hair salon. He paid €10,000 for his license and opened his salon. He loved the job and said he was able to run it because he learned everything in Turin from his uncle. However, he was not satisfied with the work because he said he did not to earn enough money. B. managed to earn about 3,000 euros a month but had to pay €900 rent for the salon as well as €900 rent for the apartment. He lived there with his 21-year-old girlfriend, also from Zhejiang, who worked in a Chinese café. After closing their small textile company for the second time (because of the crisis and high taxes, he says) his parents also opened a hair salon in downtown Milan.

Young Chinese migrants usually send money back to kinship networks in their country of origin. Business develops in the country of immigration, establishing channels for the distribution and sale of economic objects in transnational transaction spaces. Here economic norms inherited from a diverse range of societal contexts are superimposed and the borders of cosmopolitan existence are delineated. This gives rise to "bazaar economies" embedded in market and non-market economies, taking increasingly diverse forms in international cities. In European cities, low-skilled young Chinese migrants find work as street vendors, create micro or small businesses and develop economic activities which for the most part are informal. While the migratory experience may lead to a loss of expertise and qualifications, it also provides an opportunity to repurpose and mobilise diverse resources in micro economic spaces where "small-scale urban production" emerges (Roulleau-Berger, 1999). For example, when young poor Chinese migrants in France fail to find jobs, some turn to practices such as illegal selling and suitcase trading to sell various goods such as toys, counterfeit products, handbags, amongst others. Bazaar economies are organised by expertise in maintenance, salvaging and the trading of skills and goods. We can observe how macro and micro economies develop, in a constant state of being embedded and disembedded.

Destitute young Chinese migrants and new globalised "hobos" circulate in these poor-to-poor markets, already stratified by international migration, stripped of all social and public recognition as well as all goods, resources and identity. These bazaar economies emerge in neighbourhoods where young Chinese transmigrants tend to group together by community affiliation. At the same time, they develop inter-ethnic relations to expand their own economic services and activities by mobilising their individual and group resources. One can find restaurants, small shops, hairdressers, international money exchange booths, brothels, bars, etc. These spaces are the result of collective recognition and ethnic and inter-ethnic relationships of solidarity.

If, with the Chinese presence, the faces of European metropolises have been largely "cosmopolitanised", Near-Eastern and Middle-Eastern capital cities have become either major places of deliberate and negotiated international migration or gateways to the West.

For example in Sofia (Bulgaria) the peripheral districts of Sofia have been the scene for the organisation of a wholesale market called Ilientzi in which ethnic businessmen from the Near and Middle East and Chinese businessmen have created ethnic enclaves employing Bulgarian workers. Sportswear, lingerie, household linen, watches, toys, electrical goods, etc can be found in this market [...] Moreover, the Chinese traders are purchasing nearly all the shops except those owned by the local mafia who hold the covered and renovated areas of the market. Transnational spaces, bazaar economies and poor-to-poor markets can also come into contact in African cities.

Since the beginning of 2000, millions of Chinese have moved to North Africa, to Africa, and more recently, their presence has not stopped growing in South Africa. Young Chinese migrants from rural and urban lower social classes, have massively left middle school and integrated the Chinese labour market, where they have rapidly experienced situations of social and economic disqualification. For example, in bazaars of Dakar Chinese merchants sell new clothes, belts, scarves, bags, bracelets, calculators, etc in central districts (Bredeloup, Bertoncello, 2008). Thereby, they decided to try their chance towards the 'African Dream', thanks to familiar networks or social relations with entrepreneurs who had previously settled in Africa. In African cities, they integrate the sectors of activity where competitions, conflicts and urban accommodations between young Chinese migrant salesmen and young African sellers or craftsmen are less likely to occur. For instance, Cina Gueye (2021) has outstandingly shown how the transnational economic device based on street commerce and shoemaking in Dakar illustrates the dynamics of 'bottom-up globalisation'. A new relationship between poor-to-poor markets and a cosmopolitan merchant capitalism which has emerged in African cities from recent Chinese migrations. This shows how different sectors of economic activity are restructured through complex commercial transactions, which are concomitantly local and global. For example, we see how, inside a sub-regional space, Chinese salesmen have become the huger supplier for local street salesmen. The multiplication of Chinese commercial counters in the regional and sub-regional spaces illustrates the multipolarity of Chinese migration in the 'Global South'.

Since Chinese and international cities are involved in the globalisation process, new internal boundaries and new cosmopolitanisms with transnational territories are being produced simultaneously. This simultaneity reflects twin phenomena of closed local spaces and opened global territories (Sassen, 2006), which in turn reflects a dual process of multiple inequalities in international cities and new economic and social links between international cities.

If globalisation is a multi-dimensional process, if we have already seen several globalisations, then present-day globalisation is more a phenomenon in which the relationships between the local and the global, are endlessly being reconfigured. Transnational spaces are the scene of a proliferation of new combinations which can be seen in the increasing differentiation of areas which were formerly a part of the national and supranational fields. Adopting the terms of Saskia Sassen (2007b), we can say that we are moving "from a dynamic centripetal force which characterised the Nation-State to a dynamic centrifugal force in which the multiplication of specialised assemblages" demonstrates how the access to these territorialities is constructed from diverse and varied *capabilities*. Locality, commerciality and ethnicity construct assemblages between polycentric economies (Zukin, Kasinitz, Chen, 2015) and hierarchically organised economies beyond the Nation-States, conjunctions between economic forms of unequal value. For example in eight-storey buildings of Dashatou Street in Guangzhou, there is a multitude of small workshops and shops housing the activities of tailors, fabric sellers, haberdashers, curtain sellers [...] In the city center the Pearl Market, the Jade Market and the semi-precious gem market are frequented by Chinese, African, Indian and Brazilian traders who come to purchase stock as well as to have stones cut in China.

Transnational economic networks linking cities compete with or even engulf national economies. The nearer international cities become to being "global cities" the more this phenomenon can be observed. Different facets of economic globalisation reveal new hegemonies, competitive forces and rivalries between the international cities. These economies form networks out of hegemonic dynamics or the dynamics of resistance which, for example, are visible in the transnational circulations of poorly qualified populations. Processes of re-composition, segmentation and diffraction of the local and global labour markets find expression in the multiple constructions of arrangements between the diversified and hierarchically organised forms of labour which influence the mobilities and circulations within and between international cities.

Consequently, a new map can be drawn, a map of new transversal anchor points for both economy and identity, points which are linked by more or less visible lines along which the more or less qualified populations circulate in the Chinese and international cities. Young Chinese migrants, which are compelled to follow the injunctions of mobility and which are subjected to numerous displacements, are positioned according to plural modes within economic spaces of weak or strong legitimacy. These plural positioning modes emphasise the inclusions and separations between commercial and non-commercial markets, between official and natural markets and between formal and informal markets, on both local and global scales.

China is fully engaged in the process of globalisation, from which have emerged phenomena of deterritorialisation/reterritorialisation that reveal disjunctions and associations between social, political, economic and symbolic spaces of variable legitimacy. Saskia Sassen (2006, 2007a) shows how spatio-temporal frameworks and normative orders are becoming diversified, reconfigured and recodified beyond the boundaries of Nation states as a result of internationalisation and cosmopolitisation. The migratory flows of the new 'elites' and traders within the international space, as well as those of 'discredited' populations, and the increasingly visible presence of Chinese entrepreneurs in different countries actively contribute to what Saskia Sassen calls the proliferation of new arrangements and to the destabilisation of established institutional arrangements between territory, authority and rights, producing emerging territorialities and associations that are neither exclusively national nor exclusively global.

CHAPTER 4

Young Chinese Migrants and World Society

As we saw in the previous chapter, in multi-compressed modernity, local cosmopolitanisms and global cosmopolitanisms are embedded. The broad spectrum of migratory forms urges us to consider local dynamics and the production of transnational economic and social spaces to understand the transformation of global labour markets. The international circulations of young Chinese reveal a double movement of transformation. On the one hand, they reflect the ethnic segmentations with the production of ethnic niches in traditional (manufacturing, care work, trade, etc) and new (Information technology, tourism, etc) branches of activity. On the other, they demonstrate the process by which local markets expand to a transnational and global level—in a more or less visible way—through the circulation of men, women, commodities, products and beliefs and where minority norms can become majority norms.

1 Work, Employment and Young Chinese Graduates in Europe

A growing number of young Chinese graduates are leaving China for Europe. According to a 2018 employment survey by INSEE (the French National Institute for Statistics and Economic Research) Chinese nationals accounted for 3.2% of immigrant arrivals in France in 2017.

Of the total, 29.7% had a secondary school certificate equivalent or no diploma, 8.1% had an NVQ-GNVQ[1] equivalent, 18% had the equivalent of a general baccalaureate diploma or a GNVQ, 5.4% had a general baccalaureate diploma + 2 years' higher education, 37.8% had a tertiary qualification higher than a general baccalaureate diploma + 2 years' higher education (Bac +2) (see table2).

Summary

31,3% Chinese employees for 32,8% African employees

23, 9% Chinese executives for 12,5% African executives

19% Chinese manual labourers for 34,5% African manual labourers

17,1% Chinese artisans, traders and company directors for 6,2% African artisans, traders and company directors

8,8% Chinese intermediate professions for 14% African intermediate professions

---

1 NVQ: National Vocational Qualification ; GNVQ: General National Vocational Qualification.

© LAURENCE ROULLEAU-BERGER, 2021 | DOI:10.1163/9789004463080_006

YOUNG CHINESE MIGRANTS AND WORLD SOCIETY

TABLE 2   Education level of immigrants by geographic origin in 2018

by %

Country	PSC, GCSE, no diploma	NVQ/ BTEC	Baccalaureate, GNVQ Advanced	Bac+2	Diploma higher than Bac+2	Have finished their first diploma
Europe	41.7	19.5	11.8	6.4	20.6	89.2
Spain	50.2	26.4	7.5	4.0	11.9	85.2
Italy	49.8	22.6	7.7	3.1	16.9	88.8
Portugal	66.4	20.6	7.2	3.4	2.3	94.2
United Kingdom	10.6	10.6	17.0	9.6	52.1	90.4
Other 28 EU countries	17.4	14.4	19.0	12.4	36.8	89.0
Other European countries	23.5	21.0	15.6	6.6	33.3	82.4
Africa	44.8	19.3	12.3	7.2	16.4	92.4
Algeria	46.6	22.5	8.8	5.2	16.9	94.1
Morocco	50.8	16.9	10.7	8.0	13.6	94.2
Tunisia	44.2	19.7	12.0	6.8	17.3	94.3
Other African countries	37.9	19.0	16.7	8.1	18.3	89.1
Asia	42.2	12.4	15.0	6.9	23.4	90.9
Turkey	62.7	19.5	12.7	1.8	3.2	94.8
Cambodia, Laos, Vietnam	43.1	11.1	12.4	11.8	21.6	95.6
China	29.7	8.1	18.9	5.4	37.8	78.7
Other countries in Asia	28.2	8.4	17.4	8.4	37.6	87.6
America, Oceania	34.0	12.0	15.9	5.2	33.0	86.1
Total immigrants	42.8	18.1	12.7	6.7	19.7	90.7
Total non-immigrants	20.5	30.7	17.6	12.9	18.3	72.1

Notes:

89.2% of immigrants from European countries had completed their first diploma. Of those, 20.6% had a tertiary qualification higher than Bac+2.

Non-immigrants include descendants of immigrants.

Scope: France except Mayotte, individuals residing in their principal residence.

SOURCE: INSEE, 2018 EMPLOYMENT SURVEY

TABLE 3   Socio-professional categories of immigrants by geographic origin in 2018

by %

Country	Agricultural workers, artisans, traders and company directors	Executives	Intermediate Professions	Employees	Manuel labourer
Europe	9.3	16.5	17.9	27.9	28.5
Spain	9.4	19.2	20.6	29.7	21.1
Italy	8.6	37.3	21.2	24.2	8.7
Portugal	8.3	4.2	10.4	33.5	43.6
United Kingdom	21.3	39.6	17.2	19.2	2.6
Other 28 EU countries	10.0	23.7	23.8	22.7	19.8
Other countries in Europe	7.8	14.8	22.2	27.0	28.2
Africa	6.2	12.5	14.0	32.8	34.5
Algeria	9.7	11.8	14.2	29.7	34.7
Morocco	6.9	13.5	14.6	28.2	36.8
Tunisia	9.3	19.7	13.3	27.6	30.1
Other countries in Africa	3.2	10.5	13.8	38.7	33.9
Asia	10.9	16.8	13.1	23.2	35.9
Turkey	11.6	4.3	6.4	13.6	64.1
Cambodia, Laos, Vietnam	8.1	22.4	17.6	20.7	31.2
China	17.1	23.9	8.8	31.3	19.0
Other countries in Asia	10.9	20.2	15.5	29.0	24.4
America, Oceania	10.7	20.2	19.5	31.5	18.1
Total immigrants	8.2	14.9	15.5	29.8	31.7
Total non-immigrants	7.7	18.6	27.2	27.1	19.4

Notes:

16.5 % are European immigrants aged 15 to 64 years and currently employed are executives.

Non-immigrants include descendants of immigrants.

Scope: France except Mayotte, workers aged 15 to 64 years residing in their principal residence.

SOURCE: INSEE, 2018 EMPLOYMENT SURVEY

YOUNG CHINESE MIGRANTS AND WORLD SOCIETY

In comparing Chinese and African immigrants Chinese immigrants occupy more qualified professional positions and are strongly invested in the creation of businesses and companies (see table 3).

Young Chinese who move to Western Europe, especially France, develop highly proactive strategies for finding employment. They look for work in French companies and must hold an employee's residence permit. They face many hurdles, to the extent that certain individuals have been forced to launch legal proceedings. Some decide to return to China where they have a guaranteed job and the support of family and friends.

> Last year due to the policy restricting migrant workers, many students could not transfer their student visa to an employee's residence permit and had to return to their country of origin. I personally struggled for a year. I couldn't find a job after graduating. The XX association made me an offer, so I continued to work there. I went to the prefecture to renew my work permit with this employment contract. However, they didn't even assess my application; it was rejected for no reason. With the help of a lawyer friend, I took legal action. After a six-month trial, we won the case and I was finally granted my residence permit. But then, at this time my employer—the XX association—closed down. I didn't know what to do. YY's boss offered me a job so I had to reapply for a visa with the new work contract. I was forced to wait for months on end. All up the process went on for a year, back in 2010. This is the same approach immigration policies: priority access to employment for French citizens in a context of high unemployment and strict control over access to employment for foreigners. More and more Chinese nationals are launching legal action against the prefecture in response to their rejected residence permit applications. Many equally return directly to China as they have other options there.
>
> LIN, woman, 29 years old, interview conducted in Paris in 2015

Young skilled Chinese migrants are victims of a toughening stance in French and European migration policies, forcing some of them to leave Europe. These Chinese youth express worry at the idea of returning to China after having lived in what has become their second home. The CMIRA research programme, already mentioned, conducted from 2012 to 2015 in Paris and Lyon, found that one of three young Chinese graduates had kept their first job, 66.18% had stable employment with a permanent contract, 25% had a short-term contract and 4.41% were temporary workers. Of the young Chinese working in France, 54.76% reported that their first job after graduating was in a foreign company,

14.29% in a Taiwanese or Hong Kong company, 14.29% in a Chinese company, 13.10% in a state-owned company and 5.95% in a governmental structure. Those with work experience prior to their current role had advanced in their careers in the fields of teaching, purchasing, communication and finance, information system, audit and accounts managing. One of two young Chinese cited dissatisfaction with wages and lack of self-fulfilment as reasons for leaving, one of three highlighted poor work conditions linked to stress and difficult professional relationships. Some graduates, especially those who complete training offering fewer employment prospects, face precarity and downward social mobility. Workplace discrimination in French employment markets drives some young Chinese to find employment in Chinese companies that are part of the Chinese community and where they can take advantage of their network of interpersonal relationships. For example, a young 33-year-old woman with a bachelor's degree found her first job in a company specialising in the import and sale of furniture made in China. She was the only Chinese national of 20 employees.

> The company's main business activity was selling furniture in France. Of the twenty employees, I was the only one from China, the rest were French. The three partners (bosses) were from Wenzhou and were second generation Chinese women born in France. They were young, around 35 years old. The company was badly managed, which is why it later went bankrupt. It was a small company and the three young partners were not specialised in management. Their level of education was not sufficient to operate the business effectively.
>
> LI, woman, 33 years old, interview conducted in Paris in 2015

Many young migrants experience situations of linguistic instability which render their acquired professional and social expertise partially invisible. The relative absence of linguistic capital further complicates their efforts to secure economic, social and moral capital. These situations of linguistic instability can be likened to a veil placed over the professional qualifications these migrants have attained in China.

> I moved to France five years ago in 2012. I had no support network here because all my friends and former classmates are in China. Everyone in the office here graduated from leading universities. So, I don't think it is easy for a Chinese person to succeed. Even my boss told me that if I wanted to become a manager, my future was not in the company. I could have perhaps had an opportunity for career development in a Chinese

company investing in Europe, but not in a European company. The issue isn't me, it's my boss. I could also return to Asia, where social distinction isn't based on where you're from, but on the individuals themselves. For the moment, I'm starting my career as portfolio manager and not asking too many questions regarding the future, because right now I'm just learning the ropes in my occupation.

ZHANG, man, 26 years old, interview conducted in Paris in 2017

Some young Chinese in France take advantage of their personal networks to change jobs, while others look for work online. Young Chinese consider salary essential when looking for employment. However, it is clear that young Chinese are more demanding when it comes to wages in the industrial, sales, media, design and tourism sectors, for example.

2   Ethnic Niches, Violence and Suffering

European labour markets have become increasingly segmented, precarious and ethnicised, with the emergence of *ethnic niches* (Waldinger, R., 1994; Waldinger, R., Bozorgmehr, M., 1996) which are structured in a hierarchy according to cultural origins, levels of diploma, qualification and gender. As per Cédric Jolly, Frédéric Lainé, and Yves Breem (2012), Chinese migrants are highly represented in certain occupations and industries. Unlike their counterparts from developing countries, low-skilled Chinese migrants rarely find employment in personal services or the cleaning and security industries. Compared to other immigrants, Chinese migrants are poorly represented in the construction and industrial sectors. Nonetheless, there is a large concentration of low-skilled Chinese migrants of both sexes in care work, trade and manufacturing industries. In 2012, 15% female Chinese migrants worked in care work, whereas almost one 18% male Chinese migrants worked as cooks. In addition, 13% of Chinese workers were employed as vendors. Chinese migrants also find work in wholesale businesses or entrepreneurs in the textile and clothing industry.

Ethnic niches are decreasingly dominated by one ethnic group and becoming more pluri-ethnic, as successive waves of migrants from different continents find work in them. The restaurant industry, particularly the fast-food sector, and the hotel trade are emerging as true pluri-ethnic niches, in which migrants from China, sub-Saharan Africa and the Maghreb and, more recently, Eastern Europe work side-by-side (Roulleau-Berger, 2010). They face to situations characterised by harsh treatment linked to identity where solidarity might be expected. In the traditional urban enclaves, hierarchies are constructed on the basis of place of origin and length of stay in the host country.

Young Chinese have a dominant presence in certain labour market segments. These sectors play a role in shaping ethnic niches comprised of young Chinese workers, youth from central and eastern Europe and labourers from the Maghreb and sub-Saharan Africa. Ethnic niches emerge in disqualifying segments of labour markets and develop through ethnic and inter-ethnic solidarity networks to form assemblages. Interactions between employers and young Chinese are increasingly based on relationships of suspicion and contempt that contain social, ethnic and sexual domination. Ethnic niches continue to flourish with the arrival of new waves of migrants and due to employees resorting to an undocumented work force attracted by pull factors in a context of flexibility.

These different ethnic niches form through both ethnic and inter-ethnic solidarity. Nevertheless, the concept of inter-ethnic solidarity can only stretch so far as young Chinese are most often hired to carry out difficult work without a contract. For example, they accept seasonal work (fruit picking, grape harvesting) and temporary jobs in harsh conditions in the agricultural industry, for the benefit of other Chinese. Young Chinese female migrants work in beauty salons. Take Cui for example, interviewed in 2018, who worked in different nail salons in Milan.

Cui, 29 years old, is from Zhejiang, located in the countryside near Wenzhou City. She and her younger brother were brought up by her grandmother because her parents did not work in the village and often went to Russia to do business. At the age of seven, she went to Wenzhou to attend school. She lived there during the week and on weekends she returned to the village. At school she also met her boyfriend, who works for Taobao. At the age of 11, she learned that her parents had left for Italy, first her father, followed by her mother. They had told her that it is easy to earn money there and that they had to leave, but later she and her brother would join them. Her parents had travelled illegally to Florence where they had family, fellow villagers from Wenzhou: "here in Italy, all the Chinese come from Wenzhou [...] I think it's because we like to see other places, we're entrepreneurs and we like to earn money. Moreover, since we come from Zhejiang we've already seen how the foreigners work and we know how to work with them, that's why we go". Cui's father initially traded in wholesale clothing in Rome, while his mother worked in a clothing factory. They then moved to a suburb of Florence. It's a small town where there are not many Chinese, although there are many in Florence and Prato. In China, Cui went to high school for two years in Wenzhou until her father called her and told her to leave school to do a type of internship in a nail salon. This was the job she was destined for once in Italy, and in order to get a job quickly she had to have experience. After several months in the hair salon, her father sent her the plane tickets and the visa. She left with her brother. They landed in Florence. Cui cried all the way through the flight because she didn't want to leave China. When she arrived at the airport, she could not even recognise her father because she had almost never seen him. She was quickly sent to Naples by her parents. In the countryside near the city, Chinese people had opened an Italian school for young Chinese people. Cui's parents had heard that students learnt fast there, so she studied there for three months. She told about the differences between the two countries and her difficulties adapting and integrating there. "Italy is hard, Italians are not like the Chinese. I struggled to learn the language, I'm getting better now, but it's hard. They don't understand me at times [...] our ways of thinking are not the same [...]". She was then sent to live with her father's aunt who lived in a Milanese suburb. She had opened a clothing shop where Cui worked as a sales assistant. She cleaned her aunt's house (there were six of them including the children), prepared food and earned a total of €500 a month, which for her was not much. After two years, Cui returned to China for five months to see her boyfriend, then she travelled back to Florence. Her father sent her to Milan to work in a nail salon. She did not like the atmosphere at work or the accommodation given to her by the Chinese boss of the nail salon: "I didn't like it [...] the boss was arrogant, the work was hard [...] we were made to work a lot, way too much [...] I was tired and accused of complaining, I was so tired [...] polishing nails is cool, I like it, but not working at that place. As for money, I was paid very little". All eight girls lived together in a single large room above the nail salon. After three days, Cui left the salon and found herself unemployed, with no accommodation. She also spoke very little Italian. Thanks to a smartphone application for Chinese people living in Milan, she found a job in another nail salon. Her accommodation was also provided by the boss. She lived, at the end, next to a Chinese supermarket and shared the bed with another Chinese woman. The salon owner was Chinese and had made a lot of money, so he bought the salon and the apartment in which she lived with the other two girls. Cui worked from Monday to Sunday, 8 a.m. to 8.30 p.m., with no day off. She used to have a free day, but not anymore and she feels exhausted. The salary was based on the number of completed manicures, between €1,500 and €2,000. She wanted to go back to China.

Ethnic niches are connected to a "shadow economy" that exists in European labour markets where young Chinese migrants are restricted to dirty work. Ethnic niches can therefore be labelled *restrictive work spaces* where young Chinese migrants are deprived of all autonomy. Ethnic niches do not comply with the labour laws in force. As long as Chinese nationals are in an irregular situation, they are hired without an employment contract and may be forced to work up to 14 hours a day. These young migrants cannot escape the behaviour and attitudes exhibited by their employers and are forced to do dirty work. They are rendered invisible, face diminishing recognition, suffer frequent humiliation and mistreatment and are forced to accept maximum flexibility at work. Migrants lose any possibility of being autonomous and are subject to forced work, meaning they are dependent on individuals that may control them through various means in the care work, clothing workshops and in home-based work settings. These young migrants retreat within themselves, they regret moving to Europe where in lieu of living waking dreams, as defined by Strauss (1992), they experience a harsh everyday reality.

Beyond the segmentation of economic systems, strong ethnic and gender stigmatisation can be observed, creating partial segmentations (Roulleau-Berger, 2004) which strengthen and complicate the integration process for young Chinese women looking for a job. Ethnic niches are giving way to pluri-ethnic niches as young Chinese from different continents successively work in these spaces. The care service and agricultural industry are diversified pluri-ethnic niches. Labour organisation systems in these niches produce extreme symbolic violence by rendering the professional qualifications acquired by young migrants in China invisible. This also leads to physical violence and moral or sexual harassment. Labour law regulations are often flouted in pluri-ethnic niches and maximum flexibility is enforced on women forced to accept illegal work conditions in some cases (Jounin, 2009).

The transition from traditional ethnic niches to pluri-ethnic niches appears to be a recent phenomenon. It is linked to both the saturation of ethnic enclaves (Beltrane, Lopez, 2007) and to low-skilled young Chinese successfully attaining linguistic security, often by marrying a French national. Entry into ethnic niches or the transition from one niche to another defines horizontal mobilities that do not grant access to a stable job in the French employment market. Economic domination also enforces horizonal mobilities in labour market segments, spaces where young Chinese are excluded and have no professional development opportunities.

YOUNG CHINESE MIGRANTS AND WORLD SOCIETY

3   Chinese Economic Elites and the *Cosmopolitan Spirit*[2]

Chinese youth with the most social and economic capital are now more likely to turn to business activities related to China from 2013 onwards, notably the New Silk Roads in eastern and central and southern Europe where labour markets offer more opportunities than Western Europe. At the beginning of the 1990s, the southern European countries had favoured the immigration of Chinese entrepreneurs who quickly integrated themselves into the national economies. Eastern and Central Europe had also favoured the emergence of Chinese entrepreneurs, businessmen and traders by relying on *intermediate minorities*, i.e. groups that rely on cross-border networks to invest institutionalised positions in economic niches (Nyiri, 2007). These niches have changed in terms of the structure in which Chinese have employed natives; new entrepreneurial figures have emerged who then produce new arrangements in global markets from dispersed economic structures by producing international economies of material and immaterial labour.

Transnational communities cannot exist without dense social networks from individual social capital accrued in China, on migratory pathways and in host countries. Today Chinese populations with high levels of social and economic capital also occupy skilled and high-skilled segments of the labour market in the service, industrial and new technology sectors across various European countries. This Chinese presence has become institutionalised in the European and global markets via New Silk Roads. Young Chinese migrants in central and eastern Europe possess mobility capital and streamlined access to means of communication superior to those in western Europe, facilitating the maintenance and development of cooperation and trade relations with mainland China.

It should also be emphasised that young Chinese women are increasingly asserting their presence and have started travelling alone, playing an increasingly central role in ethnic economies through their active participation in building and consolidating highly-mobilised family networks. Furthermore, skilled Chinese women also develop socially prestigious transnational careers formed through networks, norms of trust and reciprocity which facilitate the coordination and cooperation to produce social capital. Chinese nationals develop types of differentiated migratory careers—in line with their economic, social and symbolic resources and the economic and political context of their host countries—which unfold in diverse modes in western and

---

2   Ciccelli, V. 2012. *L'esprit cosmopolite*, Paris: Presses de Sciences Po.

eastern European societies. The Chinese present in central, eastern and southern Europe develop distinctly transnational careers in the service and industrial sectors. We can observe transnational economic networks which produce plural forms of transnationalism interconnected by diasporic dynamics and themselves linked to economic networks formed in mainland China.

Young skilled Chinese carry out globalised work in China and Europe, which entails geographical and professional mobility. In Europe, young skilled Chinese migrants have all developed strong geographical and professional mobility by accumulating social and spatial capital with each change of situation. This ensures the right conditions are in place to produce globalised work. They also have the shared idea of creating international lives. To this end, they develop networks of friends across different cities around the world (in Europe and the United States, for example) in which they circulate and display a *cosmopolitan spirit* (Cicchelli, 2012).

> My mother comes from Tianjin and I have a lot of family in Beijing. I went to primary school, middle school, high school and university in Shanghai. I was also there for my internship in my fourth year of university. I worked in an American company specialising in public relations and more precisely in consulting on media and government relations. It was very interesting. The directors had experience working in government and at consulates. It was an international company; half of the employees were foreigners, many of them from a Chinese background. Only four or five employees were local Chinese, like me for example. My boss was from Jiangxi, and one of my colleagues from Wu Xi. This was an enriching experience for me, especially because it was my first job. I didn't care about the career, I just wanted to take advantage of this work opportunity, which I really enjoyed. I had a good salary and got along well with my colleagues. I met my best friend in this company, as well as an American girl there for her internship. We became good friends and we were in frequent contact. We met again in London, Paris, Rome and Belgium, as we both travelled a lot. One day, she told me she was going to go to Rome from the United States, so I decided to join her. She's a journalist. It's great, we met in Shanghai and we are often meeting together in other parts of the world.
>
> NIN, woman, 28 years old, interview conducted in 2016

Cosmopolitan socialisation in the workplace leads to the coexistence and direct contact of disparate cultural norms. Young Chinese all report that employees have access to social rights in terms of social protection and job security in the European employment market, which is not the case in China. However, young Chinese may face forms of distancing in French companies that may be analysed as covert ethnic discrimination. They produce globalised work and develop international micro-companies in China in the international tourism and communication industries. This is the case for JJ, director of the Asian region at PB, which is expanding in China. As a brand developer, she facilitates the company's establishment in the Korean, Singaporean and Malaysian markets. Like other Chinese, she inherited her mobility skills from her parents who were entrepreneurs in China. Entrepreneurial and circulation skills draw on the reproduction of conditions for social and spatial capital, expressed initially by local mobility and then by international mobility. For example in 2016 we met 28-year-old Na, who is Asia regional manager in a large French company:

> Most of my family members are actually entrepreneurs, so it's really a family legacy. It's a great opportunity, the fact that my parents' work is very similar to mine has helped me a lot. I am familiar with the distribution business in department stores and shopping centres. For example, I know how to assess good and bad locations. It's something I learned when I was a kid. My parents don't handle the production side of things. Ten years ago, they created a cosmetics brand in China and had a factory, but it didn't work as well as they hoped. So, they closed the factory to concentrate more on distribution in the leather goods sector, especially shoes. They managed to invest in other distribution companies and acquired several points of sale.

Young entrepreneurs produce new economic arrangements in global market sectors by combining local and international dimensions from dispersed economic structures. They play a very important role in the development of material and immaterial, e.g. digital, labour economies. These entrepreneurial skills are based here on high social capital, low economic capital and strong spatial capital, which means the ability to develop strong and weak ties from social, family and symbolic resources. We also see how immaterial labour is highly cooperative in immediately collective forms.

Global work is based on symbolic and material assemblages of transnational activities and spaces governed by similar economic conventions and standards to ensure regulated coordination. Thus, global work is defined based on shared, specific standards for young Chinese migrant business executives and entrepreneurs who play a central role in the circulation of moral and material goods. Global work is denationalised, meaning it develops in the accumulation of gaps in the national labour markets and local economic institutions, gaps which vary in different contexts. The intermediate figure of the Chinese migrant appears in this accumulation of gaps, an individual who holds *discretionary power* (Karpik, 2007) as to the orientation and circulation of material goods. Young Chinese executives and entrepreneurs are mobilising knowledge and expertise on an international scale in the circulation and distribution of commodities, collaborating to produce assemblages between economic spaces (Roulleau-Berger, 2010). Material and moral goods circulate in circulatory territories via economic transactions in unpredictable circumstances managed through trust and loyalty networks on markets of international repute.

The modes of economic inscription of young Chinese migrant executives and entrepreneurs imply that they can adapt to new international contexts. The greater their discretionary power, the greater their social prestige in their own communities and in transnational communities. Young Chinese executives and entrepreneurs must employ strong market capture strategies (Trompette, 2008) to win over new clients in local economic spaces, sites of competitive struggles. Symbolic authorities form in these spaces on a global scale, resulting in effects of domination in access to moral and material goods. This is the case for Stéphane we have met in 2015.

Stéphane was born in Nanjing in 1979 in a family that he himself described as abnormal, where he was allowed more freedom than is usual. Both his parents worked in the hotel business. They were sent to the countryside for 10 years during the Cultural Revolution. They hoped to raise a child who could go to college. His parents therefore pushed him from primary school onwards to pass a test to enter Nanjing's School of Foreign Languages. The school offered high-level language training and granted access to the country's best universities. Stéphane therefore chose French as his primary foreign language studied at the age of 12, and then continued his language studies at the Shanghai University of Foreign Languages. After finishing his studies in Shanghai, Stéphane obtained a position as a Chinese language assistant in Toulouse for three years. He then chose to apply to Sciences Po Paris to broaden his field of expertise as he felt that he was restricting himself in the sociolinguistics training he was undertaking at the time. He enrolled in a Master's of International Relations and Economic Governance. His years at Sciences Po left a strong mark on him and he had started a doctorate in economics, when he met a Chinese director at YY China. They convinced him to the step into the business world. He was hired by YY in Shanghai as a training manager. His return to China after six years of life in France and his adjustment to YY's corporate culture was not easy. His supervisor pointed out that he was probably the most highly qualified manager in the country. In 2009, Stéphane joined a training course provided by the French Fashion Institute and was hired again by YY as a product manager. Stéphane feels Chinese in France and French in China, he is often confronted with the fact that the "Asians" at YY are confined to assignments related to Asia. He is constantly reminded of his Chinese identity when he would like to move to a position that is not limited to this market. He finally managed to obtain a position as product manager for an international franchise, which he felt was as an acknowledgement of his skills.

In these transnational dynamics, young skilled Chinese migrants create convergences between economic systems situated in distinct contexts using their translation and communication abilities. This allows them to render one context visible to the other. The systems of decision-making and trust play a decisive role in local markets and the conditions in which executives and entrepreneurs participate in international economic activities. In situations of cosmopolitan socialisation at work, young skilled Chinese have integrated the social norms linked to globalised work and the injunction to be oneself, meaning they "confront" situations of economic risk and accept new responsibilities abroad.

In a context of cosmopolitan socialisation, young Chinese must face contradictory societal norms that create identity conflicts. Circulation skills reflecting an increase in the repertoires of economic, social and moral resources on migratory pathways from China to Europe may result in a decline in work or jobs with no opportunities for career development. For example, 38-year-old C. had developed a pathway to promotion in a large international company yet was implicitly asked to return to China "without a safety net". In this instance, cosmopolitan socialisation may lead to a form of cosmopolitan delocalisation in cases with an indirect injunction to return to China.

4   Discrimination, Racism and Skills

Forms of racism towards young Chinese migrants in the West are expressed in different ways according to young migrants' skills and educational qualifications. They also differ to the racism shown to migrants from African countries, Syria, Iraq and the Maghreb. In addition, the least qualified migrants are often viewed by potential employers as unskilled, unexperienced and not committed to their work. Furthermore, the issue of religious discrimination of the practice of Islam by young women in European countries is a pressing matter, rapidly becoming a barrier to employment access and recognition in the workplace. Racism at work towards young migrants from Africa or the Maghreb is fuelled by an internal colonialism, manifested by wariness and suspicion by

126   CHAPTER 4

employers and social inclusion stakeholders (Boubeker, 2003; 2018; Giraudo, 2014, 2018). They are quickly categorised as potential "troublemakers" and capable of rebelling. Some young migrants may be seen as "schemers", welfare consumers who try to fraud public institutions In contrast, young Chinese migrants are seen as "good workers" to be "used at will" and are labelled as discreet and not prone to revolt at work.

Considering young Chinese to be discreet and "passive" signifies a denial of their professional identities built throughout their migratory journey. In low-skilled labour markets, discrimination is shown through false recognition that produces violence and identity fragmentation. Young Chinese migrants are still seen as Strangers, assigned to specific places, defined by employers who deny their identity and develop strategies to camouflage their racist practices. In France, attention must be drawn to racist crimes committed against Chinese migrants in recent times, such as the fashion designer killed in Aubervilliers in August 2017 by two young French nationals.

The key challenge for young skilled Chinese in Europe and France, eclipsing the problem of disqualification, is to be able to stay and work in France, to not be forced to return to China or be distanced from French employment markets. The impact of the economic crisis and migration policies creates situations of risk and permanent insecurity for young Chinese who have developed adaptive strategies in French society and do not necessarily want to return to China. Let's hear from Jun, 30 years old, IT/Communications engineer that we have met in 2015:

> Chinese students have three choices: continue working in France, return to work in China, or continue studies in France. The most difficult choice is to stay and work in France. Age plays a role here. French students take a two-year preparatory course followed by three years of engineering school, graduating with an engineering degree at the age of 22 or 23. Chinese students study for four years to obtain their university diploma, then two or three years in France. If a Chinese person undertakes doctoral studies, they will feel the pressure of age and passing time. There also face financial difficulties as many Chinese students have limited funding. The longer the studies, the harder it is. France's economic situation is difficult at the moment and migration policies do not support access to employment for foreigners. Even the French can't find work, without mentioning the language difficulties foreigners face.

In France, young skilled Chinese, graduates of prestigious French universities such as business schools, who gain access to French labour markets, may face discriminatory practices in companies. Moreover, at a given point in their career paths, these companies create deadlock situations for internal mobility. Not having French nationality could influence their opportunities for professional advancement. When young Chinese executives reach a certain level in the corporate hierarchy, employers use strategies to deter them from staying in France and remove them from the competition. Chinese nationals do not have the professional networks required at this stage of their career paths to secure important positions in the company. They are therefore excluded from roles that interest them.

> It's never easy when you're a foreigner and, in particular, I don't know if anyone would admit it. In any case, saying this to human resources is very frowned upon. I am product manager in this company, and when you're Asian, you must try harder to prove yourself, to show that you are capable, because you're put in the "Asian" box. Most Chinese who work here, or at least those in our field, work on specific Asian jobs. So, we're not necessarily considered Chinese, we represent Asia in general, and its biggest market. To have a more international position, you must do more because there is a language barrier. Not all Chinese people speak French or English well, or at least well enough to carry out complex work involving multiple non-Chinese or non-Asian contacts. It's more difficult to move up in the hierarchy if you can't manage a region beyond China or Asia. Because today we are still told: "Yes, you are here to train and to learn the trade, but we will send you to Asia one day." It's very rare, for example, at ww at any rate, to be told: "No, you're not going to China, you're going to the USA." Nevertheless, I have to say that Asians are not trusted in the same way as French nationals or Europeans.
>
> G., man, 34 years old, interview conducted in 2015

It is clear that overqualified and overeducated young Chinese are indirectly discriminated against when the link between professional qualifications and the opportunity for professional mobility is severed. In this case, a university degree is no guarantee to secure positions that lead to vertical mobility in a company's hierarchy.

And young low-skilled Chinese migrants could be relegated to situations of exclusion and social disqualification in positions of invisibility and social marginality. Young low-skilled Chinese women may face a lack of access to employment in labour markets. Some are forced into care work. Today, a significant number of women from poor countries are housekeepers, relegated to demeaning work where they often work undeclared. These unequal situations cannot be dissociated from a process of globalisation. The disqualification and humiliation suffered by young Chinese women are particularly visible with the expansion of the world market for domestic work. Care work thus shows clearly how gender, ethnicity and social stratification can combine in a "negative" way to produce forms of contempt for women migrants. A new globalised social stratification distributes women in transnational spaces that provide access to invisible forms of work. Care work appears as a very opaque segment of the labour market that allows for constrained flexibility and is often violently imposed on women migrants; here a new form of wage exploitation in a context of economic globalisation is clearly expressed. Care work clearly shows how economies are becoming dematerialised and how women migrants play a central role in this process where the exploitation of material resources is coupled with the exploitation of emotional resources (Ehrenreich, Hoschschild, 2004). The dynamics of dematerialisation of capitalist economies combine with the effects of structural impoverishment in the countries of Central and Eastern Europe, sub-Saharan Africa and the Maghreb in pushing women to migrate. Care work reveals the social identities of wounded women who, more or less constrained, leave societies and migrate to others where they will most often be invisible.

These new forms of economic imperialism in care work produce forms of denial of recognition and an injunction to low self-esteem. Young female Chinese students who work develop care work selection strategies, while those with few personal resources are subjected to care work. Hierarchies have been constructed in care work according to the volume of personal resources, the type of work offered, whether it is more or less "dirty", and the wage conditions. There is both social and ethnic competition for access to care work which entails a degree of violence.

In 2009, Cai, 34 years old, found a house with an old Shanghai woman. She shared a room with three people and paid 120 euros a month. She always kept her passport and her money with her because thefts were commonplace. The old woman told her about a job as a nanny in a family that lived outside of Paris. Cai would take the TGV and a man would pick up her at the station and take her to the house. She looked after the children and did house chores for a week. In the end, the family asked her to leave and paid her €230 for a week's work. Afterwards, she met a couple from Shanghai. They told her that she could learn how to make clothes with them. However, during her apprenticeship, she had to pay board and lodging. She only understood later that the something was wrong, she should not have to pay board and lodging because she made clothes for them. This couple paid €320 in rent and Cai payed €160 for board and lodging. The couple told her that in order to get a residence permit she would have to be in a couple, and that it would be better if her husband came to France and worked with her. They told her she could make a fortune in making clothes. At the time, she didn't not understand the system in France at all, she bought their lie.

It is patently clear that young low-skilled Chinese women feel the full force of these new forms of economic imperialism and injustice. Care work reflects forms of injustice resulting from the combination of economic globalisation, ethnicisation of labour markets and social disaffiliation. It operates through invisibility in the workplace where professional relationships and intimate ties combine, and blocks social identities constructed in other spaces. While domestic service can lead to prostitution, Marylène Lieber and Florence Lévy (2009) showed that, faced with the closure of the labour markets (French in general and Chinese in France), Chinese women, young and old, come to perceive their bodies and sexuality as a migratory resource. This occurs in a context of economic/sexual arrangements in various ways, as if to escape from community confinement and the domination of employers in South China. Here the sale or exchange of sexuality is a way to make money by escaping a form of stigma and racism. These Chinese women are partially reappropriating their lives, with constraints to ensure an acceptable future for themselves and their children.

5   Ethnic Enclaves and Multiple Affiliations

For young low-skilled Chinese in a situation of linguistic insecurity, ethnic enclaves appear to be the first step in a process of economic integration. These ethnic enclaves arise as a result of diaspora networks that clearly rely on highly structured forms of economic organisation. However, when young Chinese are linguistically secure, they may access certain labour market segments that offer more opportunities for professional development.

Ethnic enclaves (Portes, Sensenbrenner, 1993) arise through assemblages of multi-situated economic activities in different world places. They are constructed from economic regimes founded on principles of economic and moral associations and long coordination networks in which material, social and symbolic resources circulate during migratory experiences. Ethnic enclaves have existed for a long time in diasporas, but they are now revealing a new geography of interstices in hierarchised and diverse capitalist structures and are sources of both weak and strong reticular, sexual and ethnic domination.

Ethnic enclaves form in genuine autonomy from local societies (Miranda, 2002) and, in order to reach a global scale, contain zones of strong uncertainty and weak legitimacy (Deboulet, 2012). In these spaces, relationships of trust build and structure specific forms of economic coordination governed by a reputation market and sustainable interpersonal relationships which are more or less restricted and anchored in a myriad of cultural traditions.

Currently in Paris, most undocumented Chinese migrants live Stalingrad and in Aubervilliers. They mostly come from Zhejiang or Fujian, including some young migrants from the Northern provinces. Young Chinese migrants work here in the catering, food, clothing manufacturing, leather goods, small distribution, wholesale, electronic goods and Chinese tourism sectors (founding tourism agencies). Overseas branches are established by Wenzhou bosses who hire young, recent arrivals on short-term contracts to reduce taxes and fees. Wenzhou people are labelled as "bosses" and Northerners as "black workers". Wenzhou and Fujian people want to stay in France and have their families join them, young Northern migrants, however, plan on returning to China to return to their families once they have accumulated wealth (Su Liang, 2019).

According to Enzo Mingione (2013), in 2010 the Chinese community in Italy was estimated to be the largest in Europe, accounting for 25 percent of all Chinese immigrants present in Europe; Chinesse businesses in Italy were much less concentrated in ethnic sectors (restaurants, take-aways, traditional Chinese medicine, etc) then new young Chinese migrants have developed a new sort of Chinese-Italian community in business in the luxury industries of the *Made in Italy* trademark.

How do Chinese youth access transnational enclaves? Social, family and economic networks play a key role in building systems of trust in diasporic and transnational spaces. The position of young Chinese in ethnic enclaves depends on their social capital, linguistic insecurity (no knowledge of French or Italian [...]) and professional qualifications. The strength of their position dictates the varying degree of recognition that they receive in the Chinese community and European society. Their country of origin, situations of linguistic security and insecurity dictate the modes by which positions in ethnic enclaves are divided, attributed and distributed.

Young Chinese migrants may be confronted by paradoxical situations that produce identity violence instead of the solidarity they expected. Hierarchies in traditional Chinese enclaves are based on place of origin and time spent in European cities. Migrants from Northern China often feel overlooked compared to their southern counterparts. New arrivals experience situations of violent domination and are often given inferior positions compared to Chinese women from southern China. Undocumented migrants from Northern China

(Dongbei) report being despised by Chinese from the south and are even exploited in various work situations. They therefore face double discrimination: on the one hand by certain employers from southern China, and on the other through their difficulty accessing the French labour markets. Despite being caught in situations of captivity and marginalisation, they also develop resistance and survival strategies.

The economic regime in ethnic enclaves is based on criteria that do not comply with labour laws in force. As long as Chinese nationals are in an irregular situation, most of them are hired without an employment contract and may be forced to work up very hard. These migrants cannot escape the behaviour and attitudes exhibited by their employers and are forced to do dirty work. They are rendered invisible, face eroding recognition, subjected to frequent humiliation and mistreatment and are forced to accept maximum flexibility at work. Young migrants lose any possibility of being autonomous and are subject to restrictive work, meaning they are dependent on individuals that control them through various means, in the care work, clothing workshops or in home-based work settings, for example. Unskilled young Chinese workers are trapped in indecent occupations, and "lower-class" in secondary markets and floating social networks. Cross-labour intermediaries help them to work overseas but cannot provide long-term job opportunities. Thus, when the work is finished in a place of immigration, they must return to China or move to another destination, circulating in floating social networks (Su Liang, 2019).

The weaker the links in the floating social networks, the more young migrants may find themselves overexposed to violent situations in ethnic enclaves and experience mistreatment and humiliation; in this case we will consider that they live in totalitarian worlds and produce strong local domination. Nevertheless, digital economies, the Chinese community websites publish extensive information about daily life, getting jobs, renting houses and paid translation services.

In ethnic enclaves, community work contains forms of invisible and visible work. Forms of invisible work emerge in the family space when parents of Chinese youth are forced to include their children in their personal and professional survival strategies. Many children of Chinese migrants, also migrants themselves, are asked by their parents to take on responsibilities in Chinese restaurants and businesses. Forms of visible work also arise in closed labour markets for liberal professions such as lawyers, doctors, amongst others. Highly-educated young Chinese are occupying new segments that emerge as a result of economic regimes. They are founded on principles of economic and moral association and extensive networks for coordinating the circulation of material, social and symbolic resources in the diasporic space.

Throughout my career, I met people, entrepreneurs, my parents' friends and my friends who were starting their own company, etc. who asked me to be their accountant. When I told them that I was going to leave—because I had to tell them since they were family and friends, I wasn't going to hide it from them—they said to me, if you leave, we'll go with you. I started working with my parents, my cousins and then gradually with my parents' friends, my friends, friends of friends etc. So, I worked for my parents, the first generation of immigrants and I also worked for the second generation of immigrants with my cousins who are a few years older than me. They had arrived early in their lives at 7–8 years of age and went to school in France, but they stopped studying after graduating to take over the family business. I also have other clients. For example, I have a customer who has become a friend who I met through other friends. He was born and studied in France, became a self-employed entrepreneur and set up his own company. I have quite a lot of freedom because I can bring in clients to the business and not all employees can do this. In fact, I'm the only Chinese woman! I bring in clients mostly from my community. I certainly don't have a monopoly on my own community, but let's just say that the Chinese are very supportive of each other, they don't like to go elsewhere. So, if they can work in the same community and it goes well, they stay with you. It is true that there are some Chinese accountants, but there aren't many.

RUI, woman, 29 years old, interview conducted in 2015

In Europe, young Chinese migrants may also "take their place" in the community space on a professional level. Community work develops in diasporic spaces in segments of the European labour markets which are currently evolving in European cities. In France, young Chinese migrants face *double-bind* situations at certain moments in their professional careers. They find themselves caught between working in a family space steeped in the heritage of the migratory experience and the need to position themselves in the French labour market. Chinese youth find this form of invisible work highly restrictive. It hinders their professional aspirations in France where they seek to develop pathways to professional success and upward social mobility to become or continue to be "heroes", as Anne explains:

At the time the first bar/tobacco shops were opening. My parents own one today. At the time, I came back to work there, but after a while I told them, "It's not possible, I didn't study all that time for this". It's a very, very hard work environment as well. What's more, since I had built up my professional network in China, I decided to go back to school and enrolled in a Master's degree at ESCP. So, I had to work in the bar/tobacco shop for 18 months. It was very hard and depressing, but I wasn't even allowed to be depressed because I had to work. My father still had the leather goods store and worked there with my sister while I ran the bar/tobacco shop. After 18 months, I couldn't take it anymore. My parents had closed the leather goods store, which is what I was waiting for, and my sister was finally free too. As for me, I needed to create my own professional network in France, which is why I enrolled in a Master's degree. Today I am company partner.

ANNE, woman, 29 years old, interview conducted in 2014

These spaces are formed through relationships of trust that build and order particular forms of economic coordination governed by "reputation markets", lasting interpersonal ties that are more or less constrained and rooted in Chinese traditions. Xavier's experience aptly illustrates how young skilled Chinese must have both French and Chinese cultural resources in order to create new segments in closed labour markets. It is essential for Chinese youth to have both the recognition afforded by a French university degree and professional qualifications, as well as the trust and loyalty of the Chinese community. They may then establish dual reputations linked to their dual cultural affiliations, bringing about the necessary conditions for professional success. To establish themselves in two distinct reputation markets, young Chinese must learn to organise, prioritise and structure dual repertoires of economic, social, cultural and moral resources that coexist but rarely intersect.

I graduated in 2008, and in 2009 I was sworn in. I first worked in a French law firm as an associate, but I only worked there for three months, the reason being that at the time, the main idea was for me was to work as a freelancer. This meant having the possibility and freedom to go to work at 11 a.m. and leaving at any time, even midnight. But, above all, it meant having my own clientele. I tried to build my own client base. In fact, I had a part-time contract with my former boss to have a little more time for myself. At that time, I already had two clients, they were friends and family members who came to see me. That's why I thought of finding myself an office to sublet and establishing the firm there. The Chinese community in France is quite active in the field of repurchasing, buying, selling, this kind of thing. A total of 80% of my activity, that's right, is the commercial purchase of shops and restaurants. I was able to gradually develop my clientele in this way and it is really thanks to word of mouth that I was able to get to where I am today. When I started in 2009, I was the only one, I think. One of the first, anyway. But there are also two friends with me, one from Wenzhou and the other from Shanghai. There are more and more of us because young people are studying law, which is quite popular in the Chinese community. Now there are different groups of Chinese: there are those from Wenzhou, who represent most of the customers in this field, and then there are those who buy and sell ready-to-wear stores, for example in the 11th arrondissement and in Aubervilliers.

XAVIER, man, 25 years old, interview conducted in 2014

Social, family and economic networks play a key role in building systems of trust in diasporic spaces. Chinese youth must mobilise resources from communities they are part of in order to form these modes of coordination. The position of young Chinese in these spaces depends on their social capital, linguistic security and professional qualifications. The strength of their position dictates the varying degree of recognition they receive in the Chinese community and in French society. The presence of young qualified Chinese on closed labour markets in Europe reveals the formation of new ethnic enclaves that participate in their internationalisation.

CHAPTER 5

The *Compressed Individual* and *Polygamic Biographies*

In a context of multi-compressed modernity, multipolar Chinese migrations entail reversible, pendular and continuous mobility between China and the rest of the world. As such, migratory pathways are continuously diversifying, producing a range of itineraries which take the place of continuous and stable biographies, itineraries that are decreasingly linear, increasingly divided, diverse and complex. Young Chinese migrants have become emblematic of the *Compressed Individual.* To define more the Compressed Individual, we will analyse the relationship between social and spatial capital and migratory careers, and the effects of family governance in the individualisation process. While Ulrick Beck (2006) explored the concepts of the cosmopolitisation of biographies and geographically polygamic, this chapter will explore *polygamic biographies* organised around the amplification and intersectionality of social, ethnic, generational and gender-based inequalities. In polygamic biographies, biographical crossroads linked to migration and re-migration open onto a diversity of multi-situated mobility spaces and a kaleidoscope of aspirations. The effects of collisions inherent to multi-compressed modernity prevent young Chinese migrants from permanent adjustments and identity conversions accelerated at each biographical crossroads. This in turn raises constant questions of self-ownership, self-preservation and loss of self. Also, it must be borne in mind that in emotional capitalism, aspirations are quickly transformed into *emodities* that favour the loss of social, economic and moral resources, processes of social disqualification and identity trauma.

1 Social Networks, Spatial Capital and Migratory Circulations

Thomas Faist (2004) defined transnational social spaces as the product of combinations of non-static ties and networks and organisational positions locatable in at least two geographically and internationally distinct spaces. He introduced the notion of various forms of capital, the volume thereof and their mode of transferability. Some trajectories of migration are constructed on the basis of networks and norms of trust and reciprocity that facilitate coordination and cooperation to produce social capital (Putnam, 2000). Spatial capital

(Lévy, Lussault, 2003) also plays a role in the reciprocal exchanges with other resources. These interactions, however, are fluid, depending on the incentives offered by the social or societal context. When spatial and social capital is increased diasporic and transnational spaces, it has a strong activating effect on entrepreneurial strategies. The professional experience and skills of young Chinese migrants have indeed proliferated over the course of their two-way or multipath transnational migrations that facilitated the circulation of knowledge and expertise. Success in the form of entrepreneurship adopted by these migrants depends on the form of solidarity on which it is based. While activities based on strong solidarity (moral economy) or weak solidarity (opportunism) do not always seem able to guarantee economic success, limited solidarity seems to confer advantages over competitors. This is by virtue of the trust relations it engenders while at the same time limiting the obligations that accompany solidarity (Steiner, 1999).

Some Chinese sociologists, namely Bian Yanjie (2010) and Zhang Wenhong (Bian Yanjie, Zhang Wenhong, Cheng, 2012), studied the importance of social networks in accessing employment during the transition from a planned to a market economy. Bian Yanjie (2012) converted Granovetter's concepts of weak and strong ties into weak and strong *guanxi*. He showed that Granovetter's theory of weak ties is questionable in the Chinese context where the strength of guanxi (social networks) through familial and clan history outweighs weaker ties. Zhong Yunhua (2007) added the idea that strong ties play a major role in the public employment sector, whereas the strength of weak links allows access to private employment. However, at the time of hiring, the strength of strong ties over weak ties is clearly visible. In China, networks are analysed in terms of how the transmission of information relating to job offers, contacts, and places to go, but more precisely in terms of the introduction of a close relative to an employer. For example, an employer may ask a migrant to introduce him to trustworthy friends and relations. These relationships of trust vary in intensity according to a combination of ties and resources, but appear to be central to accessing employment. While access is organised around systems of exchange, offers and counter-offers, influence, and information, it also largely depends on capacity for professional and geographical mobility. The relative ease with which interpersonal ties link individuals despite the very large distances between Chinese provinces demonstrates the strength of family ties and the connection of places in migratory spaces in which families circulate.

Additionally, young Chinese migrants develop strong individual and collective strategies and entrepreneurial dynamics. These are based on networks of solidarity, family and community exchange in international contexts in which opportunities are present. As the process of ethnic discrimination on

European labour markets produces resistance expressed in the creation of self-employment, young Chinese entrepreneurs and traders of diverse cultural backgrounds draw up new global markets through transnational movements in which "bottom up" and "top down" globalisations intersect. These movements are organised according to ethnic, and even inter-ethnic, solidarities; economic systems founded on principles of economic and moral associations; and long coordination networks in which material, social and symbolic resources circulate during migration. For example, young Chinese migrants, open travel agencies, IT firms, and ready-to-wear clothes shops, etc., in European cities. Spatial movements become embedded in social relations specific to Chinese society, and young migrants rely on acquired or inherited resources by manipulating the spatial capital that enables them to integrate into transnational networks.

Space does not always appear as a resource; it can also be a constraint. As a resource, it promotes the circulation of young Chinese migrants along long social, economic, and transnational networks. When it appears as a constraint, it moves to shorter social, economic and transnational networks both in China and in Europe. The conditions needed for visibility and the mobilisation of personal resources play on irregular and hierarchical access to socialisation spaces within European and Chinese societies linked to reciprocal increases and decreases in social capital. In Europe, the level of inequalities faced by migrant populations may be doubled or tripled depending on age, gender, and the distribution and volume of resources and the extent to which they can be transferred. The likelihood of increased or decreased inequalities is dependent on the various economic, social, ethnic and symbolic resources available to individuals (Roulleau-Berger, 2010). Multi-compressed modernity and transnationalism have given rise to a proliferation of complex inequalities due diverse social, economic and symbolic resources acquired or developed in different societal contexts.

The lower the expansion and intensity of their social and symbolic ties, the less young Chinese will invest in activities in different socialisation spaces, and the less these ties connect them. When local and transnational coordination between economic spaces are reduced, individual resources repertoires diminish in terms of the exchange of goods, capital, people, information and cultural practices. In addition, the transferability of individual resources also decreases. The greater the breadth of social and symbolic ties, the more local and transnational interactions are maintained and strengthened, and thus the more personal resources are partially transferred. Further, when the intensity of social and symbolic ties is greater than their expansion, exchange and cooperation are strengthened at given point in time and space, ensuring the conditions for circumstantial resource transfer.

2   *Compressed Individual* and Family Governmentality

The fabric of the Compressed Individual is also influenced by the evolution of Chinese familial governmentality and geography of feelings with the rise of emotional capitalism and the injunction to be a "hero". During the Mao era, Chinese families sought economic stability, security and social protections above all. Parents of young migrants grew up in this context, internalising ideological and materialistic norms. The 1978 reforms profoundly overwhelmed familial structures in Chinese society. Emancipation from ideological and economic constraints was progressive; strong economic growth lead to improved living conditions for Chinese families. The changes brought by a growing GDP, mass education and a decline in patriarchy destabilised traditional societal structures in China (Wang Tiannan, 2014), particularly in rural areas. From the 1980s, the younger generation began to assert a desire for freedom from familial constraints, for social autonomy and a focus on developing their own individual identities. Modernisation in China saw the emergence of a generation gap between a majority of young migrants and their parents in terms of world views; their relationship with themselves and others; and other social norms produced by distinct moments in Chinese social, economic and political history.

For Aiwa Ong, the Chinese family is managed by a familial governmentality (Ong, 2002) drawing on productive bodies liable to sell themselves in labour market and bringing economic resources back to their family. In multi-compressed modernity, and an economy founded on injunctions of flexibility and productivity, there is extremely high demand for the bodies of young migrants. Everything starts within the family, be they located in China or France. However, as Li Yong (2016) demonstrated, the Chinese family has become the site of the formation of a new dynamic. The relationship between the individual and their family during the Mao era (1949–1976) was lessened in favour of their relationship with the state. The state freed individuals from their family and clan ties, and from local communities to integrate them into new social structures.

For Ji Yingchun (2018) contemporary Chinese society has witnessed ongoing complex institutional and cultural reconfiguration, driven by the transition from the socialist planned economy to marketisation and later its deep engagement in globalisation and neoliberalism. In the reshaping of Chinese society—in this gigantic mosaic—tradition and modernity, the resurgence of Confucianism, the socialist version of modernity, the capitalist version of modernity, and the socialist heritage are interwoven. Facing the increasing economic uncertainties, Chinese parents heavily invest in their children and

THE *COMPRESSED INDIVIDUAL* AND *POLYGAMIC BIOGRAPHIES*

continue to support them in their adulthood; whereas, the youth is under great obligation to providing old age care for their parents. Thus, *mosaic familialism*—in the sense of Ji Yingchun—is characterised by a sequential symbiosis between parents and children in a context of reactivation of patriarchal Confucianism and of production of the neoliberal discourse articulating personal choice and responsibility.

Over time, this individual-state relationship evolved into an individual-market coupling. The Chinese family structure actively participates in the production of this individual: exploited at will, generally young and a migrant from a rural area. It privileges the movement from a "partial individualisation" (Yan Yunxiang, 2010), to a compressed individuation which accompanies the cult of excellence ideology through feelings of scholastic and social success. The majority of youth from agricultural backgrounds aim to reach a higher socio-economic status than their parents. Work is overrepresented as a source of potential social success and access to the middle classes for less qualified graduates.

Young migrants, in their race to achieve economic and social success, may also draw on their family to overcome their individual challenges. Among those living and working in Shanghai, those receiving the lowest salaries may receive financial support from their parents. In highly competitive job markets, social origins and family networks play a decisive role in the professional careers of young migrants. Following experiences of "professional failure" in large Chinese cities, the majority will remobilise family and social resources to re-enter the labour market.

As their parents age, young migrants must care for their parents and siblings. Young migrants with less social capital are restricted by the need to meet their parent's needs, particularly in terms of health expenses and educational expenses for their siblings. They therefore internalise the injunction to accept work for which they are over-qualified at the start of their career in response to urgent situations and the economic survival of their families. Additionally, confronted by the risk of economic uncertainty, young migrants internalise the injunction to become a "hero of Chinese society":

> To be honest, when I arrived in Shanghai, I was aware that the crisis was in full swing, especially because I didn't have any resources, including networks, and I had no family or friends there. It still feels the same today. To get ahead here you have get in first—first in, first served. You always have to think ahead, to know when to stay and when to move on, that's what I said to myself when I arrived in Shanghai.
>
> BAI, man, 28 years old, interview conducted in 2016

Inequalities between more and less qualified youth are built on the different rate which expected and sought-after social positions are accessed. The most qualified can manage their time and develop strategies to anticipate the position they would like to reach, in comparison the those who are less qualified. This latter must support their families and adopt strategies that are simultaneously hasty and cautious, and which may place them in positions that do not correspond to their professional skills and social qualifications. The least qualified know that they are overexposed to the risk of failing in their professional endeavours.

In compressed modernity, family relations are reconfigured in a contradictory sentimental geography between a desire for autonomy and submission to parental authority, and between access to self and caring for others. This sentimental geography is built on tensions and conflict with parents. Mei's parents, for example were employed in work units in Wuhan. They enjoyed stability and hoped their daughter would join them. However, Mei appreciated her work environment in Shanghai and was satisfied with her personal success. As a result, she consistently refused to return to her birth village to work, even if her job in Shanghai was stressful: "I could never have imagined that they would expect me to follow their way of seeing things. I didn't think it would be a problem, and I didn't think they would expect me to ask their advice. My business is my business". The conflict between Mei and her parents heightened when she returned home for Chinese New Year. Her parents forced her to stay in Wuhan and to take a job at a security firm, confiscating her ID card and locking her in the house. After a month of being held captive, she finally gave in and accepted to remain in Wuhan. But Mei continued to refuse to take up the job they had chosen for her, and instead passed the exam to become a public servant. She then worked several months for a local council while secretly preparing to leave her stable job to return to work in Shanghai.

The family sentimental geography linked to compressed modernity also concerns young migrants of both sexes who do not want to return to their home regions and to their children who remain in the countryside known as 留守儿童 *liu shou er tong* (left-behind children). According to a 2017 report on the 2015 1% National Population Sample Survey, "China's Children Population: facts and figures", 68.7 million children aged between 0 and 17 years old are 'left-behind children', that is to say at least one of their parents is absent (due to migration), 40.5 million of these children reside in rural areas. At the heart of sentimental geographies linked to migratory experiences are several forms of separation and breaks in family ties. These are an ongoing threat to the individual and collective identities of young migrants.

THE *COMPRESSED INDIVIDUAL* AND *POLYGAMIC BIOGRAPHIES*

In multi-compressed modernity, the intergenerational conflicts between young migrants and their parents reveal fundamental differences in perceptions of Chinese society that correspond with societal breaks provoked by China's economic and social transformations. Before the implementation of reforms and the opening up of China, society was dominated by charismatic, traditional style leaders. Following the reforms, the emergence of consumerism in society destroyed traditional rural societal and social structures by creating conflict between generations (Zhou Xiaohong, 2008) and geographical separations that fuelled social conflicts. The family life of young migrants from rural areas was routinely marked by intergenerational conflict and tensions. Xu, for example, was born to a poor family in rural Zhejiang province. While he did well at school, he did not pass the university entrance exam. He has never consulted his parents regarding his career: "Only students from the city can consult with their parents. Parents of students from rural areas don't know so much about this. I've never asked my parents for career advice. I found a job myself, they never told me what to do." Parents, who are to a degree cut-off from modern urbanism, lose all influence over their children who carry out their plans far from any parent-child dynamic. Wu, a small business owner in Shanghai originating from a poor rural family, feels his parents are too conservative and that they have a "narrow" mindset and "have achieved nothing". By following through on his migration plans by which he gained financial resources, he has acquired a position of authority in his family.

During secondary socialisations, young migrants, most of them with no siblings, find themselves bound up in strong identity tensions between family obligations and their desire for social mobility. Caught in a double-bind between their plans for migration and "social success" and—as the only children of ageing parents—staying, the choice of these young migrants is often reduced to two options. They must either return to their home villages to live with their parents, or invite them to live with them in Shanghai. The double-binds in which these young migrants without siblings find themselves is particular to the compressed modernity of Chinese society.

In 2016 we met Tang, 30 years old, who was married in 2012. She was pregnant and wonders how to find a balance between her parents and her future child: "Once my mother retires, I can invite my parents to move here, I will buy them an apartment and I'll offer the same to my parents-in-law. My father-in-law is in poor health. My mother-in-law takes care of him but maybe in the future she will live with my parents. All of this puts pressure on me, especially because my son is due to be born soon". Tang and her husband considered themselves successful in their professional careers; their jobs were well-paid and provided financial stability. They planned on staying long-term in Shanghai: "We purchased an apartment in Shanghai and we plan on staying there, and maybe emigrating abroad if the opportunity comes up". They needed to take care of their parents requires them to save substantial amounts of money. Financial pressure was therefore strong, all the more so as they were expecting a child.

In China, the "injunction to become a hero" has gained strength as much in the family space as it has in the societal space. This triggers ruptures, conflicts, distance and loss of hope between young migrants and their families, while also maintaining inherited solidarities with family histories and reconstructing relational configurations in the context of modern China. An image is thus drawn of a sentimental geography fed by moments from childhood and rural, urban and work life.

3 Polygamic Biographies and the Translation of Resources

In polygamic biographies of young migrants in China, spatial capital comes into play in reciprocal exchanges with social capital. Multi-migrations in China produce spatial capital which is "positive" or "negative" depending on the context of an individual's arrival. The extent and size of social and family networks appears to play a decisive role in the production of spatial capacity along migratory routes linking labour markets. The greater the spread of a network, the more "positive" the spatial capital appears on migratory routes. Spatial capital takes on a different value according to the context of departure, economic practices, the value of goods in circulation and the expertise, qualifications and skills on migratory routes. For example, as seen in the migratory pathway of Meng, the nature and varying strength of family and social ties contributes to increases and decreases in available resources, and the conditions for their transfer, over the course of domestic and international migrations. But above all, we can observe how she positioned herself for mobility from a young age moving between Beijing and Guangxi, before studying in Hunan and later migrating internationally.

Meng was born in 1979, we met her in 2015. Her mother was among those sent to the countryside for "re-education" during the Cultural Revolution because of her poor class status. Her father remained in Beijing. Meng travelled back and forth throughout her childhood between Guangxi, a rural province in southern China where her mother lived, and Beijing. When she was seven years old, her mother filed for divorce because the situation was untenable. Meng moved to live with her mother and continued her studies at a high school in Hunan, a

THE *COMPRESSED INDIVIDUAL* AND *POLYGAMIC BIOGRAPHIES*

neighbouring province. As her parents lived in two different provinces, Meng had the option of sitting the *gaokao* in Hunan or Beijing. Her mother encouraged Meng to sit it in Beijing to have easier access to the best universities in the country. Just before Meng sat the exam, her father died of cardiovascular disease. Meng lost her sense of certainty: "It seemed to me that all my plans had gone up in smoke, that my life was over". She returned to Hunan to sit the *gaokao* and scored high enough to enter a good university in Harbin, in Northeast China. Meng describes her childhood as being very hard: "I had a lot of bad things [happen]." She has no regrets, however, because her experiences, such as being able to travel, visiting different places and meeting people later helped in her career. Meng insists that she has never felt free to make her own life choices. Speaking of her decision to study pharmacology at a university in Harbin, she says: "At that time we studied pharmacology because it was easy to find a job afterwards. I didn't even think about whether I liked it or not, I never thought about it". After graduation, her uncle offered her a job in his company as an assistant, a position unrelated to her studies, which she accepted. Meng has always had the impression that until her arrival in France, she was carried away by events. She thinks this is the case for all of her generation who, like her, were born during the Cultural Revolution. After leaving her uncle's business, Meng moved to Shenzhen to be more independent. She sought job in a large company: "It was still a typical, predictable choice. Everyone wants to work in a big company, so I wanted to as well." After a period spent in the Research and Development department of a large company, Meng, again dissatisfied, decided to move abroad. She arrived in France and studied communication in Lyon.

When personal resources and social capital combine in opposing directions (one shrinks while the other grows), it can be said that spatial capital plays a "negative" role in the migration experience. On the contrary, when personal resources and social capital combine in the same direction, spatial capacity plays a "positive" role. That being said, if spatial capital appears "positive" with a growing social network, it can become less so when young migrants access a less qualified position in a different city. It can therefore be positive or negative depending on the spaces to which it provides access.

Young Chinese migrants with less resources move within horizontal networks while those with greater personal resources move more often within vertical networks. As demonstrated by Su Liang (2019), low-educated multinational migrant workers have achieved horizontal mobility in global labour markets via legal transnational labour intermediaries and illegal visa agents. This produces a possible "macro-opening" but, once they arrive at their destination, they become illegal workers and are engaged in a process of eroding social status, possible marginalisation, and become trapped in migration. In international migration, the translation of resources results in varying degrees of over qualification and social disqualification as personal resources and skills attained during the migratory experience become invisible.

The careers of Chinese migrants are constructed from bifurcations that correspond to the conjunction of migration steps, i.e. changes in space systems through geographical mobility, and changes in economic regimes in the form of professional mobility. In the biographical process, these bifurcations can produce affiliations by multiplying points of contact with local host societies. Conversely, they can reduce integration where differences with the local host societies have accumulated.

We met Qiong in 2016. She was born in 1991 in a rural village in Henan province. Her parents moved to Fuzhou, in Fujian province, to work in factories and so grew up with her grand-parents and sister. At the age of fourteen, she left the countryside and migrated to the city of Shenzhen. There she moved between several jobs in textile and electronics factories. Within a one-year period, she changed jobs seven times, living and working in seven different factories. Every time she decided to change job, she had to move to a different neighbourhood where the factories were located. From Bao'an, she moved to Longhua, Huiyang, Longwu and Tianzhen. And every time, she needed to learn a different job and adjust to the factory routines, working environment and the house rules for living in the dormitories. Spatial bifurcations were thus accompanied by professional and economic bifurcations. Despite the similarities between the companies, Qiong had to adjust to the regulations of each and adapt her skills to the work routines and tasks she was employed to perform on the assembly line. After a year in Shenzhen, sick of repetitive work and hoping to gain upward social and professional mobility, she decided to re-migrate to Guangzhou: "Shenzhen is full of migrant workers, and many of them come from Anhui, like me [...] When you stay in a factory, around the assembly line with people like you [...] you cannot learn much [...] I wanted to find a nice house, get married, work in an office [...] I had changed several jobs there but every time I was asked to do the same repetitive things [...] The tasks were different since every factory was in charge of a different kind of production, but I felt bored [...] That is why I moved to Guangzhou. I had a friend there who suggested that I work as a salesperson in a market, and I accepted [...]."

Qiong moved to Guangzhou, where she started working as a salesperson in a market with a couple of co-villagers. Despite the stressful working schedule and hard work pace, Qiong felt less frustrated than in Shenzhen. She had the impression of she was achieving a different social status: through spatial

THE *COMPRESSED INDIVIDUAL* AND *POLYGAMIC BIOGRAPHIES* 145

mobility by moving to Guangzhou and through professional mobility by moving to a different role.

> We woke up at 4 am everyday [...] We lived in a urban village which was quite far from the market. The market was close to the river and we lived far away [...] real estate is crazily expensive in Guangzhou and we couldn't do it any other way [...]. We worked all day long selling clothes, talking to customers, receiving new boxes full of clothes and textile products to sell [...]. But I was happy! I met a lot of people there, and my Mandarin also improved since I was talking to many people and I had to speak in Mandarin [...]. When I was in Shenzhen, I always spoke the Henanese dialect [...]. Also, my communication skills improved, and I became more confident [...]. I used to be so shy before. I was young and I did not want to speak much, but there I had to. I felt that I was becoming emancipated [...].
> QIONG, woman, 25 years old, interview conducted in Zhongshan in 2016

At each bifurcation, events and social structures influence an individual's repertoire of resources which in turn rearrange to reflect the status, places and social identities of individuals. However, reflexive skills, that is the degree to which situations of change can be predicted, influence the modes and forms of reconfiguring resource repertoires. When bifurcations are unexpected or when there are emergencies, capabilities are developed to manage the effects of interference or identity shocks. Social and moral inequalities appear at these points, built around migratory experiences and the ratio between biographical bifurcations, social and personal resources and reflexive skills.

To achieve upward social mobility, Qiong gradually realised that she had to move again. She therefore decided to join her sister in Shanghai and to work in local restaurants there. Her language competency had improved, and she felt more confident and ready to perform new professions in order to improve her skills and her economic status. She worked for few years in Shanghai in local restaurants, canteens and in a cafe. After improving her financial position, Qiong decided to take evening classes to learn how to use a computer. Having completed the course, she re-migrated to Zhongshan, Guangdong province, where she currently lives and works. Here, she met her boyfriend (from Shandong province), and she currently works for IQC company, which produces surf boards. However, unlike her first migratory and professional experiences in Shenzhen, Qiong is no longer a factory worker. Having improved her skills, she is now in charge of recruitment and is responsible for conducting interviews and for work contracts on a daily basis.

Migrants' repeated mobilities increase social inequalities and can be defined as multi-situated. They represent irregular, and hierarchical access to labour markets in different societal contexts. Bifurcations can be imposed, negotiated and controlled. Social, cultural and symbolic capital influence the effects of biographical discontinuity and how resource repertoires are organised. The larger the resource repertoire, the more organised it will be, thus enabling individuals to better cope with the effects of biographical discontinuity. The pathways of young migrants from the middle classes are generally built on professional experiences in line with their initial studies. The biographies of migrants from lower classes or from rural areas tend to be built on multiple or combinations of professional activities (poly and pluriactivity). The majority of young Chinese migrants develop access to mobility through polygamic biographies interspersed with challenges for the self. Practical skills are gained along migration routes through biographical transitions and will be partially transferred and utilised upon arrival at their destination.

At each stage of migration, social capital increases or decreases leading a reassembly of the different personal resources available to young Chinese migrants, be they economic, social, linguistic or symbolic. If, during a migratory stage, an opportunity presented by migratory spaces is secured by a migrant, their economic, social and symbolic resources will increase or decrease as they move from one employment and location to another. As individuals pass from one space to another, and from one economic regime to another, available individual resources reposition themselves. Additionally, status, places and social identities reconstruct themselves in response to an individual's capacity for action in sequential biographical changes.

This is illustrated by the example of Hu, who we met in Paris in 2015- a young manager in a multi-national business whose qualified migrant pathway has taken place within a sole Chinese telco giant operating in over 140 countries. Originally from Chengdu where he studied science and technology, Hu commenced work in the R&D department of HW in his home town. He then moved to Shanghai, where he continued to work for HW and undertook an internal training program to move into marketing. By doing so, he was presented the opportunity to work for HW's Russian subsidiary in Moscow. He stayed in Russia for only 6 months due to security risks caused by the xenophobic protests that were taking place there at the time. Thanks to his experience and his work performance, he earned the possibility to work for HW's German subsidiary. In this way, he continued to gradually work his way up within the company. He finally decided to leave for France, where he currently works as head of operations. With this role, as young well-travelled Chinese man, Hu

THE *COMPRESSED INDIVIDUAL* AND *POLYGAMIC BIOGRAPHIES* 147

found himself in charge of a Franco-Chinese team, which requires him to constantly adjust his management methods and his approach to his work in response to various situations. He clarifies that, until this point, when working overseas his primary contacts and work colleagues had been exclusively Chinese. In his new role in France, however, where the desire to not push out local workers is prioritised, he is obliged to change his point of view to perceive individual mobility as international mobility, and not only as internal mobility within a company.

Migrants with low social, linguistic and economic resources quickly interiorise the effect of being assigned to captive situations and consequently develop weak skills for reconstructing repertoires and resources for action. Nevertheless, when they develop skills to resist these situations, they can induce upward mobility trajectories to ethnic enclaves and, as a result, bifurcations may then become sources of affiliation. Ethnic enclaves and niches are forms of economic inscription that express biographic trajectories made of strong bifurcations and not particularly integrative in nature. Migrants are assigned to locations in low economic legitimacy spaces which produce low integration socialisations and situations of great unpredictability and social insecurity.

In the migratory experience, the translation of resources remains a dynamic, irregular and reversible process. The translation of social capital and individual resources is built around steady increases which move from a strong recognition of skills and expertise to their invisibility which must be brought down to forms of ethnic discrimination and stigmatisation experience by young Chinese migration in the differing arrival contexts. In the combination of resources, linguistic skills play a decisive role in translation conditions. The stronger the language skills, the better the conditions for translation and vice versa. Linguistic resources also play a decisive role in the visibility of individual resources. As linguistic resources increase, the more a resource repertoire can increase in scope and reach a certain economic value.

For translation to take place, the ordering of repertoires and decontextualistion/recontextualisation of resources must take place. Depending on the strength or weakness of gaps between the departure and arrival contexts, resources and skills will be rendered invisible to varying degrees, and difficulties in translating social capital and personal resources will increase or decrease depending on the degree of capability (Roulleau-Berger, 2011). Resources can only be ordered or decontextualised/recontextualised in migratory careers once visibility of resources and skills fluctuate. When arrival contexts are richer than those of departure, young migrants with symbolic, economic and social resources at hand can gain social qualifications. Resource repertoires can increase in range and order themselves depending on the context of arrival, and skills and experiences can be transferred almost in their totality.

Lastly, the role of emotional resources in terms of how repertoires of roles are organised and their effects on other roles should be considered. If emotional resources are experienced as being too negative, resource repertoires cannot be activated and remain invisible. Emotional resources participate in the construction of social capital within migration experiences as they are always lost and where, according to their intensity, they restrict social capital to a certain extent.

The young Chinese migrant appears as a multi-situated Compressed Individual in both local and global spaces. Where young Chinese migrants lose material, social, economic and symbolic goods in a diversity of spaces with poor legitimacy, and where their social and spatial capital diminishes in access to low valued places, we speak of *bottom-up multi-compressed individuation*. Where they accumulate material, social, economic and symbolic goods in a diversity of spaces with strong delocalised legitimacy, and where they acquire increasingly more social and spatial capacity by accessing highly valued spaces, we speak of *top-down multi-compressed individuation*. In these two types of multi-compressed modernity, subjectivities contract and create identity lesions in top-down and bottom-up multi-compressed individuations.

4   Multi-Compressed Modernity and the *Spiral of Downward Mobility*

Multi-compressed modernity is also built on what Louis Chauvel (2016) called the formation of a "systemic spiral of downward mobility" in globalisation which contributes to the production of the *Compressed Individual*. Since the 2000s, possibilities for upwards mobility in China have regressed and a proletariat of white-collar workers has appeared (Li Peilin, 2020).

When migrating internationally, the social, salary and status qualifications of young Chinese are not fully recognised, as though migration has indebted them towards to the host society. If this downward social mobility can be considered objectively, it must also be considered subjectively in terms of migratory situations which weaken the emotional resources mobilised in difference phases of migratory pathways. On a subjective level, downward social mobility results from identity trauma which can anaesthetise *capabilities*, or the ability to mobilise moral resources to self-replace in the social spaces of destination societies. These situations can impede inherited social resource acquired in socialisations in China from being converted to active resources in transit and

THE *COMPRESSED INDIVIDUAL* AND *POLYGAMIC BIOGRAPHIES*

destination cultures. Many young Chinese, having held a high social position in China with vertical mobility, will experience situations of professional disqualification, which will subsequently be felt more strongly.

For example, in France, the existence of open and closed employment raises questions of disqualification. In France, several types of employment are closed to foreigners. According to data from the Inequality Observatory of 19 August 2019, in 2018 more than one in five jobs (5.4 million positions) in the public and private sectors remain closed to non-EU foreigners. This equates to more than 20% of the workforce. For the most part (4.3 million), they are public service roles, but more than one million in the private sector are also difficult for foreigners to access, due to the educational requirements or pre-authorisation procedures needed to exercise these roles. Jobs non-European foreigners are excluded from holding include drink sellers, tobacconists, managers of security companies, notaries, merchant navy officers, bailiffs. Among the professions where only French diplomas are recognised are: nurses outside hospitals, medical laboratory technicians, opticians, speech therapists, paramedics, psychometricians and occupational therapists, pedicures, dieticians, speech therapists, hearing aid acousticians, medical electro radiology handlers. Among the trades requiring prior authorisation: doctors, pharmacists, lawyers, dentists, architects, midwives, accountants, auditors, veterinarians, surveyors.

The exclusion of young Chinese migrants from these roles in the private and public sectors places them in situations of unequal treatment and injustice compared with nationals and foreign EU members. This exclusion also limits them to positions of social invisibility expressed by a lack of recognition of their skills, training and professional experience. European labour markets rest on the principle of egalitarian non-distribution of jobs between nationals, foreigners and people born abroad.

Furthermore, while emotional skills influence the mobilisation of social, economic and moral resources, differing levels of linguistic security play a major role in the ways people take their place in societies of arrival. As per P. Bourdieu (1987), all linguistic exchange contains a potential act of power and linguistic competency is not a simple technical capacity but also one of status. Once arrived, many migrants find themselves in a situation of linguistic insecurity and are therefore denied a place and status in their host society. Linguistic insecurity therefore invalidates individuals but also imposes the conversion of professional, migratory and social skills. It casts a veil over all the skills acquired in professional careers. In addition, once arrived in France, migrants are confronted by a system which does not recognise tertiary studies undertaken in their home country.

This situation produces symbolic violence, it signifies a denial of initial training and an obligation to participate in training that is disjointed from that undertaken along migratory routes. It can also create a feeling of social uselessness which leads to strong identity tensions. The imposition of downward mobilities represents a loss of resources that can lead to the resignation of not being able to legitimise their qualifications and professional experiences gained in both China and along migratory routes. Furthermore, the imposition of forms employment with no opportunities for professional development reveals violent economic domination founded on ethnic differentiations and distinctions. A majority of migrants find themselves restricted to mourning past and future dreams. The maintenance of experience capital in migratory pathways appears to be an exception to the rule. The challenge of downward social mobility imposes a reinvention of self, and a confrontation with in injunction to rewrite their own history in a foreign society.

5   Ownership, Maintenance and Loss of Self

In a diversity of polygamic biographies, young Chinese migrants face crucial questions of ownership and loss of self. The more the situations they encounter are disjointed and contrasting, the greater the retrospective loss. Subjective identities are configured around these social and moral goods; confidence in the Other and self-confidence; social respect and respect for self; social esteem and self-esteem. This phenomenon thus actively contributes to the risk of distorted identity. Confronted with identity conflicts, reassessments and readjustments, young Chinese migrants find it increasingly difficult to adjust to their different "selves" that rapidly collide with multi-compressed modernity (Roulleau-Berger, 2010). If self-esteem and shame appear as aspects of reversible and dynamic self-identity, there are saturation levels from which they will no longer be reversible and where migrants lose their reflexive and mobilisation capacities. Loss of self generates social and psychological trauma that can direct young Chinese migrants to psychological or psychiatric care that can promote a process of reconciliation with oneself (Wang Simeng, 2017). These levels incorporate repetition phenomenon and repeated situations of disqualification, humiliation, and racism that produce irreversible feelings of shame and even self-hatred.

The question of self-ownership, loss of self, and even maintenance of self, in different temporalities is thus asked in all migration spaces. For example, young Chinese migrants develop horizontal mobility disturbed by biographical bifurcations, roughly maintaining themselves to produce partial social integration in their destination society. In each migratory experience, they will never access the same recognition, and must confront different local and societal norms and position themselves to adhere to these norms in order to find a place in their destination society. Finding a place symbolises conforming to normative expectations of institutions, in particular the injunction to rewrite stories of self in line with largely legitimated moral figures, such as entrepreneurs or transnational citizens.

The effects of collisions linked to movements around differentiated societies inherent to multi-compressed modernity provoke growing gaps between the order of social and public recognition. They also trigger a reduction in forms of recognition and even contempt where subjects struggle to become actors. Young Chinese migrants are confronted by identity reversals between social recognition and contempt, caution and confidence in others, and between self-esteem and shame. In multi-compressed modernity, the migratory experience is organised around situations of incertitude and collisions which can generate strong tensions between physical and moral identities which are put to the test. As we already have mentioned, the migratory experience contains of social distorsion situations between individuals'subjective feelings about themselves and their real identities, including between self-identities and attributed identities by others.

Young migrants with more resources have integrated the injunction to a form of *negotiated autonomy* and *autonomy in tension* (Schmoll, 2020), which will be restricted for those with less resources. The latter, in particular those that are undocumented, have neither the right to singularity, nor to the justice system which defines them as "illegitimate". They are condemned to life of shame, fear of being found or denounced, and to being stuck between a denial of their existence and attempts to attain a certain status. These individuals struggle to survive. Among the less-qualified young Chinese migrant populations in Europe who live with high social and economic insecurity, a new *hobo* identity appeared: the *left-behinds of globalisation*, or new supernumeraries, objects of invisibility and public and social non-recognition, forced into lost lives(Bauman, 2003). The *left-behinds of globalisation*, voiceless, placeless, and without any positive recognition, remain forced to be themselves against and despite domination, noise and powerful racism, being assigned to invisibility, and marginalised into spaces with no rights (Roulleau-Berger, 2007). Young Chinese migrants see themselves limited by a denied existence, to lives "wasted" by significant moral and material uncertainty. They also find themselves lost, cut off from their families, wives, husbands and children.

The maintenance of self can be partially facilitated by digital economies that allow migrants to stay connected to their families, in tension with several spaces and temporalities. To reference Dana Diminescu (2014), these migrants are connected. Information and communication technologies (ICT) are now a daily part of life for migrants. They are a means for previously unheard-of opportunities for exchange and communications with loved ones who have stayed behind. Smartphones, online applications, and digital platforms, etc., simultaneously maintain links with Chinese society and create transnational links. With the development of ICTs, migrants' lives were transformed, both migrants in general and Chinese migrants who in particular adopted this technology early on. They are no longer confronted by the *double absence* (Sayad, 1999) but are inscribed in a connected presence. This is comprised of different forms of potential and actual presence (Diminescu, 2019) on ethnoscapes linked to regimes of high-compressed modernity for China and low-compressed modernity for Europe. The maintenance of self via emotions and affects and is partially facilitated by digital resources which combine with social, economic and moral resources. Digital technologies help migrants survive.

6 *Compressed Individual*, Re-migration in China and to China

Many young Chinese domestic migrants have dreamed of going to Shanghai, Beijing, Shenzhen, Guangzhou, etc. and they have all had the same rude awakening. Having imagined an urban fairyland and a highly valued job, they are thrown into economic competition and confronted by high living standards, expensive rent and professional difficulties. Some of these young migrants will decide to leave big cities after several years for other Chinese cities, while a minority will return to their home villages and perhaps even re-migrate once more to Shanghai.

The 19th National Congress of the Communist Party of China on October 2017 put forward a strategy to implement the revitalisation of rural areas. The strategy offered unprecedented opportunities to encourage young university graduates to return to their home cities and to set up businesses as part of this revitalisation. While some graduates are attempting to create their own company, they do not benefit from economic and political support. Some villages, like that of Jiupu, have implemented a policy to aid the development of new businesses by young graduates (Zhang Zhen, Ma Dong, 2019). Youth who re-migrate are seen as likely to actively participate in the process of rural revitalisation. A survey conducted in Henan (He Huili and Su Zhihao, 2019)

identified three categories of young migrant-entrepreneurs who have returned to rural areas:
- Those establishing companies in the rural sector.
- Those seeking to reconcile their professional and family lives.
- Those seeking to reconcile rural and urban development.

Young migrants who return to their *laojia* after years of urban life find themselves caught in a contradictory socialisation process built on conflict between high-compressed modernity and the low-compressed modernity that they must re-learn. In order to re-locate their place in the space of return, young migrants are forced to make do with situations of tension between urban and traditional lifestyles, urbanity and rurality, and contractual and interpersonal relationships, etc. They no longer recognise the locals with whom they grew up during their first socialisations (Liu Yana, Dong Qiyuan, 2019). The means of returning in rural society for young migrant workers who have left the major cities also depends on their relationship with themselves and their choice of life partner. The new generation draws on personal and social networks to form socially homogamic couples and integrate into their 老家 *laojia* (hometown).

Moreover, some young low-skilled migrants are not able to live in large Chinese megalopolises due to exorbitantly high rents and the impossibility for their children to attend public schools. Their only option is private schools which are very expensive and do not guarantee access to higher education. These young migrants want to escape a life of poverty in order to survive and aspire to set up different business ventures to recover some dignity in the workplace. They return to their home cities to build a house and a business and set up small enterprises in new economic and political conditions. Yangchun, 25 years old, resident of an urban village in Guangzhou, was tired of working 11 hours a day for seven years in various factories for a low wage. In 2018, he decided to return to his home town to sell roast meat:

> My life is not satisfactory, I would like to do business, I'm tired of being a *dagong*, I want to go into my *laojia* to do business. There are a lot of people doing this kind of business, and so you have a lot of costs. Going back to *laojia* to do business is more profitable because the material, the meat, is cheaper [...] In town, houses are very expensive [...] and when you return to the village, your status is no longer that of the *dagong* as in cities, but you become a *laoban*. Also, when you are a *laoban*, there is no one controlling you, you are not a *dagong*. Because here, when you are a *dagong*, others mistreat you. Last week, we took a 5-minute break from work because we were exhausted, and they insulted us. They look down on you, because if you have no money, nobody cares about you.

154 CHAPTER 5

If young migrants return to their home province, they must present a fictional account of the success of their migratory experience. The obligation to save face directs this biographical crossroad on their behalf. In China, when returning to their home province they are faced with a new moral challenge (Li Nan, 2010) where they must compromise with material, social and moral uncertainties. The return quickly becomes an ordeal which prescribes the heavy price of reassessing their identity at the heart of this pivotal biographical moment in the re-migratory experience of young Chinese people. Forms of urban expulsion are the product of multi-compressed modernity, which forces young migrants to leave high-compressed modernity regimes and reposition themselves in weak-compressed modernity regimes where they return to spaces of economic activity linked to more tradition systems of economic production.

Han Jia-Ling and Yu Jia-Qing (2020) recently have described how the transformation of the *hukou* system in small and medium-sized cities and the new educational policies for migrant workers led to expulsions from big cities and are producing a new phenomenon of 离城不回乡与回流不返乡 *Li cheng bu hui xiang yu huiliu bu fan xiang* (leaving for the Metropolises without returning to their home villages). Among the qualified migrants, some do not go to their *laojia*, but in the province where their family is registered, they do not return to their home town. In this re-migration they find themselves cut off from rural life and have to reintegrate into small or medium-sized towns in different Chinese provinces.

Finally, in China, the production of multi-compressed modernity also contains stories of re-migration that reveal hidden aspects. These become visible in areas of abstract poverty, corruption and crime. Stories of hardship related to internal Chinese migration reveal how the confiscation of self generates a chain of suffering, humiliation and sadness that may lead to suicide. Only one such story was included in this work to avoid painting a bleak image of Chinese society, yet the story is emblematic of the figure of the new poor and the new hobos (Anderson, 1993) in the context of multi-compressed modernity.

Wen, interviewed in 2016, comes from a village in Shandong. She was born in 1990 and is four years younger than her brother. She comes from a very poor farming family. She was educated between the ages of 8 to 14 but did not attend school regularly and failed to finish primary school. At 14, her brother took her to Qingdao to find work for her. He found her a job at a supermarket where she also received food and board along with three other girls. Wen was fired, she had no identity papers and found herself in the street in the middle of winter without a home or job. She knocked on the door of a textile factory and got a job there, she worked from 8 am to 10 pm in difficult conditions. She had to

THE *COMPRESSED INDIVIDUAL* AND *POLYGAMIC BIOGRAPHIES* 155

place her hands in freezing liquid all day. After several weeks, the skin on her hands was badly damaged and she could no longer stand working there. She had no further contact with her brother, had no financial resources and felt completely abandoned. She stole 1 yuan to call her father who came to pick her up. Wen returned to her parents where she accepted a job offered by her aunt in Weifang for a breeder and fur manufacturer. For 400 yuan a month, she had to look after the animals and clean their cages. She was often bitten by the animals, had little sleep and always smelled. After the new year, her parents would not allow her to return to the job and her father finally took her to a temp agency to find work. She secured a job at Tianjin in a factory that man-ufactured mobile phones. Her boss required her to work quickly and late into the evening. She earned between 1,400 and 2,000 yuan. After one year, she had been able to save some money and resigned without returning to her family's home. Wen wanted a job that was not exhausting and offered a decent wage but she was constantly told she wasn't sufficiently qualified. In a restaurant she met a young lady who, like her, was looking for work and decided to follow her. Together, they met a young man who worked for a work agency and he offered to help them. He offered her a job as a waitress in a karaoke bar which she accepted. Her job was to accompany the clients who selected her, and to drink and sing with them for 100 yuan a night. She was raped by this young man and fled, finding another job in another KTV bar. She did not return home for Chinese New Year in 2007. Several months later, her father fell seriously ill and passed away from a stroke. Wen felt very guilty that she had not returned home for the New Year, and for not sending more money home. She criticised her boyfriend for not giving her money to see her family. When she learned he was married, she attempted suicide and they separated. She returned to her village, got married, and was once again raped. She got divorced and today sells clothing at a market.

Wen 's experience is likened to one of hardship due to the series of situations in her personal and private life which stripped her of more of herself each time. Confronted on multiple occasions by her subordinate position in situations of extreme violence, she lost herself in each biographical sequence.

Young or unskilled migrants, after internal migrations, may also attempt international migration followed by *re-migration* to China. Young Chinese female migrant workers' migrations notably pluralise and take international directions. Movements are multiplied according to the opportunity and con-straints young migrant women can negotiate and adjust to. When the urban and labour regimes of the city and urban factories in China become oppres-sive, for example some women negotiate cross-border marriage and migration with a Taiwanese national (Zani 2018). After few years in Taiwan, a portion of these women might consider re-migrating back to China to their society of origin. In this respect, when constraints and obstacles inhibit the achievement of this plan, re-migration can be produced. Taiwan can become a new land to depart from. Moving back to their society of origin does not equate to a process of return for Chinese migrant women. Re-migration unlocks possibilities for new navigations and re-mobilities, translocal journeys and moorings, which makes movement potentially endless (Zani, 2019).

Multi-compressed modernity places low-educated international migrants in captive migration. The coexistence of legal labour intermediaries and illegal visa agents have insufficient control over overseas job opportunities. Some migrants are forced to return to China and leave again several times, accessing low-cost transnational opportunities, including short-term overseas labour contracts and illegal access to overseas countries. Others, however, will remain in China. Young, low-educated Chinese migrants are locked into overseas, instable employment and circulate in floating social networks which are manifested not only in multiple transnational migrations, but also in multiple regional changes within a country (Su, 2019).

When young re-migrate to China from Europe, the obligation to maintain honour directs this biographical crossroad for them as much as for young international migrants. They have not necessarily chosen their destination but, for example, the idea of moving to Paris corresponds with a successful migration experience. Some, having lived in Europe and experienced disappointment or having come to the conclusion their careers were stagnating and they had reached the ceiling of success (Li, 2016), decide to return to China to embark on a different professional pathway.

> As Asia regional manager in this French company I can't imagine retiring to a foreign company in China, because in China they don't let you retire. If you're over forty and you haven't reached a very important position, you're fired! [...] If you don't move up, if you don't stand out, there's no reason why we should pay a forty-year-old employee who's expensive, especially when we could very well recruit a 28-year-old. He might have a little less experience, but [...] too bad! Yes, we quickly get rid of employees who are over forty, we don't care anyway, maybe I'll go back to China and look for a job in a state-owned company or [...] but I can't imagine going to China with O. I can see myself better in France or in another country. I can ask the company to put me on a local contract. I would lose my expatriate benefits, but at least I will stay in France. I want to secure my job because I have a family and a husband. This return is destabilising for me,

THE *COMPRESSED INDIVIDUAL* AND *POLYGAMIC BIOGRAPHIES*

if I can't move up in the hierarchy, what will I do in five years? They say that you have to leave room for young people, that you have to help them succeed, but I can't succeed because there's no job! The Chinese are starting to cost a lot. Because if they pay you a good salary, it means your job is important, it's difficult, it's high risk. It's like in investment, the higher the return, the more risk you take. In France, €5,000, €6,000 a month represent big salaries for important positions at the top of the hierarchy. If you sign contracts that are not terminated overnight, you can even consider retiring in this company. In China today, if you don't have an annual salary of one million, you are poorly paid! You're very poorly paid! A million is nothing, but it's considered a good salary. But then you have to change jobs all the time because you're easily fired. It's high-risk. At a certain age, when you're thirty, you can take it, and it's not serious, you can change jobs! But at forty [...] you can no longer change jobs every two years.

CHEN, woman, 38 years old, interview conducted in Paris in 2016

In the collective representations of these young migrants, returning to China can only be a "victory" in their eyes and in those of their family and partners. These are young executives of European companies who develop plans to return once they have reached the "glass ceiling" due to ethnoracial boundaries in European society. The more diverse their experiences abroad, the more their return is likely to be trying as they redefine their identity for themselves and others. As per Li Yong (2020) identity crises affect many young Chinese who came to Europe with a project of self-transformation, and when they return to China, they are facing several risks: biographical ruptures, namely in their family or romantic lives; social risks due to difficulties re-adapting to a China that has greatly evolved since they last lived there; environment and supply risks; and political risks from a system that they no longer know from the inside.

Young international migrants returning to China also face a new moral challenge. They must arrange themselves around moral and social uncertainty on both an objective and subjective level. The return home quickly becomes an ordeal. It involves the heavy burden of reassessing their identity at the heart of this pivotal biographical moment in the migratory experience of the young Chinese that have migrated to different provinces in China or to foreign megalopolises: the return (Roulleau-Berger, Yan Jun, 2017).

Conclusion

In this book we have seen how, in intra-continental migrations in China, young unskilled Chinese migrants, often of rural origin, suddenly entered in a "multi-compressed modernity" in the large Chinese cities, how young skilled Chinese migrants were accessing it in a more gradual way. In the first case, the effects of collision between traditional culture, industrial culture and compressed modernities produce plural situations of subalternity which provide young migrants with little social and public recognition in Chinese society. In the second case, the collision effects between different regimes of compressed modernity produce injunctions to become "heroes" of Chinese society and adhesions to emotional capitalism. These two faces of the young Chinese migrant appear in the intertwining between different compressed modernities in China. We have seen how internal migrations and international migrations meet each other and are embedded to produce hierarchical economic cosmopolitanisms, where Chinese internal migrants and international migrants invent local and global economic and social apparatuses at the same time, bringing about a *multi-compressed modernity*.

Compressed modernities contain effects of economic and social collision when social, economic, moral processes linked to forms of premodernity, modernity and postmodernity clash, revealing conflicts and social inequalities. The young Chinese migrant embodies a *Compressed Individual*, confronted with a variety of situations of uncertainty in a multiplicity of local and global spaces, accelerated temporalities and diversified situations. For example, in their internal migratory paths, low-skilled Chinese migrants generally move from a regime of "low compressed-order modernity", which is linked to a traditional rural culture, to a regime of "compartmentalised compressed modernity" or "high-order compressed modernity" during their mobility in Chinese or international cities. In international movements, in Asia, Europe or Africa, migrants have to compose with the different regimes of compressed modernities which all produce plural inequalities.

Chinese internal and international migrations produce diverse local and global cosmopolitanisms. However, at the end of this book, we can raise the question of the presence of hierarchies and inequalities between hegemonic cosmopolitanisms linked to the Wests and non-hegemonic cosmopolitanisms linked to the Easts. Young Chinese migrants show how non-hegemonic economic transnationalisms are interconnected and with non-Western spaces. It is through local cosmopolitanisms that we understand how the roads of globalisation on which young Chinese migrants circulate in the world are organised.

© LAURENCE ROULLEAU-BERGER, 2021 | DOI:10.1163/9789004463080_008

CONCLUSION 159

From the production of this compressed individual embodied by the figure of a young Chinese capable of intracontinental, transnational migration, of re-migration we have contributed to a sociology of globalisation by showing how accelerations and telescoping of mobilities inform of the production of economic transnationalisms, of the construction of migratory careers and of processes of subjectivation. We have grasped the relations between migrations and multi-sited inequalities on the basis of social and ethnic discrimination on the Chinese labour market. If the relationships between Chinese intra-continental/international migrations and economic inequalities can be appre-hended through the lens of social and ethnic discrimination, these also appear in a diversity of hierarchical economic transnationalisms between them.

Thereby, we have distinguished:
- *Transnationalism from above* with the training of young migrants who belong to the new Chinese middle classes or new international elites.
- *Intermediate transnationalism* in Chinese ethnic commerce and entrepreneurship.
- *Transnationalism from below* with the appearing of new young Chinese "hobos", the forgotten ones of globalisation.

In these intra-continental or international mobilities, the question of the intentionality of individuals is raised, and it is often translated by the notion of migratory project. Yet, our empirical research has forced us to use the notions of bifurcation, event, transition or rupture to understand migratory careers in their dimension of unpredictability and reversibility. Young Chinese migrants mobilise repertoires of social, educational, economic, symbolic and even reli-gious resources which are constructed in sequences of actions that are more or less predictable in the context of compressed modernity. The collision effects peculiar to multi-compressed modernity also produce bifurcations, unpredict-ability and reversibility in individual and collective biographies. Each time young Chinese people move, a new biographical crossroad generates a wide spectrum of possible choices, this produces uncertainty. Individuals build their migratory careers from a multiplicity of roles and affiliations linked to heterogeneous socialisation spaces. In this regard, we have talked about *bio-graphical polygamy* and *global individuation* to define the plural identities that are both located and global of young Chinese migrants.

However, multi-compressed modernity involves capabilities in that it leaves little time and space to develop practical anticipation. Consequently, young Chinese migrants can only partially mobilise their past this is integrated into a present which constantly expands in ever-changing conditions. Multi-compressed modernity drives migrants to position, move and reposition them-selves in multi-situated spaces in China or abroad through their participation in the process of local and global socialisation. Additionally, it encourages the interlocking of socialisations and their continuous contraction. The intensity of regimes of compressed modernity has an impact on the degree of continuity of contracted socialisations. The weaker the compressed modernity is, the more continuous the process will be, although it may contain discontinuities, i.e. short breaks. The stronger the compressed modernity regime is, the more unremitting may be the process. The *hysteresis* of dispositions is widely questioned, and later socialisations may trigger each other at each stage of mobility by taking precedence over earlier socialisations. We can consider that dispositions, skills and contexts of action are present in all human societies (Lahire, 2012). In the context of multi-compressed modernity, however, their presence does not vary according to the type of society or within a given society. The contexts of action contract and give rise to dispositions and skills which can be mobilised in different societies. Multi-compressed modernity fragments the assumed order of young Chinese migrants' aptitudes. Skills developed in recent socialisations may hide or render invisible the skills acquired in previous learning experiences. The effects of collisions inherent in multi-compressed modernities affect the chronology and the expected intersectionality between social, economic, ethnic and gender inequalities, i.e. the way in which they combine into a plurality of spaces and of temporalities. Young Chinese migrants are participating to produce emergent global classes: an international class of powerful elites, new cosmopolitan middle-classes and new underclasses; these global classes are "partially denationalized classes"(Sassen, 2007).

To produce the theory of the Compressed Individual, we have created theoretical conjunctions between European, American, Chinese and Korean located knowledge about what makes modernity and what means individuation, globalisation, what about subalternity and resistance.

Shamuel Eisenstadt (2000) produced the theory of "multiple modernities" to describe through a comparative civilisational perspective the plural forms of modernities in the diverse historical and structural contexts.

Göran Therborn (2003) has considered the different varieties of modernity and non-modernity, and the different cultural contextualisations of the contrast between the past and the future. He looked at the ways these do not simply co-exist and challenge each other, but also at how they are entangled with each other in various ways. Therefore, reflecting with Therbörn we have considered non-modernity.

Saskia Sassen (2007) has produced a theory of sociology of globalisation by establishing the complexity and multiscalar character of various globalisation processes and by making clear the hegemonic globalisation is but one

CONCLUSION 161

of several. In this perspective the global economy contains both the capabilities for enormous geographical dispersal and mobility, emergent global classes are emerging. In multi-compressed modernity partially denationalised classes entails transnational, discontinuous, more or less legitimated economic, social, symbolic networks.

Li Peilin (2015) largely introduced the concept of Eastern modernisation to open a space where theoretical thinking together and not separated manner, as has often been the case between Chinese society and modernisation. Proposing Eastern modernisation is because "oriental society" almost had no relation to modernisation in the past several centuries, it seemed to many people that the possibility of oriental modernisation can only be a suspension. So, the Eastern modernisation should include all development paths of new experiences in providing world modernisation deferent from the West.

In this sense, modernity can be plural not only across different national societies, but also within each national society. Chang Kyung-Sup has advanced the emergence of an *internalised reflexive cosmopolitisation* which builds a bridge compressed modernity to Beck's endeavour in *methodological cosmopolitanism* (Beck and Grande, 2010). Therefore, we have grasped the theory of compressed modernity proposed by Chang Kyung-Sup by retaining the different forms of compressed modernities, the hierarchies between them and the processes of transition from one to the other, the interactions among multiple modernities in Chinese internal and international migrations.

Alain Touraine (2007) alludes to the unity of modernity and the multiplicity of paths to modernisation when he defines modernity in terms of adherence to rational thought and respect for individual rights. He advances the hypothesis that several types of society exist. There are those that combine modernity and modernisation, those that combine instrumental modernisation with a strengthening of apparatuses of domination and integration and those that fail either to achieve modernity or to find a path to modernisation. The concept of modernity is here based on the use of universalistic judgements; rational knowledge is superior to all other ways of explaining phenomena, the notion of rights applies to all individuals and the notion of subject must be seen as lying at the heart of the question. Then for Alain Touraine (2005) modernity is defined in terms of adherence to rational thought and respect for individual rights; the notion of Subject is conceptualised in conjunction with modernity. It remains associated with social movements and collective actions. So, to some extent, we have used this conception of the Subject to define the compressed Individual.

In China, individuals remain heavily dependent on the authoritarian state and continue to think of themselves as part of the state, even while developing strategies of individual or collective emancipation. Shi Yunqing (2018) has identified the *compressibility* between tradition and modernity, the coexistence of socialism and capitalism, as well as the social and political emancipation of individuals subjected to an authoritarian state. What is at stake here is the question of the production of an "Eastern-style" individuation linked to an authoritative state. A process of "partial individualisation" (Yan Yunxiang, 2010) is defined by Chinese sociologists under the control of the central state when individual/local government/central government relationships are part of circles linked to interpersonal networks, of which the boundaries are more or less permeable and more or less enable the self-empowerment of individuals. In the sense of Chang Kyung Sup (2010) individualisation should mean people's active management of such individual-level compressed modernity, regardless of their attitude and performance at other units of life.

In combining Chinese, Korean, American and European sociological theory we have introduced the definition of *the Compressed Individual* via the subjectivation's process where the place of the *self* is situated within a process of individuation and being linked to the *We*. In this vein, we have mobilised the work of Paul Ricoeur (2004) on the narrative identity has been and still is a major influence in the definition of what enables a plurality of *selves* to coexist. We have integrated the interactionist theories of the individual revisited in French sociology by thinking of the social structures, societal contexts, interactions, as well as individual and collective capabilities. We were invited to reflect on the sociological theories of recognition inspired by the German sociologist Axel Honneth and the sociology of emotions invented by Eva Illouz to understand how adhesions to emotional capitalisms are built, and how these are transformed into emotional socialism in China.

We also have used transnational knowledge, i.e. concepts produced by European or American sociologists and reinterpreted by Chinese sociologists in the Chinese context. For example, we adopted the theoretical point of view of Chinese sociologists like Sun Liping and Guo Yuhua (2003) who showed that the state trains and informs the frameworks of action and the practical processes of civil life by considering that the modes of domination are not continuous and permanent between ordinary situations of civil life and the state. If the work of Scott (1990) was mobilised to analyse the "weapons of the weak", the daily resistance of subaltern groups, in particular Chinese migrant workers, Shen Yuan (2011) introduced Alain Touraine's theory on the production of society to think of the collective mobilisation strategies of Chinese migrants and Michael Burawoy's (1979)one based on the "second great transformation" which

CONCLUSION 163

results in the production of labour regimes inherited from Chinese socialism and globalised capitalism. In her work, Shi Yunqing (2020) has adopted the perspective of social psychology to see the production of citizens with subjectivity as adjustment strategies to the state-individual relationship. Moreover, we have focused on the "arts of doing with" (De Certeau, 1980) and the voices of subordinate groups and their ability to produce their own societal narrative.

By constructing the figure of the young Chinese migrant as a *Compressed Individual* in a context of global emotional capitalism, we have re-actualised Michaël Burawoy's thesis on the emotional labour produced by migrants who undergo strong injunctions to interiorise standards in order to become "heroes" of Chinese society and/or world society. If the less endowed migrants are deprived of positive emotions and aspirations, yet the more endowed can internalise such injunction to produce a self-optimisation narrative that actualises a form of "emotional socialism". This young Chinese migrant, in this multi-compressed modernity, also knows how to develop capacities for reflexivity, action, mobilisation and resistance by accumulating gaps with the imposition of the emotional capitalism.

Finally, to construct this theory on the Compressed Individual and the global condition from figures of the young Chinese migrant, we have produced a non-hegemonic, non-western-centred, mixed by making nomadic concepts produced in European, Chinese contexts and Korean from an experience of multi-located research and crossed perspectives. From the production of an epistemology shared with Chinese, Korean and Japanese sociologists, we produced a *Post-Western Sociology* to enable a dialogue—on a level– on common concepts and concepts situated in European and Asian theories (Roulleau-Berger, 2016; Xie Lizhong, Roulleau-Berger, 2017; Roulleau-Berger, Li Peilin, 2018). This helps to consider the modes of creation of continuities and discontinuities, the conjunctions and disjunctions between knowledge spaces situated in different social contexts, as well as to work on the *gaps* between them. In a context of the easternisation of the westernised East we have advanced the idea of the multiplication, the complexification and the hierarchisation of new epistemic autonomies vis-à-vis Western hegemonies in social sciences. Then we defined the Post-Western Sociology, and identified some knowledge niches in which situated concepts are produced, and we have analysed how transnational theory could be used in different ways in China and in Europe.

By creating conceptual arrangements between European, American, Chinese and Korean sociologies in this book, by co-producing mixed knowledges, this work represents a major contribution to what we have called *post-Western sociology*. If post-Western sociology is based on several empirical and theoretical materials, as well as societal and civilisational forms, yet it also imposes a permanent epistemology of translation (Laplantine, 2009), of the conjunctions and the disjunctions, as well as a sense of intellectual and aesthetic creation to produce and co-produce.

Bibliography

Abdelnour, S., Bernard, S. 2019. Quelles résistances collectives face au capitalisme de plateforme, in Abdelnour, S., Méda, D. (dir), *Les nouveaux travailleurs des applis,* Paris: PUF.

Aglietta, M., Guo, B. 2012. *La voie chinoise. Capitalisme et empire.* Paris: O. Jacob.

Ambrosini, M. 2007. *Employment and working conditions of migrant workers.* Report to the European Foundation for the Improvement of living and working conditions.

Ambrosini, M., Cinalli, M., Jacobson, D. (eds). 2020. *Migration, Borders and Citizenship.* London: Palgrave MacMillan.

Anderson, N. 1993. *Le Hobo. Sociologie du sans-abri.* Paris: Nathan.

Appaduraï, A. 2013. *Condition de l'homme global,* Paris : Payot.

Barraud de Lagerie, P., Sigalo Santos, L. 2019. Les plateformes du micro-travail: le tâcheronnat à l'ère du numérique, in Abdelnour, S., Méda (dir), *Les nouveaux travailleurs des applis,* Paris: PUF. pp. 33–46.

Bastide, L. 2015. *Habiter le transnational. Espace, travail et migration entre Java, Kuala Lumpur et Singapour,* Lyon: ENS Editions.

Bataille, P. 1997. *Le racisme au travail,* Paris : Ed. Seuil.

Bauman, Z. 2003. *Vies perdues. La modernité et ses exclus,* Paris: Payot.

Beck, U. 1992. *Risk Society: Toward a new modernity.* London: Sage Publishers.

Beck, U. 2006. *Qu'est-ce que le cosmopolitisme?* Aubier: Paris.

Beck, U., Grande, E. 2010. Varieties of second modernity: the cosmopolitan turn in social and political theory and research, *The British Journal of Sociology.* 61(3). pp. 409–444.

Becker, H.S. 1963. *Outsiders: studies in the sociology of deviance.* New York: The Free Press of Glencoe.

Bellot, M. 2019. *Faire entendre les voix en Chine: jeunesse qualifiée, autoritarisme négocié et civisme ordinaire,* Thèse de doctorat de sociologie, Université Lumière—Lyon 2, février 2019.

Beltrane, A. Saiz Lopez. 2007. Sortir des niches ethniques: les Chinois au sein et en marge du marché du travail espagnol, in L. Roulleau-Berger (dir), *Nouvelles migrations chinoises et travail en Europe,* PUM : Toulouse. pp. 207–229.

Berger, P., Luckmann, T. 1986. *La construction sociale de la réalité,* Paris: PUF.

Bessin, M., Bidart, C., Grossetti, M. 2010. *Bifurcations. Les sciences sociales face aux ruptures et à l'événement.* Paris: La Découverte.

Bian Yanjie. 2010. Guanxi shehui xue jiqi xueke diwei (Network sociology and its position among other disciplines). Xi'an Jiaotong Daxue Xuebao. *Journal of University of Xi'an Jiatong* (5). pp. 1–6.

Bian Yanjie, Wang Wenbin et al. 2012. Kua tizhi shehui ziben jiqi shouru huibao (Institution-crossing Social Capital and Its Income Returns). *Zhongguo shehui kexue.* 2012(2). pp. 16–18.

166 BIBLIOGRAPHY

Bian Yanjie, Zhang Wenhong, Cheng Cheng. 2012. Qiuzhi guocheng de shehui wangluo moxing: jianyan guanxi xiaoying jiashe. (A Social Network Model of the Job-Search Process: Testing a Relational Effect Hypothesis) *Shehui, Society*. 2012(3). pp. 24–37.

Boltanski, L., Esquerre, A. 2017. *Enrichissement: une critique de la marchandise*, Paris: Gallimard.

Bottazzi, C. 2016. *L'appropriation des questions environnementales au sein de trois entreprises sociales à Kunming (Chine)*, Mémoire de Master 2, septembre 2016, ENS Lyon.

Boubeker, A. 2003. *Les mondes de l'ethnicité. La communauté d'expérience des héritiers de l'immigration maghrébine* Paris: Balland.

Boubeker, A. 2018. Ethnicity and individuation: the victim, the tricker and the hero, in Roulleau-Berger, L., Li Peilin (eds), *Post-Western Sociology-From China to Europe*, London & New York: Routledge.

Bourdieu, P. 1978. Classement, déclassement, reclassement. *Actes de la recherche en sciences sociales*. n° 24: 2–22.

Bourdieu, P. 1987. Espace social et pouvoir symbolique, in *Choses dites*. Paris: Minuit. pp. 147–166.

Bredeloup, S. 2008. L'aventurier, une figure de la migration africaine, *Cahiers internationaux de sociologie*, 125 (2). pp. 281–306.

Bredeloup, S. 2013. African migrations, work and new entrepreneurs: the construction of African trading-posts in Asia In Li Peilin, Roulleau-Berger, L. (eds), *China's internal and International Migration*. London and New York: Routledge Publishers. pp. 202–211.

Burawoy, M. 1979. *Manufacturing Consent: Changes in the Labor Process under Monopoly Capitalism*, Chicago: University of Chicago Press.

Cabanas, E. 2019, Les « psytoyens » ou la construction des gens heureux, in E. Illouz, *Les marchandises émotionnelles,* Paris: Editions du Premier Parallèle.

Cai He, Li Chaohai, Feng Jianhua. 2009. Liyi shousun nongmingong de liyi kangzhen xingwei yanjiu—jiyu zhu sanjiao qiye de diaocha (On Migrant Workers' Conflict Behaviors against Benefit Damages: A survey of enterprises at Pearl River delta). *Shehuixue Yanjiu (Sociological Research)*, n° 1. pp. 1–24.

Casilli, A. 2019. *En attendant les robots,* Paris: Seuil.

Castel, R. 1995. *Les métamorphoses de la question sociale*. Paris: Fayard.

Castel, R., Haroche, C. 2001. *Propriété privée, propriété sociale, propriété de soi.* Paris: Fayard.

Cefaï, D. 2007. *Pourquoi se mobilise-t-on?* Paris: La Découverte.

Chan, A. and Zhu Xiaoyang. 2003. Disciplinary Labor Regimes in Chinese factories. *Critical Asian Studies*, 2003: pp. 35–4, 559–584.

Chang Kyung-Sup. 2010, "The second modern condition? Compressed modernity as internalized reflexive cosmopolitization". *The British Journal of Sociology*. 61(3). pp. 444–465.

BIBLIOGRAPHY

Chang Kyung-Sup. 2017, China as a Complex Risk Society. Risk Components of Post-Socialist Compressed Modernity, *Temporalités,* n° 26. pp. 1–17.

Chang Kyung-Sup. 2020. Compressed modernity in South Korea: constitutive dimensions, manifesting units, and historical conditions, in Kim, Y. (ed), *The Roultegde Handbook of Korean Culture and Society,* New York, Routledge Publishers. pp. 75–92.

Chauvel, L. 2016. *La spirale du déclassement*, Paris: Seuil.

Chen Mei Hua. 2012. Sexualité et ethnicité dans le tourisme sexuel. Les consommateurs taïwanais de sexe à Dongguan, in Angeloff, T. Lieber, M., *Chinoises au XXIe siècle*, Paris: La découverte. pp 195–213.

Chen, Qi, Wu, Yi. 2014. Quntixing shijian de qinggan luoji yi DH shijian wei kexin anli jiqi yanshen fenxi. (The Logic of Emotion in Mass Disturbances: Based on an Analysis of -the Case of DH Event and Its Extensions). *Shehui (Society)* 2014(1). pp. 75–103.

Choplin, A., Pliez, O. 2018. *La mondialisation des pauvres*, Paris: Seuil.

Ciccelli, V. 2012. *L'esprit cosmopolite*, Paris: Presses de Sciences Po.

Colomy, P., Brown, J.D. 1996. Theoretical Perspectives on Goffman: Critique and Commentary *Sociological Perspectives.* September, n° 39. pp. 383–391.

Deboulet, A. 2012. Villes convoitées et inégalités, *Idées Economiques et Sociales*, vol. 1, n° 167. pp. 37–47.

De Certeau, M. 1980. *L'invention du quotidien*, Paris: Ed. Flammarion.

Deleuze, G. 1980. *Mille Plateaux,* Paris: Éditions de Minuit.

Diminescu, D. 2014. Traces of dispersion: Online media and diasporic identities, *Journal of Migration and Culture,* Volume 5, Number 1, March 2014. pp. 23–39 (17).

Diminescu, D. 2019. Les risques et les opportunités de la migration « connectée »: Entretien avec Dana Diminescu, *Socio-anthropologie*, n° 40. pp. 203–213. https://doi.org/10.4000/socio-anthropologie.6330.

Dubet F., Cousin, O., Macé, E., Rui, S. 2013. *Pourquoi moi? L'expérience des discriminations*, Paris, Ed. Seuil.

Dubar, C. 1992. Formes identitaires et socialisation professionnelle, *Revue française de sociologie*, XXXIII, vol. 33, n° 4. pp. 505–529.

Dubar, C. 2001. *La Crise des identités*, Paris: PUF.

Du, Hui, Lu Yini, Li Ding, 2013. Empirical study -based on hierarchical linear modeling-on the factors influencing the feeling of deprivation among employees, *Science and Management*, n° 3.

Ehrenberg, A. 1998. *La fatigue d'être soi,* Paris: Odile Jacob.

Ehrenberg, A. 2010. *La Société du malaise,* Paris: Odile Jacob.

Ehrenreich, B., Hochschild, A.R. 2004. *Global woman: nanies, maids and sex workers in the new economy.* New York: Owl Books.

Eisenstadt, S. 2002. *Multiple modernities*, New Brunswick: Transaction Publishers.

Faist, T., Özveren, E. 2004. *Transnational social spaces: agents, networks and institutions*. Farnham: Ashgate Publishing Company.

Favereau, O. 2015. Arrogance de l'économie et économie de l'arrogance in Enriquez, E. (dir), *L'arrogance. Un mode de domination néo-libéral*, Paris: Editions in Press. pp. 147–164.

Fei Xiaotong. 2012. *From the Soil–The foundations of Chinese Society*, Berkeley: University of California Press.

Foucault, M. 1975. *Surveiller et punir*. Paris: Gallimard.

Froissart, C. 2011. NGOs Defending Migrant Workers' Rights. Semi-union organisations contribute to the regime's dynamic stability. *China Perspectives,* n° 2. pp. 18–25.

Geertz, C. 2007. Traduit et présenté par D. Cefaï, *Le souk de Sefrou. Sur l'économie de bazar*. Paris: Bouchêne.

Giraudo-Baujeu G. 2014. *Travail et racisme. Carrières d'intérimaires d'origine maghrébine et africaine et épreuves de la discrimination*, Thèse de doctorat de Sociologie, Université Lumière Lyon 2.

Giraudo-Baujeu, G. 2018, L'épreuve du racisme dans le travail: faire avec ou faire face?, *Les mondes du travail*, n° 21. pp. 61–73.

Goffman, E. 1963. *Stigma. Notes on the management of spoiled identity*, Englewood Cliffs, New Jersey: Prentice-Hall.

Gransow, B. 2014. Se réapproprier le quartier. Redéveloppement urbain, activisme citoyen et conflits de reconnaissance à Canton, *Perspectives chinoises*, n° 2. pp. 17–27.

Grossetti, M. 2004. *Sociologie de l'imprévisible. Dynamiques de l'activité et des formes sociales,* Paris: PUF.

Gueye, C. 2021. *Migration chinoise et reconfiguration économique à Dakar*, Lyon: ENS Editions.

Guiheux, G. 2012. Travailleurs migrants du prêt-à-porter en Chine. Flexibilités et opportunités, *Revue européenne des migrations internationales*, 2012, 28 (4). pp. 27–42.

Guo Yuhua, Sun Liping. 2002. Suku: yizhong nongmin guojia guannian xingcheng de zhongjie jizhi (Denouncing sufferings: an intermediary mechanism producing the notion of State for peasants). *Zhongguo xueshu (Academic Research in China)*, n° 4. pp. 130–157.

Guo Yuhua, Shen Yuan, Pan Yi, Lu Huilin. 2015. *Dangdai nongmin gong de kangzheng yu zhongguo laozi guanxi zhuanxing (The struggle of migrant workers and the transformation of Labor-Management Relations in China)*. pp. 1–7.

Hannerz, U. 1983. *Explorer la ville*, Paris: Ed. Minuit.

Harvey, D. 2006. *Spaces of Global Capitalism: Towards a Theory of Uneven Geographical Development,* London : Verso.

He Huilin, Su Zhihao. 2019, Fanxiang qingnian heyi fanxiang? Jiyu zhu tixing shijiao de kaocha (Why Do Young People Return to their Hometowns? An Investigation from

BIBLIOGRAPHY

the Perspective of Subjectivity). *Guizhou shehui kexue (Social Sciences of Guizhou)*, (10). pp. 72–78.

Han Ka Ling, Yu Ka Hing. 2020. Li cheng bu hui xiang yu huixiang yu huiliu bu fan xiang—xinxing chengzhen hua Beijing xia xinsheng dai nongmingong jiating de zinu jiaoyu jueze (Leaving the city without going home and returning home without coming back—Educational choices for the children of the new generation of migrant workers' families in the context of new origin) *Beijing Shehui Kexue (Social Sciences of Beijing)*, n° 6. pp. 4–13.

Haroche, C. 2015. La peur et l'insécurité psychique aux origines de l'arrogance, in Enriquez, E. (dir), *L'arrogance. Un mode de domination néo-libéral*, Paris: Editions in Press.

Higgins, E.T. 1987. Self-discrepancy: a theory relating self and affect. *Psychological Review*, vol. 94 (3). pp. 319–340.

Honneth, A. 2000. *La lutte pour la reconnaissance*, Paris: Editions du Cerf.

Huws, U. 2003. *The making of a cybertariat. Virtual work in a real world*, New York: New York University Press.

Illouz, E. 2019. *Les marchandises émotionnelles*, Paris: Editions du Premier Parallèle.

Illouz, E., 2006. *Les sentiments du capitalisme*, Paris : Seuil.

Ji Yingchun. 2018. A Mosaic Temporality: New Dynamics of the Gender and Marriage System in Contemporary Urban China, *Temporalités*, no. 26 (2017). pp. 1–16.

Jounin, N. 2009. *Chantier interdit au public*, Paris: La Découverte.

Karpik, L. 2007. *L'économie des singularités*, Paris: Gallimard.

Kokoreff, M., Lapeyronnie, D. 2013. *Refaire la cité. L'avenir des banlieues*, Paris: Ed. Seuil.

Lahire, B. 1998. *L'homme pluriel. Les ressorts de l'action* Paris: Nathan.

Lahire, B. 2012. *Monde pluriel*, Paris: Seuil.

Laplantine, F. 2009. *Anthropologies latérales*, Paris: Liber.

Lee Ching Kwan. 1999. From Organized Dependence to Disorganized Despotism: Changing Labour Regimes in Chinese Factories, *The China Quarterly*, 157. pp. 44–71.

Levy, J., Lussault, M. (dir). 2003. *Dictionnaire de la géographie*, Paris: Belin.

Li Chunling. 2008. Migrations villes-campagnes et mobilité sociale. In *La société chinoise vue par ses sociologues. Migrations, villes, classe moyenne, drogue, sida.* Edited by Rocca, J.-L. Paris: Presses de Sciences Po. pp. 47–75.

Li Chunling, Wang Boqing. 2010. College Graduate Employment and Skilled Survey Report in *The China Society Yearbook*, Volume 4. pp. 123–141.

Li Chunling, Meng Lei, Lu Peng, Shi Yunqing, Chen Xin, 2011. Xin shidai de xin zhuti: 2007–2010 Nian qingnian yanjiu zongshu (New Themes of the New Era: A Review of Youth Studies from 2007 to 2010). *Qingnian yanjiu (Studies on Youth)* (3). pp. 87–93.

Li Chunling. 2012. Social Mobility and Social Class in China: A comparative study of intragenerational mobility models before and after the economic reforms, in L. Roulleau-Berger and Li Peilin (eds), *European and Chinese Sociologies. A New dialogue*, Leiden-Boston: Brill Publishers. pp. 117–127.

Li Chunling. 2013. Institutional and Non-institutional Path: Different Processes of Socio- economic Status Attainment of Migrants and Non-migrants in China, in Li, Peilin, Roulleau-Berger, L. (eds), *China's internal and International Migration*. London and New York: Routledge Publishers. pp. 26–40.

Li Chunling. 2017. Qingnian qunti zhong de xinxing chengxiang fenge ji qi shehui yingxiang (New urban-rural division and its social impact among youth groups). *Beijing Gongye Daxue Xuebao*. 2017(2). pp. 1–7.

Li Chunling. 2019. Gaige kaifang de haizimen: zhongguo xinsheng dai yu zhongguo fazhan xin shidai (The new generation and new period of development), *Shehuixue Yanjiu (Sociological Research)*, n° 3. pp. 1–24.

Li Lulu. 2008. Transition et stratification sociale dans les villes chinoises, in Roulleau-Berger, L., Guo, Yuhua, Li, Peilin, Liu, Shiding (eds), *La Nouvelle Sociologie chinoise* Paris: Editions du CNRS. pp. 119–145.

Li Zhengang, Zhang Jianbao. 2020. Zhenggui yu fei zhenggui: Jiuye moshi dui nongmingong gongzuo pinkun de yingxiang—laizi ba ge chengshi de jingyan zhengjiu (Formal versus informal: the impact of employment patterns on migrant worker work poverty -Empirical evidence from eight cities), *Beijing Gongye Daxue Xuebao (Journal of Beijing University of Technology)*, vol. 20, n° 6. pp. 29–44.

Linhart, Danièle. 2015. *La comédie humaine du travail*, Paris, Eres.

Li Nan. 2010. Nong cun wai chu lao dong li liu cheng yu fan xiang yi yuan ying xiang fen xi,. (Analysis of factors affecting the willingness of rural migrant workers to return to their homeland), *Zhong guo renkou kexue (Chinese Journal of Demography)*, n° 6. pp. 102–108.

Li Peilin. 2008. Les villages urbains de la Chine en mutation: le cas de Yangcheng à Canton, in L. Roulleau-Berger, Guo Yuhua, Li Peilin, Liu Shiding (dir.), *La nouvelle sociologie chinoise*, Paris: Editions du CNRS. pp. 237–267.

Li Peilin. 2012. *Chinese Society-Change and transformation*. London/New York: Routledge.

Li Peilin, Roulleau-Berger, L. 2013. *China's Internal and International Migration*. London & New York: Routledge.

Li Peilin, Li Wei. 2013. The Work Situation and Social Attitudes of Migrant Workers in China under the Crisis", in Li Peilin, Roulleau-Berger, L. (eds), *China's internal and International Migration*. London and New York: Routledge Publishers. pp. 3–26.

Li Peilin. 2015. La modernisation orientale et l'expérience chinoise. *Socio n° 5*. pp. 25–45.

Li Peilin. 2018. China's 40-year experience in managing the movement of migrant workers. *Chinese Journal of Sociology*, 38(6). pp. 45–55.

BIBLIOGRAPHY

Li Peilin. 2018. The Great Change in the Past 40 Years of Reform and Opening Up and the Contemporary Mission of Chinese Sociology—Study & Exploration, *Sociology Research* (09). pp. 1–8.

Li Peilin. 2019a. Changes, Problems and Countermeasures of Class Structure in China in the Past 40 Years of Reform and Opening Up. *Journal of the Party School*, 21(06). pp. 5–16.

Li Peilin. 2019b. *Cunluo de zhongjie yangcheng cun de gushi wu nong de cunluo* (*The End of a Village: The Story of Yangcheng Village*). Beijing: Shangwu Yinshuguan Publishers.

Li Peilin, Cui Yan. 2020. The Changes in Social Stratum Structure From 2008 to 2019 in China and the Economic and Social Impact, *Jiangsu Social Sciences*, 04. pp. 51–60.

Li Qiang, 2012. Social stratification and institutional change. In *Chinese Society. Change and Transformation.* Edited by Li, Peilin. London and New York: Routledge. pp. 193–117.

Li Zhang. 2002. Spatiality and Urban Citizenship in Late Socialist, *Public Culture*, vol. 14, n° 2.

Li Zhigang, Laurence J.C. Ma, Desheng Xue. 2013. The making of a new transnational urban space: the Guangzhou African enclave, in Li Peilin, Roulleau-Berger, L. (eds), *China's Internal and International Migration*. London and New York: Routledge Publishers. pp. 150–174.

Li Yong. 2016. *Condamnés à réussir. Insertion professionnelle des diplômés chinois en France, Nouvelles dynamiques migratoires et identitaires*, thèse de sociologie soutenue en juin, Université de Rouen.

Li Yong. 2020. The identity crisis of Chinese graduates in France, in Liu Yue, Wang Simeng (eds), *Chinese immigrants in Europe: image, identity and social participation*, Berlin-Boston: Walter de Gruyter. pp. 101–126.

Lian Si. 2009. *Mazu* (*Ants*), Cuilin: Guanxi Normal University Press.

Lieber, M., Lévy, F. 2009. La sexualité comme ressource migratoire. Les Chinoises du Nord à Paris, *Revue française de sociologie*, n°4, vol. 50. pp. 719–746.

Liu Haifang. 2013. Mapping the New Migrants between China and Africa: Theoretical and Methodological Challenges, in *China's internal and International Migration*. Edited by Li, Peilin, Roulleau-Berger, L. London and New York: Routledge Publishers. pp. 234–245.

Liu Jiankun, Xu Hongzhi. 2019. Liyi weixie, zhengfu gongzuo manyi du yu shiming dui jin cheng nongmin de jiena yiyuan—Jiyu CSS2011 shuju de shizheng fenxi (Interest Threat, Satisfaction of Government Work and Citizen's Willingness to Accept Farmers into Cities—Empirical Analysis of CSS2011 Data), *Shehui, Society* 2019 (2).

Liu Linping, Li Chaohai. 2009. Behavioral Convergence and destimatization. A study on the legitimization of prostitution, *Chinese Sociology and Anthropology*, vol. 41 (3).

Liu Yana, Dong Qiyuan. 2019. Xinshengdai nongminggong de chengshi rongru yu fanxiang tiaoshi- jiyu zai jing wugong renyuan ze'ou wenti de guancha" (Urban Integration and Relocation Adjustment of the New Generation of Rural Migrant Workers—Based on the Observation of Spouse Selection in Beijing). *Lilun yuekan.* n° 7. pp. 139–146.

Liu Shiding. 2012. Three types of discrimination against migrant workers in the labor market and logical consequences, in L. Roulleau-Berger and Li Peilin (eds), *European and Chinese Sociologies. A new dialogue,* Brill Publishers, Leiden-Boston. pp. 283–293.

LIU Ziqin. 2014. *Les jeunes diplômés chinois à l'épreuve de la précarité. Mobilités, accès à l'emploi et rapport au travail. Le cas des jeunes migrants qualifiés dans les villages-urbains à Pékin.* Thèse de sociologie soutenue à l'ENS de Lyon.

Lu Xueyi. 2002. China's modernization process: urbanization of rural areas, *Social Sciences of China,* vol. XXIII, n° 1. pp. 109–116.

Luo Jarde and Yeh K. 2008. Shehui wangluo he shehui ziben (Social networks and social capital), in Li, Peilin, Li, Qiang, Ma, Rong (eds.), *Shehuixue he zhongguo shehui (Sociology and Chinese Society),* Shehui kexue wenxian chubanshe, Beijing (Academic Press of Social Sciences, Peking). pp. 341–363.

Luo Jarde and Yeh K. 2012. Neither Collectivism Nor Individualism. Trust in Chinese Guanxi Circles, *Journal of Trust Research,* vol. 2, n° 1. pp. 53–70.

Meng Fanqiang, Xiang Xiaomei. 2019. Zhiye geli, gongzi qishi yu nongmin gong qunti fenhua (Occupational Segregation, Wage Discrimination and Differentiation of Peasant Workers). *Journal of South China normal University,* 51(3). p. 102.

Merle, A. 2014. Homeowners of Beijing, Unite! The construction of a collective mobilisation, *China Perspectives,* 2014/2. pp. 7–15.

Mingione, E. 2013. New migrants in Europe: the Chinese in Italy in comparative perspective, in Li Peilin, Roulleau-Berger, L. (eds), *China's internal and International Migration.* London and New York: Routledge Publishers. pp. 245–259.

Miranda, A. 2002. Les Chinois dans la région de Naples. Altérités et identités dans une économie locale en mutation, in M. Péraldi (dir), *La fin des norias? Réseaux migrants dans les économies marchandes de la Méditerranée,* Paris: Éditions Maisonneuve & Larose. pp. 76–99.

Nyiri, P. 2007. Transnationalisme et minorité intermédiaire: les entrepreneurs chinois en Hongrie, in L. Roulleau-Berger (dir), *Nouvelles migrations chinoises et travail en Europe,* Toulouse: PUM. pp. 91–121.

Ong, A. 1999. *Flexible Citizenship: The Cultural Logics of Transnationality,* Durham: Duke.

Paradeise, C. 1984. La marine marchande française: un marché du travail fermé, *Revue française de sociologie,* vol. 25, n° 3. pp. 352–375.

BIBLIOGRAPHY

Park, R. 1926. The urban communauty as a spatial pattern and a moral order, in Park, R., Burgess, E.W., *The urban community*, Chicago: University of Chicago Press. pp. 118–127.

Pieke, F. 2007. Les migrations chinoises contemporaines: nouveaux régimes et nouvelles activités en Europe, in L. Roulleau-Berger (dir), *Nouvelles migrations chinoises et travail en Europe*, Toulouse: PUM. pp. 91–121.

Pollak, M. 1993. *Une identité blessée : études de sociologie et d'histoire*. Paris: Éditions Métailié.

Portes, A., Sensenbrenner, J. 1993. Embeddedness and immigration: notes on the social determination of economic action, *American journal of sociology*, vol. 98, n° 6. pp. 1320–1350.

Portes, A. 1999. La mondialisation par le bas. L'émergence des communautés transnationales, *Actes de la recherche en sciences sociales*, n° 129. pp. 15–25.

Pun, N. 2005. *Made in China. Women Factory Workers in a Global Workplace*, Durham, NC: Duke University Press.

Pun, N. 2007. The Dormitory Labor Regimes: Sites of Control and Resistance for Women Migrant Workers in South China, *Feminist Economicus* 13(3). pp. 239–245.

Pun, N. 2016. *Migrant Labor in China*, Cambridge: Polity Press.

Qin Cong. 2013. Nongmin weiquan huodong de lifa kangzhen jiqi lilun jieshi liang qi zhengdi anli de qishi (Fighting with Rationality and Legality in Peasants' Right—Protection Activities and a Theoretical Interpretation: Insights from Two Cases of Land Expropriation). *Shehui (Society)*. 2013(6). pp 1–7.

Qiu Zeqi, Zhang Maoyan. 2014. Comment la mise en œuvre d'une technologie peut-elle échouer? Le dévidage mécanique dans deux deltas en Chine (1860–1936) (How can the implementation of a technology fail? Mechanic unwinding in two deltas in China (1860–1936), in Roulleau-Berger, L., Liu, Shiding (dir), *Sociologies économiques française et chinoise: regards croisés*. Lyon: ENS Editions. pp. 346–369.

Ricoeur, P. 2004. *Parcours de reconnaissance*. Paris: Stock.

Roulleau-Berger, L. 1991, réed. in 1993. *La Ville Intervalle: jeunes entre centre et banlieue,*Paris : Méridiens Klincksieck.

Roulleau-Berger, L. 1999. *Le travail en friche. Les mondes de la petite production urbaine*, La Tour d'Aigues : Editions de l'Aube.

Roulleau-Berger L. 2003. La production d'espaces intermédiaires, *Hermès*, n° 36. pp. 147–156.

Roulleau-Berger, L., Shi, Lu. 2004a. Inégalités, disqualification sociale et violences symboliques à Shanghai: l'accès à l'emploi urbain des provinciaux *Journal des Anthropologues*. n° 96/97. pp. 233–252.

Roulleau-Berger, L. 2004b. Insertions segmentées, travail et discriminations des femmes immigrantes et de leurs filles, in *Femmes d'origine étrangère. Travail, accès à l'emploi, discriminations de genre*, Paris: La Documentation française. pp. 13–70.

Roulleau-Berger, L. 2006. Insécurité morale, brouillage des engagements et propriété de soi", in Guillaume, J.F. (dir), *Engagement, participation et responsabilité dans le parcours biographique*, Bruxelles: Editions de Boeck.

Roulleau-Berger, L. 2007a. Grammaires de reconnaissance, individuation et ordres sociétaux, in Caille, A. (dir), *La quête de reconnaissance,* Paris: La Découverte.

Roulleau-Berger, L. (dir). 2007b. *Nouvelles migrations chinoises et travail en Europe,* Toulouse: PUM.

Roulleau-Berger, L. 2009. Circulation, disqualification, autonomie des migrants en Chine continentale *Espaces, populations et sociétés*, n° 3. pp. 419–438.

Roulleau-Berger, L. 2010. *Migrer au féminin*. Paris: PUF.

Roulleau-Berger, L. 2011. *Désoccidentaliser la sociologie, L'Europe au miroir de la Chine*). La Tour d'Aigues: Editions de L'aube. Translated in Chinese by *Social Sciences Academic Press* 社会科学文献出版社 （中国), 2014.

Roulleau-Berger, L. 2013. Migration, plural economies and new stratification in Europe and in China, in Li Peilin, Roulleau-Berger, L. (eds), *China's Internal and International Migration,* London&New York: Routledge. pp. 259–275.

Roulleau-Berger, L. 2015. Incertitudes, inégalités et rapport au travail des jeunes en Chine, in Sobel, R., Séhier, C. (dir)*, La transformation du rapport salarial dans la Chine contemporaine.* Lille: Presses Universitaires du Septentrion. pp. 143–159.

Roulleau-Berger, L. 2016. *Post-Western Revolution in Sociology. From China to Europe,* Leiden-Boston: Brill Publishers.

Roulleau-Berger, L., Yan Jun. 2017. *Travail et Migration. Jeunesses chinoises à Shanghai et Paris,* La Tour d'Aigues: L'Aube.

Roulleau-Berger, L. 2018. Temporalités, espaces et 'Individu compressé' en Chine, *Temporalités,* n° 26. https://doi.org/10.4000/temporalites.3819.

Roulleau-Berger, L., Li Peilin. 2018. *Post-Western Sociology-From China to Europe,* London & New York: Routledge.

Sassen, S. 2006. *Territory, Authority, Rights: From Medieval to Global Assemblages,* Princeton: Princeton University Press.

Sassen, S. 2007a. *A sociology of globalization*. New York.: W.W. Norton & Company, Inc.

Sassen, S., (ed.). 2007b. *Deciphering the global: Its spaces, scales and subjects.* New York and London: Routledge.

Sassen, S. 2014. *Expulsions: Brutality and Complexity in the Global Economy,* Harvard: Harvard University Press.

Sayad, A. 1999. *La Double Absence. Des illusions de l'émigré aux souffrances de l'immigré,* Paris: Seuil.

Scholz, T. 2016. *Uberworked and Underpaid.How workers are disrupting the Digital Econmy, Cambridge*, Polity Press.

BIBLIOGRAPHY

Schmoll, C., 2020. *Les damnées de la mer. Femmes et frontières en Méditerranée*, Paris: La Découverte.

Scott, J. 1990. *Domination and the Arts of Resistance: Hidden Transcripts*. Yale: Yale University Press.

Sen, A. 1992. *Inequality Re-examined*. New York: Russell Sage Foundation, and Cambridge, MA: Harvard University Press.

Shen Yuan. 2011. *Nongmingong jieji de lishi miongyun* (*Historic destiny of migrant workers' class*), in Zheng, G.H, Zhu, J.A. (eds), *Xingonren jieji: guanxi, zuzhi yu jiti xindong* (*New Working class: relationship, organizing and collective actions*). Guangzhou: Zhongshan University. pp. 109–116.

Shen Yuan. 2013. *Social Transformation and the New Generation of Migrant Workers*. Beijing: Social Files Publishing House.

Shen Yuan, Guo Yuhua, Lu Huilin, Fang Yi. 2010. Nongmingong and dust pulmonary disease in Shenzhen. *21th Century International Review*. Volume 1.

Shen Yuan, Wen Xiang. 2014. Recherches sociologiques sur les transformations des marchés du travail chinois, in Roulleau-Berger, L., Liu Shiding (dir), *Sociologies économiques française et chinoise: regards croisés*, Lyon: ENS Publishers. pp. 141–171.

Shi Yunqing. 2015. *"Selective* Firming" of the Self-Boundary: Social Movements and the Reshaping of the State-Individual Relationship during China's Transformation: A Case Study of a Collective Litigation Caused by Demolition in City B, *The Journal of Chinese Sociology* volume 2, number 2, April 2015. pp. 1–28.

Shi Yunqing. 2018. Individualization in China under Compressed and Contradictory Modernity, *Temporalités*, n° 26. https://doi.org/10.4000/temporalites.3853.

Shi Yunqing. 2021. *Becoming citizens in China*, Leiden-Boston: Brill Publishers.

Steiner, P. 1999. *La sociologie économique*. Paris: La Découverte.

Strauss, A. 1959. *Mirrors and masks: the search of identity*. Glencoe: Free Press.

Su Liang. 2019. *Mobility and deskilling low-educated transnational migrants' decision-making, trajectory and consequences in multiple migration*, Thesis in sociology, Shanghai University.

Sun Liping. 2003. *Duanlie: Er shi shiji jiushi niandai yilai de Zhongguo shehui* (*Fractures: Chinese society since the 1990's*). Beijing: Shehui kexue wenxian chubanshe (Social Sciences Academic Press).

Sun Zhongwei, Liu Mingwei, Jia Hailong. 2018. Neibu laodongli shichang yu zhongguo laodong guanxi zhuanxing (Internal Labor Market and Transformation of China's Labor Relations). *Zhongguo shehui kexue* (*Chinese Social Sciences*) n° 7. pp. 81–105.

Tarrius, A. avec Missaoui, L. 2000. *Les nouveaux cosmopolitismes. Mobilités, identités, territoires*, La Tour D'aigues: Ed. de l'Aube.

Tassin, J. 2020. Une éthique alimentaire ? Redéfinir l'agriculture paysanne dans la Chine contemporaine. *Journée d'études du GIS Asie, l'Asie à lère de l'Anthropocène*, 19 novembre 2020.

Therborn, G. 2003. Entangled modernities. *European Journal of Social Theory*, 6 (3). pp. 293–305.

Tian Feng, Ni Chengzhang. 2017. Nongmingong shehui jingji diwei de shi nian bianhua 2006–2015 (Reverse Growth: Ten Years of Socioeconomic Status of Rural Workers 2006–2015). *Shehuixue Yanjiu (Sociological Research)*, n° 3. pp. 121–143.

Thireau, I., Hua Linshan. 2010. *Les ruses de la démocratie*. Paris: Seuil.

Tong Xin. 2008. Continuity of the cultural socialist tradition: collective action and resistance in State-owned companies in Roulleau-Berger, L., Guo, Yuhua, Li, Peilin, Liu, Shiding (dir). *La nouvelle sociologie chinoise*, Paris: Editions du CNRS. pp. 217–237.

Tong Xin. 2012. Three Decades of Chinese Women. State, Family, Women: Comments on the Last Two Decades of Women or Gender Related Sociological Studies, in *European and Chinese Sociologies. A new dialogue*. pp. 309–319. Edited by Roulleau-Berger, L., Li, Peilin. Leiden-Boston: Brill Publishers.

Tong Xin. 2014. Identités professionnelles des femmes propriétaires d'entreprises privées en Chine, in Roulleau-Berger, L., Liu, Shiding (eds), *Sociologies économiques française et chinoise: regards croisés* Lyon: ENS Editions. pp. 207–233.

Tong Xin, 2015. The Labor Relation in Chinese Internet Business, *Social Sciences of Jiangsu*, n° 1. pp. 16–24.

Touraine, A., Khosrokhavar, F. 2000. *La recherche de soi*. Paris: Fayard.

Touraine, A. 2005. *Un nouveau paradigme*. Paris: Seuil.

Touraine, A. 2007. *Penser autrement*. Paris: Fayard.

Trompette, P. 2008. *Le marché des défunts*, Paris: Presses de Sciences Politiques.

Veltz, P. 2008. *La grande transition*, Paris: Seuil.

Wang Chunguang. 2001. Xinshengdai nongcun liudongrenkou de shehui rentong he chengxiang ronghe wenti (The Social Identity and Urban-Rural Integration of the New Generation of Rural Migrant Population). *Shehuixue Yanjiu (Sociological Research)*, n° 3.

Wang Chunguang. 2017. *Yimin Kongjian de jiangou (The construction of the migratory space)*. Peking: Shehui kexue wenxian chubanshe (Peking: Press of Social Sciences).

Wang Ou. 2019. Liushou jingli yu xingbie laodong fenhua—jiyu nongmin gong shuchu de he dagong di de shizheng yanjiu (Left-behind Experiences and the Formation of Gender Division of Labor: An Empirical Study Based on Fieldwork at Sites of Origin and Destination for Migrants). *Shehuixue Yanjiu (Sociological Research)*, n° 2. pp. 123–146.

BIBLIOGRAPHY

Wang Simeng. 2017. *Illusions et souffrances. Les migrants chinois à Paris*, Paris: Editions rue d'Ulm.

Wang Tiannan. 2014. Inglehart's Theory of Intergenerational Value Transformation and Its Real Significance. *Wuhan keji daxue xuebao, Journal of Sciences and Technology of Wuhan*, vol. 1. pp. 60–66.

Wang Yifan. 2017. Qingnian laowu paiqian gong quanyi kunjing yu baozhang lujing (The Dilemma of Rights and Interests of Young Lab or Dispatch Workers and the Guarantee Way). *Huaibei shifan daxue xuebao. Journal of Huaibei* (Normal University), vol. 38, n° 4. pp. 42–45.

Wei Wanqing, Gao Wei. 2019. Tongxiang wangluo de ling yi fu lian kong: Guzhu—gongren tongxiang guanxi dui laogong geti quanyi de yingxiang (A Different Face of Social Network: Employer-based Enclave and Migrant Workers' Rights and Interests). *Shehui (Society)*, n° 2.

Wieviorka, M. 2008. *Neuf leçons de sociologie*. Paris: Lafont.

Wu Fulong. 2013, Informality and the Development and Demolition of Urban Villages in the Chinese Peri-urban Area, *Urban Studies*, 50 (10). pp. 1919–1934.

Wu Fulong. 2016. Housing in Chinese Urban Villages: The dwellers, Conditions and Tenancy Informality, *Housing Studies*, vol. 31, n° 7. pp. 852–870.

Wu Qingjun, Li, Zhen. 2018. Fenxiang jingji xia de laodong kongzhi yu gongzuo zizhu xing -Guanyu wang yue che siji gongzuo de hunhe yanjiu (Labour Process Control and Job Autonomy in Sharing Economy: A Case Study of Online Car-hailing Drivers' Work). *Shehuixue Yanjiu (Sociological Research)*, n° 4. pp. 137–162.

Xie Lizhong, and Roulleau-Berger, L. (eds). 2017. 社会学知识的建构.后西方社会学的探索, *The Fabric of Sociological Knowledge: The Exploration of Post-Western, Sociology*, Beijing: Beijing University Press.

Xiong, Y. (2015). The Broken Ladder: Why Education Provides No Upward Mobility for Migrant Children in China. *The China Quarterly, 221*. pp. 161–184. DOI:10.1017/S0305741015000016.

Xiong, Yihan, Li Miao 2017. Citizenship education as NGO intervention: turning migrant children in Shanghai into 'new citizens'. *Citizenship Studies, 21*(7). pp. 792–808. DOI:10.1080/13621025.2017.1353741.

Xu Tao. 2013. The social relations and interactions of black Afriican migrants in China's Guangzhou province, in Li Peilin, Roulleau-Berger, L. (eds), *China's internal and International Migratio*n. London and New York: Routledge Publishers. pp. 133–150.

Yang Juhua, Zhang Zhao, Luo Yuying. 2016. Liudong shidai zhong de liudong shidai: Jin 30 nian zhongguo qingnian liudong renkou tezheng de biandong qushi (The Mobile Generation in the Mobile Era: The Changing Trend of the Characteristics of China's Youth Floating Population in the Past 30 years"). *Zhongguo qingnian yanjiu (Research on Chinese Youth)*. pp. 53–62.

Yan Jun, 2014. The individualization of Young Skilled Migrants in Shanghai, in Lu Feiyun (ed), *Urban Social Development Report of Shanghai and Yangtze River Delta, Shanghai :* SDX Joint Publishing Company. pp 159–175.

Yang Yiyin. 2009. Guanxilization or Categorization: Psychological Mechanisms Contrib uting to the Formation of the Chinese Concept of us. *Social Science in China,* vol. XXX, n° 2. pp. 49–67.

Yang Yiyin. 2012. Guanxilization and Categorization: Theoretical Considerations Based on Two Case Studies, in *European and Chinese Sociologies. A new dialogue.* pp. 163–177. Edited by Roulleau-Berger, L., Li, Peilin. Leiden-Boston: Brill Publishers.

Yan Yunxiang. 2010. The Chinese path to individualization, *The British Journal of Sociology,* vol. 61, Issue 3. pp. 489–512.

Yan Yunxiang. 2010. Introduction: Conflicting Images of the Individual and Contested Process of Individualization, in Mette H.H. and Rune, S. (eds), *China: The Rise of the Individual in Modern Chinese Society.* Copenhagen: NIAS Press. pp. 1–38.

Yan Yunxiang. 2009. *The Individualization of Chinese Society.* Oxford: Berg.

Yiu, Lisa., Luo Yun 2017. China's Rural Education: Chinese Migrant Children and Left-Behind Children. *Chinese Education & Society,* 50(4). pp. 307–314. DOI:10.1080/10611932.2017.1382128.

Zani, B. 2018. Trapped in Migration. Migratory Careers and Entrepreneurial Creativity of Chinese Migrant Women in Taiwan, *China Perspectives,* n° 1–2. pp. 75–85.

Zani, B. 2019. In-between. Re-migration, Emotional Circulations and New Cosmopolitan Biographies" Special Issue" *The Invisible Within. Actors, Relations and Activities in Chinese Migrant Family*", Guest edited by L. Momesso and I. Cheng, Asia Pacific Viewpoint. DOI: 10.1111/apv.12254.

Zani, B. 2020. We Chat, We Sell, We Fee: Chinese Migrant Women's Emotional Petit Capitalism, Special Issue Migration, Digital Media and Emotion, Guest edited by S. Ponzanesi and D.D. Alinejad, *International Journal of Cultural Studies* 23(5). pp. 803–820. DOI: 10.1177/1367877920923360.

Zhang Jing. 2012. Dual integration of social order: analysis of a case of property right dispute, in Roulleau-Berger, L., Li, Peilin (eds), *European and Chinese Sociologies: A new dialogue.* Leiden: Brill Publishers. pp. 223–235.

Zhang Shun, Cheng Cheng. 2012. Shichang hua gaige yu shehui wangluo ziben de sho-uru xiaoying (Market Reforms and the Income Effects of Social Network Capital). *Shehuixue Yanjiu (Sociological Research),* n° 1. pp. 130–151.

Zhang Yulei, Ma Dong. 2019. College Students' Returning to Their Hometown to Start Up Business under the Strategy of Rural Revitalization—Based on the Case Analysis of Young Entrepreneur in Jiupu Town, Xuyi Country. *Journal of Huaihai Engineering College,* vol. 17, n° 7. pp. 119–123.

Zhao Dingxin. 2008. Jiqunxingwei yu shehui yundong (collective action and social movements), in Li, Peilin, Li, Qiang, Ma, Rong (eds), *Shehuixue he zhongguo*

BIBLIOGRAPHY 179

shehui (*Sociology and Chinese sociology*). Beijing: Shehui kexue wenxian chubanshe (Beijing: Social Sciences Academic Press). pp. 766–798.

Zhao Yeqin. 2009. Les illusions perdues d'une Chinoise du Nord à Belleville, *Terrains & Travaux*, n° 2. pp. 195–211.

Zhao Yeqin. 2012. *Building Urban Spaces and Renovating a District in Shanghai: The Problem of Migration and Social Change.* Shanghai: Sanlian Shudian.

Zhao Yeqin. 2018. Fa wai zhufang shichang de shengcheng luoji yu juzhu de bu queding xing: Yi shanghai cheng zhongcun chai wei wei li (The Logic of the Extra-Legal Housing Market and the Uncertainty of Living: A Case Study of the Demolition of the Village in Shanghai). *Huadong shifan daxue xuebao* (*Journal of East China Normal University*, n° 4. pp. 124–130.

Zhong Yunhua. 2015. Daxue biye sheng zhiye liudong de yingxiang yinsu fenxi (Analysis of Factors Influencing College Graduate's Occupational Mobility). *Gaodeng jiaoyu yanjiu.* (*High-Education research*), vol. 36, n° 6. pp. 33–41.

Zhou Xiaohong. 2008. La classe moyenne chinoise: réalité ou illusion?, in Rocca, J.-L. (dir), *La société chinoise vue par ses sociologues.* Paris: Les Presses de sciences Po. pp. 141–161.

Zhuang Jiachi. 2018. Cong bei guanli de shou dao bei guanli de xin—Laodong guocheng shiye xia de jiaban yanjiu (From Managed Hands to Managed Hearts—Overtime Work in the View of Labor Process). *Shehuixue Yanjiu* (*Sociological Research*), n° 3. pp. 74–92.

Zukin, S., Kasinitz, P., Chen X. 2015. *Global cities, local streets. Everyday diversity from New York to Shanghai*, New York: Routledge.

Index

assemblages 8–9, 106, 110, 118, 123, 129

bifurcations 2, 12, 52, 54–55, 57, 65–68, 70, 74–75, 82, 88, 144–147, 151, 159

capitalism 2–3, 8, 12, 16, 25, 30, 35, 66, 76, 78, 81, 109, 162–163
care work 33–34, 112, 117, 120, 127–129, 131
collective action 13–15, 17, 41, 43–45, 48, 81, 161
compressed individual 1–2, 4, 11–13, 15–17, 59, 75, 77, 135, 138, 148, 152, 158, 160, 162–163
contempt 13, 33–34, 36, 50, 63, 74, 79, 118, 128, 151

danwei 8, 17, 19, 81–83
deterritorialisation 34, 111
dirty work 32, 85, 120, 131
discrimination 11, 15–16, 20, 31, 61, 63–65, 72, 88, 102, 105, 107, 116, 123, 125–126, 131, 136, 147, 159
domination 8–9, 21, 35, 40, 53, 65, 81, 118, 120, 124, 129–131, 150–151, 161–162

economic networks 34, 94–95, 104, 110, 122, 130, 134
economic niches 26, 31, 121
emotional capitalism 1, 8–9, 11–12, 15–16, 39, 41–42, 59, 78, 88–89, 135, 138, 158, 162–163
emotions 9–10, 12, 15, 34, 39, 42–43, 50–51, 64, 78–79, 81, 152, 162–163

flexibility 8, 27, 34–35, 41, 43, 60, 71, 75–76, 78–80, 118, 120, 128, 131, 138
floating labour 15, 34–35

globalisation x, xi–1, 11, 25, 93, 95, 100–101, 105–106, 109–111, 128–129, 137–138, 148, 151, 158–160
guanxi 39–41, 45, 47, 49, 80–81, 136

hegemonic labour regimes 9–10, 15, 34, 37, 39, 42, 51

hukou 5, 17, 19, 22, 27*f*1, 26–28, 28*f*2, 31, 52, 56–57, 61–62, 107, 154

identities 10, 14–16, 70, 73, 75–77, 79, 82, 92, 126, 128–129, 138, 140, 145–146, 150–151, 159
identity 10, 12–16, 25, 34–35, 59, 63, 73–75, 77, 80, 88–90, 105, 108, 110, 117, 125–126, 130, 135, 141, 145, 148, 150–151, 154, 157, 162
individuation 1, 10–12, 26, 35, 65, 73, 139, 148, 159–160, 162
inequalities 1–2, 8, 11, 14, 16–20, 42, 45, 53, 57, 64, 66–67, 78, 109, 135, 137, 140, 145–146, 149, 158, 160
informal employment 18, 33, 54, 59–60
injustice 20, 35, 43, 47, 61, 72, 85, 129, 149
internal migration 1, 5, 14, 59, 93, 155, 158
international migrations x–1, 4, 7, 11, 16, 101, 108–109, 142, 144, 155, 158, 161

justice 35, 46, 72, 151

labour markets 6, 8–9, 15, 21, 25–26, 28, 31, 34–35, 39–41, 43, 51–52, 54–55, 61, 63, 65–67, 70, 74, 80–81, 85, 96, 104, 110, 112, 117–118, 120–121, 123, 126–127, 129, 131–134, 137, 142–143, 146, 149, 159
laojia 23, 29, 36, 153–154

marginalisation 18, 22, 24, 72, 81, 84, 131, 144
market economy 3, 11, 18, 25, 53, 64, 78, 136
megalopolises 6, 25, 59–60, 153, 157
middle-class 3, 20, 33, 61, 76, 160
multi-compressed modernity 2, 4, 9–13, 15–16, 30, 35, 37, 39, 42, 50–53, 55, 57, 77, 112, 135, 137–138, 141, 148, 150–151, 154, 156, 158–159, 161, 163

nongmingong 15, 41

poverty 3, 18, 29, 33–34, 100–101, 107, 153–154
professional relationships 40–41, 65, 76, 80–81, 116, 129
professionnal mobilities 12, 17, 32, 56, 60, 64, 84, 122, 127, 144–145

INDEX

181

recognition 9, 12, 15, 20–21, 33, 35, 43, 46, 62–63, 65, 73–75, 77–78, 87, 89, 92, 97, 104, 106, 108, 120, 125–126, 128, 130–131, 133–134, 147, 149, 151, 158, 162

secondary markets 25, 131
sex work 13, 34
social differentiation 53–54, 61, 79, 99
social reproduction 17, 53
social rights 5, 18, 20, 35–36, 40, 47, 122
social stratification 3, 17, 33, 61, 128
socialism 11–12, 16, 162–163
spatial mobilities 19, 53, 60, 145

stigmatisation 13, 20, 120, 147
structural disqualification 24, 43, 61, 65, 85
subalternity 10, 15, 17, 25, 36, 49, 54$n1$, 54$n1$, 54–56, 158, 160

underclass 3, 21, 45, 48, 102, 160
urban enclaves 21, 24, 118
urban segregation 15, 21
urban villages 21–25, 42, 145, 153

workplace 10, 20, 27, 31, 36–37, 39–41, 43, 50, 61, 63, 65, 72, 78, 80–81, 85–86, 88, 116, 122, 125, 129, 153

Printed in the United States
by Baker & Taylor Publisher Services